A Life in Medicine

A Life in Medicine

A Literary Anthology

edited by

ROBERT COLES, M.D. AND RANDY TESTA

with Joseph O'Donnell, M.D.
Penny Armstrong, C.N.M., M.S.N.
and M. Brownell Anderson

THE NEW PRESS
NEW YORK

Published in the United States by The New Press, New York, 2002
Distributed by Perseus Distribution

Pages 325-329 constitute an extension of this copyright page.

ISBN 978-1-59558-780-0 (e-book)

LIBRARY OF CONGRESS CATALOGING-IN-PUBLICATION DATA

A life in medicine : a literary anthology / edited by Robert Coles and Randy Testa with Joseph O'Donnell, Penny Armstrong and M. Brownell Anderson.
p. cm.
ISBN 978-1-56584-729-3 (hc.)
ISBN 978-1-56584-849-8 (pbk.)
1. Medicine—Literary collections. I. Coles, Robert. II. Testa, Randy-Michael.

PN6071.M38 L54 2002
808.8'0356—dc21 2001055827

The New Press publishes books that promote and enrich public discussion and understanding of the issues vital to our democracy and to a more equitable world. These books are made possible by the enthusiasm of our readers; the support of a committed group of donors, large and small; the collaboration of our many partners in the independent media and the not-for-profit sector; booksellers, who often hand-sell New Press books; librarians; and above all by our authors.

www.thenewpress.com

Book design by Kathryn Parise
Typesetting by Westchester Book Composition

Printed in the United States of America

Contents

PART THREE
Physicians Must Be Skillful

To the memory of Dr. William Carlos Williams,
whose words and thoughts inspired and
helped so many of us in medicine;
and to my family with much love.
—Robert Coles

Acknowledgments

This book is the result of many people's generous efforts and much grace. Accordingly, we thank Joe O'Donnell, Penny Armstrong, and Brownie Anderson for their wise assistance; Tom Mellers for permissions help; and Samita Sinha and Diane Wachtell at The New Press for their direction, help, advice, and humor.

—Robert Coles and Randy Testa

Preface

A beginning medical student struggling to obtain a medical history is delighted by the story his elderly patient tells him instead. A mother whose child has just been diagnosed with cancer walks into the pediatric oncology unit for the first time and the ground drops out from under her. A nurse/poet meditates on the secret moments she has shared with patients, just before and just after their deaths. This anthology collects moments like these, gleaned from a life in medicine, moments rendered poignant through stories, poems, and essays. Each in its own way examines the relationship between patients and health care professionals. Some pieces are by doctors, nurses, and residents; others are by laypeople. Some pieces are filled with outrage, others with gratitude. Some offer prescriptions. All offer perspective.

In the literature and medicine courses taught by those of us compiling this anthology, we frequently hear students of our disciplines complain bitterly that, although they love reading literature, they don't really have time for it. They must learn "hard science," they insist, and they become fearful that time spent with literature is time spent away from medicine. Sadly, this view often originates with their teachers, who are not only entrusted with teaching medicine, but with determining the very structure of medical education.

Dr. Rita Charon of Columbia University's College of Physicians and Surgeons points out that, for all its emphasis on scientific knowledge, "the work of medicine in considerable part rests on the doctor's ability to listen to the stories that patients tell; to make sense of these often chaotic narratives of illness; to inspect and evaluate the listener's personal response to the story told;

to understand what these narratives mean at multiple (and sometimes contradictory) levels, and to be moved by them." Ron Carson, director of the Institute for Medical Humanities at the University of Texas Medical Branch, Galveston, offers further justification for literature in the education of health care professionals: learning to read with care stories about patients helps health care professionals become careful readers of their patients.

In 1996 the Association of American Medical Colleges (AAMC) embarked on a major new initiative to assist medical schools in their efforts to educate medical students more fully. Titled the Medical School Objectives Project (MSOP), it identified *altruism*, *knowledge*, *skill*, and *duty* as the four attributes necessary for medical school graduates to thrive in the current and future health care environment.* We have organized the selections in *A Life in Medicine* using these four objectives as section headings, and have provided the AAMC's full definition of each objective at the opening of each section of readings. It is our hope that multiple perspectives will allow for deeper insight into the implications of the four objectives, as well as what Dr. Coles has described as a moral education.

One goal of the MSOP is to provide a blueprint or framework upon which medical schools and educators can build unique approaches to medical education. Our goal is to offer narrative knowledge as a means for examining with fresh perspective the daily responses we have to those on whose behalf we work. We hope this book represents a fundamental tool—for dialogue, debate, insight, and clarification—for all of us who find ourselves engaged by a life in medicine.

*"Report 1: Learning Objectives for Medicine Student Education—Guidelines for Medical Schools." Association of American Medical Colleges: Washington, D.C., 1998.

INTRODUCTION

The Moral Education of Medical Students

ROBERT COLES

In *Middlemarch,* George Eliot's greatest novel, she remarks at one point that "character is not cut in marble—it is not something solid and unalterable." She pointedly amplifies that observation with a medical simile (in a novel that tells, among other things, of a doctor whose moral values go through a marked transformation): "It is something living and changing, and may become diseased as our bodies do." Indeed, throughout her writing career, Eliot struggled hard with moral questions—she was constantly posing them to her fictional protagonists and, thereby, to her readers. The physician, Dr. Lydgate, who figures prominently in *Middlemarch,* starts out as an intensely idealistic young man, determined to use his professional skills on behalf of needy people, no matter their background, and determined, as well, to advance his profession's knowledge, through research, as best he can. Yet, in a few short years, he is a society doctor, all too cynically catering to those who can buy his time. "He had gained an excellent practice," we are told at the story's end, "alternating, according to the season, between London and a Continental bathing-place; having written a treatise on Gout, a disease which has a good deal of wealth on its side. His skill was relied on by many paying patients, but he always regarded himself as a failure: he had not done what he once meant to do."

That second sentence is especially important. Eliot had no interest in being a scold. Rather, she meant to explore the manner in which, not rarely, we disappoint our own selves, forsake certain ideals or principles that helped shape our lives at crucial moments—only to relinquish their hold on us. She wondered why—how it comes about that we lose our moral moorings, shift the moral direction of our lives, end up doing things we once regarded as unworthy of our own standards of behavior. A half-century later an American novelist, F. Scott Fitzgerald, worried over the same matter. He gave us, in *Tender Is the Night*, the physician Dick Diver, whose last name conveys the essence of the novel's action: a steep decline in a person's self-respect, never mind his responsibility to the ethical norms of his chosen profession. Like Eliot, Fitzgerald had no great interest in wagging his finger at his readers or at doctors in general. He was a talented storyteller who knew that moral irony abounds in our lives; that we can claim an integrity which we gradually let slip by us, an integrity undermined in small, day-by-day ways that may seem inconsequential—until, in their sum, they have had their unmistakable effect. Not that either Dr. Lydgate or Dr. Diver suffers any great pangs of conscience as a result of the personal change that befalls each of them—and therein lies the unnerving reminder to us who get to know them, page by page: we, too, have agile minds that are quite capable of fooling us, that spin webs of rationalizations and self-deceptions, to the point that we're unself-consciously caught in a life whose implications we have long ago stopped examining, never mind judging.

How to call upon such novelists (they at times become moral visionaries) in our lives, in our work, if we are doctors at medical schools who are trying to teach the young men and women in our classes what it means to be a good doctor? To be sure, factual knowledge counts a lot; we have to impart it constantly, and our students are mightily challenged by the demands on their memory as they absorb blackboards full of information, textbooks full of explanations, and as they try to keep in mind what they have learned in long laboratory sessions. All too often, though, those students will wonder what the point of such an experience is, especially in the first two years of their medical school education, and they will resort to gastrointestinal imagery as they try to gain any possible perspective on a relentlessly demanding, exhausting, unnerving experience: ingestion, regurgitation. Some students will utter terse lines of poetry that stress the attitude of utter compliance required ("ours not to reason why, ours but to do and die") or stress the desired outcome as a justification for what seems to be an arbitrary kind of force feeding meant to test tenacity ("survival is all").

But medical school need not be an episode worthy of Tennyson's well-known description in "The Charge of the Light Brigade," nor a spell of melancholy resignation such as Rilke evoked in one of his elegies. Some medical schools have tried hard to emphasize ideas and ways of thinking, so that an ever-expanding mass of detailed information can be fitted to a broad understanding of how things work in our bodies. Of course, such efforts of reform have had to contend with the so-called Boards, the gateway to certification for state licensing. And so, despite curricular reforms, medical students will still have to cram and cram in order to get through multiple-choice tests that are not exactly designed to do justice to the complexity of things, nor to encourage independent or reflective thinking. Indeed, in medicine especially, with its emphasis on human particularity and on individual idiosyncrasy (the old refrain "each patient is different"), the use of multiple-choice tests, with their frequent emphasis on yes or no, right or wrong, is both ironic and not likely to encourage medical students to think broadly, make connections across various academic fields of inquiry, or develop any kind of wide-ranging, open-eyed responsiveness to patients in all their puzzling, surprising variation. One of my medical students, thrilled to be discussing ideas and examining trends, excited to be asked to write thoughtful, probing essays that connect concepts taught in various courses, stirred by the chance to contemplate apparent inconsistencies or paradoxes, the mysteries that science only gradually and incompletely banishes, at the end of her second year of medical school had this to say: "To turn from the New Pathway [Harvard's effort at curriculum reform] to learning lists and more lists (it's rote learning, and you forget what you've memorized five minutes after you take the exam)—that's very sad, and very confusing."

I mention such familiar aspects of medical school education because they are not without moral implications. Students told to stuff their heads with information, the more obscure the more likely to be queried, students told they are in a rock-bottom sense competing against one another on one "curve" after another, are not being encouraged to think about the truly consequential or to do so in alliance with one another. Moreover, in the course of teaching at seven medical schools in different parts of this country, and in doing many interviews with medical students, I have heard the usual stories about certain teachers, their displays of arrogance, condescension, mean-spiritedness, even vengefulness; and, too, the usual stories about students, their extreme competitiveness, their decline into a dog-eat-dog attitude—a continuation, alas, of what not uncommonly occurs among pre-medical students (whose professors of chemistry, physics, and biology are not always sensitive, thoughtful, let alone kindly or inspiring individuals).

No wonder, in the 1970s, Lewis Thomas (in "How to Fix the Pre-Medical Curriculum," a chapter in *The Medusa and the Snail*) was prompted to such intellectual alarm, such moral indignation, as he surveyed pre-medical life on our campuses: "The influence of the modern medical school on liberal arts education in this country over the last decade has been baleful and malign, nothing less." He documented that assertion with many observations made while working at Yale Medical School as its dean, and talking with undergraduates in New Haven and elsewhere. He wanted the MCAT test done away with, and an emphasis put on literature and history and philosophy (and yes, the study of Latin and Greek) as a means of broadening and deepening the inner life of men and women who, after all, hope one day to attend their fellow human beings, understand and connect with them heart, mind, and soul. Perhaps he exaggerates when he describes the "premeds" as "that most detestable of all cliques eating away at the heart of the college"; and perhaps he is similarly a little overwrought when he describes "today's first-year medical students" as already "surfeited by science"—not out of an ardent love for it, but a fiercely contentious desire to prevail over others, and at all costs "get in" to this or that or any medical school. Still, I suspect that many of us continue to read his brilliantly provocative essays (which graced the *New England Journal of Medicine* for many years) with nods of recognition—and especially so those essays in which he kept worrying about the ethical consequences of the undergraduate and graduate education of late-twentieth-century American physicians.

All the time we medical school teachers send moral signals to our students. As Lewis Thomas kept insisting, we let them know by our admissions practices what kind of person (educated in which way) we desire. Once those young people are admitted, we let them know (by how we teach what we teach) the kind of people we are, never mind the kind of people we expect them to be. Another physician who wrote (novels as well as essays), Walker Percy, also addressed in a moral and philosophical way the matter of scientific education. His essay "The Delta Factor" in *The Message in the Bottle* reminds us how bored and jaded and drearily submissive we can become as we take in a subject mindlessly, fearfully, in order to "get in," or "get by," those clarion-call phrases that inform so much of what gets called "pre-med" and then medical school education. He wryly suggests strategies of surprise—efforts to undermine the juggernaut of resigned compliance, of anxious boredom that informs so much of university life. He would have our students coming to a laboratory, now and then, to find Shakespeare or the words of a novelist, a moral philosopher such as William James (another physician who worried about the way science is taught to doctors and others). He worries, really, about the stifling of the moral imagination—which is our capacity to assume responsibility for what we learn, fit it into our notion of how we ought live, what we ought do (and in what manner) with what we have come to know.

We can, of course, surprise not only our students but ourselves. We can, for instance, take passages from George Eliot's *Middlemarch* to heart—follow Dr. Percy's advice, put those moments of wisdom in our laboratories for our students, but also ponder them in our own minds and hearts, let them influence the way we teach, what we have to say to, or better, ask of our students. Dr. Percy was, however, as wary of literature as he was of science—he knew that we can pay mere lip service to either (rote memorization, clever interpretations, then a hurried consignment to oblivion, so that new "stuff" can be "imprinted" on those poor brain cells). He would have us putting ourselves on the line, connecting what we read and believe to how we act, a kind of "medical ethics" that is expressed, for example, in community service. He would have us integrating *Middlemarch* or *Tender Is the Night* or Raymond Carver's "A Small Good Thing" or Chekhov's "Anyuta" or William Carlos Williams's constantly challenging "Doctor Stories" into the entire range of medical school education. He would have us connect those serious "texts" to clinical teaching so that they might have an impact on how we address and regard and respond to the people we aim to heal—so that a patient's presence before us in a hospital or office setting becomes for us a moral occasion, a measure of our moral life as it is lived moment to moment.

PART ONE

Physicians Must Be Altruistic

PHYSICIANS must be compassionate and empathetic in caring for patients, and must be trustworthy and truthful in all their professional dealings. They must bring to the study and practice of medicine those character traits, attitudes, and values that underpin ethical and beneficent medical care. They must understand the history of medicine, the nature of medicine's social compact, the ethical precepts of the medical profession, and their obligations under law. At all times they must act with integrity, honesty, and respect for patients' privacy, and respect for the dignity of patients as persons. In all of their interactions with patients, they must seek to understand the meaning of the patients' stories in the context of the patients' beliefs and family and cultural values. They must avoid being judgmental when the patients' beliefs and values conflict with their own. They must continue to care for dying patients even when the disease-specific therapy is no longer available or desired.

Rosalind Warren

OUTPATIENT

In this wry opening selection, a middle-aged hypnotist named Luisa, suspecting that she might have bronchitis, goes to the doctor for a checkup. When the examination is both "dehumanizing and demoralizing," Luisa decides to use her profession to teach her doctor a thing or two about "ethical and beneficent" care.

ROSALIND WARREN is an attorney living in Philadelphia. She has had stories published in *Crosscurrents, Fantasy and Science Fiction*, and *Seventeen*.

The waiting room is crowded. Mothers watch fidgety children, couples sit together on drab sofas, adult children talk in soothing voices to elderly parents. Everyone in the waiting room has someone with them. Luisa has come alone.

"New patient?" the receptionist asks. Luisa nods.

The receptionist hands her a clipboard that holds a form. "You'll have to fill this out," she says. When Luisa returns it a few moments later, the receptionist looks it over. "You haven't filled in your occupation," she says.

"Hypnotist," says Luisa.

"Oh?" The receptionist meets Luisa's eyes. They're unusual eyes. Clear blue, almost violet. They often remind people of deep bodies of water.

"It's the family business," says Luisa. "Both my parents were hypnotists. As were two of my grandparents."

"How lovely," says the receptionist.

"The doctor will see me right away," says Luisa, still looking into the receptionist's eyes. She enunciates each word slowly and carefully.

"But we call people in the order they arrive."

"I arrived first," says Luisa.

"You arrived first," agrees the receptionist.

Luisa has barely glanced at *Life* magazine's special Winter Olympics issue when a nurse calls her name. She follows the nurse down a corridor to a small examining room. The nurse hands her the usual skimpy garment, telling Luisa to remove her clothes and put it on. When the nurse leaves, Luisa strips, puts the thing on, and sits down on the edge of the examination table. It's cool. Almost immediately she has goose bumps.

Luisa doesn't look great in the drab shapeless garment, but she looks better than most. She is of an indeterminate age. Certainly past forty. She would probably be described as "well preserved." She is tall and strong-looking and has longish red hair. Not beautiful but striking. The nurse comes back in and smiles when she notices that Luisa's fingernails and toenails are painted cherry-blossom pink.

"Stand on the scale," she instructs. Luisa gets on the scale, and the nurse adjusts the indicator back and forth, minutely, until it finally rests on 130.

"One hundred thirty," she says.

Luisa turns to look at her. "What about my eyes?" she asks.

"Hmmm?" the nurse says, writing. She looks up and meets Luisa's eyes. "Oh!" she says. She gazes at Luisa for a moment. "They're such a nice color," she says.

"Really?" asks Luisa. "Tell the truth."

"They're a little weird."

"Scary?" asks Luisa.

"Nope." The nurse smiles. "I like them."

Luisa smiles. "I weigh one fifty-seven," she says. The nurse glances down at her clipboard and frowns. She erases the 130 and writes 157.

"But I carry it well," says Luisa. "Don't I?"

"You certainly do," says the nurse. "Now I have to take your blood pressure." She straps the arm band on, pumps it up, and looks at it. "One hundred ten over sixty," she says.

"One twenty over seventy," Luisa says. The nurse gazes at her blankly. "I'm sorry," says Luisa. "But these silly games are quite harmless, and they're crucial if I'm to stay in practice. I'll stop if it disturbs you."

The nurse smiles. "It doesn't disturb me." She writes 120 over 70 on Luisa's chart. "I think it's interesting."

"What happens now?" Luisa asks.

"You wait for Dr. Heller."

"I probably don't even need Dr. Heller," says Luisa. "I'm ninety percent sure I've got bronchitis. Everyone in my family has bronchitis. Everyone on my *block* has bronchitis. But I can't just write myself out a prescription for antibiotics, can I?"

"No," says the nurse. "You can't."

"What's Dr. Heller like?" Luisa asks.

"He's very nice."

"Tell the truth."

"He's a complete jerk," says the nurse. Then she looks startled, and they both burst out laughing.

"But he's a very competent doctor," the nurse says. "He can diagnose your bronchitis as well as the next doc."

"Thanks for putting up with me," says Luisa. "You will feel happy for the rest of the day. You will walk around thinking life is a piece of cake."

"I certainly look forward to that," says the nurse.

Luisa snaps her fingers. The nurse blinks, then moves quickly to the door. "Dr. Heller will be right with you," she says as she leaves. She has left the clipboard with Luisa's chart on the table, and Luisa quickly changes her weight and blood pressure to the correct numbers.

Time passes. Ten minutes. Twenty minutes. Nothing happens. The nurse had left her with the impression that the doctor would be right in. Clearly, he won't be. There is nothing to distract her. She should have brought her magazine with her. She imagines parading out into the waiting room dressed as she is to retrieve her copy of *Life*. She decides against it.

She looks around the room. It's a generic examination room. No windows. No pictures or photos. Nothing interesting or unusual to hold her attention.

Luisa hasn't much interest in things, anyway. Things rarely hold surprises; people do.

Another twenty minutes pass. Luisa is beginning to think they've forgotten all about her. She's starting to feel woozy. It angers her. Sitting here half dressed is the last thing she needs. She knows that in examining rooms up and down this hallway sick people sit in skimpy hospital garments waiting for the doctor. It's more convenient for him this way. She tries to calm herself. This treatment isn't life-threatening, she tells herself. It may be dehumanizing and demoralizing, but it won't kill you. They only do it this way because they can get away with it.

Finally the door opens and a big man in a white coat breezes in. He's in his mid-thirties, large and bearded. He looks like a lumberjack. His blue eyes are intelligent but not particularly kind. He moves in a rush.

"Well, Luisa," he says loudly, glancing down at the clipboard, "I'm Dr. Heller. What's the trouble?"

"Sorry to keep you waiting," says Luisa.

"Hmmm?" he says, scanning her chart.

"I said I was sorry to keep you waiting."

He looks up at her. "Symptoms?" he asks.

"Fever," she says. "Sore throat. Bad cough. I think I have bronchitis."

"*I'm* the doctor," he says, making notations on her chart. He places his stethoscope on her back. "Cough!" he barks.

Luisa coughs as he moves his stethoscope about on her back and then her chest. His movements are all precise and quick, and his touch is firm and cold. He looks into the distance, concentrating. He doesn't look at her.

"It began two weeks ago," Luisa says. "I woke up with a bad sore throat. Three days later I began running a slight fever." She stops. He isn't listening.

"How much pain have you caused your patients by not listening to them?" she asks quietly.

"Hmmm?" He takes a thermometer from a drawer. "Open," he says, angling the thermometer toward her mouth. Luisa pushes it away.

"Listen to me!" she says.

He stops and looks at her, his eyes dark and angry. Their eyes meet. It's a struggle. But Luisa is angry.

"You will slow down and give me a good, thorough examination," she says finally. "You will take your time, pay attention, and explain the reason for each procedure. You will listen to me when I speak. Not only am I older than you and deserving of your respect for no other reason, but I live in this body. I may know something about it that can help you."

The doctor gazes at her, unblinking.

"I'm not just a body with an illness," says Luisa. "I'm a person. You care about my feelings."

"I care about your feelings," he says. He sounds doubtful.

But he continues the examination at a much slower, kinder pace, and Luisa is surprised at how good he is. His cold hands even seem to warm up slightly. But it's clear that he's fighting the impulse to race through the exam and get on to the next patient.

"Why are you in such a hurry?" she asks.

"I have so many patients. I hate to keep them waiting."

"You don't care about that. Tell the truth."

"You've got a fabulous body," he says. "I love older women with big breasts."

"Not about that," she laughs. "Why are you in such a hurry?"

"This way I stay in control."

"What if you aren't in control?"

"I have to be in control."

"Why?"

"I'm the doctor."

"And you're the doctor because you have to stay in control," says Luisa. "Right?"

"Yes," he says. "I do like your eyes. They're . . ."

"What?"

"Calming."

He finishes the examination. "You have bronchitis," he says. "I'm writing you a prescription for 500 mg of ampicillin."

"What would make you listen to your patients?" she asks. "What would make you care?"

"Nothing," he says. He is writing the prescription. "Take this four times daily with plenty of water." He hands it to her and turns toward the door.

"Wait," she says.

He stops. "Take your clothes off," she says. He turns around and stares into her eyes. He begins to unbutton his shirt.

As he removes his clothing, Luisa puts hers back on. By the time he's naked, she's fully clothed. He stands there looking very pale. He has goose bumps. She hands him the hospital garment. He puts it on.

"You will sit here and wait," she says, "until the nurse comes looking for you. You'll see what it's like."

He sits down on the edge of the examination table and sighs.

She pauses at the door. "When the nurse comes, you'll forget about me."

"I'll forget about you." He sounds happy about that.

"But you'll never forget the next half hour."

As Luisa leaves the room, she sees the nurse heading toward her with a clipboard. "Dr. Heller is in the examining room," she tells the nurse. "He asked not to be disturbed for at least a half hour. But he wanted you to explain to the patients who are waiting that there'll be a delay. And to apologize."

"That's new," says the nurse.

"That's right," says Luisa. She meets the nurse's eyes. "Have an interesting day," she says.

Albert Schweitzer

from FIRST SERMON ON REVERENCE FOR LIFE

In an era marked by celebrity-driven fund-raising, Albert Schweitzer's name has become synonymous with sustained humanitarian effort on behalf of others—effort that eschews the limelight for a practical ethics based on help and love. Awarded the Nobel Peace Prize in 1952, Schweitzer is best known for his journeys to Africa, where he practiced medicine and established hospitals; Schweitzer also held degrees in philosophy and theology. In his own time, Schweitzer was regularly featured in magazines like *Time* and *Life*. Today Schweitzer's legacy is less familiar, and, by modern standards, aspects of his life are viewed as suspect by some: his patronizing, if not racist, attitudes toward some of his African patients and the moodiness those who went to work with him sometimes encountered. Perhaps this is all the more reason today to consider the words of one who understood himself only too well, who wrote about his own limits and who struggled to connect thought, word, and deed in his writing and in his service to others.

This excerpt is taken from the first of twelve sermons Schweitzer preached between February and April 1919 in Strasbourg, France, at Saint Nicolai Church. In this sermon Schweitzer first defined his well-known phrase "reverence for life." The subtitle of the sermon is "What Does It Mean to Be Good?"

ALBERT SCHWEITZER'S (1875–1965) Sermons on Reverence for Life were compiled into a book, translated by David Larrimore

Holland, titled *A Place for Revelation*. Schweitzer's 1947 anthology *The Spiritual Life* has recently been reissued.

Desire for knowledge! You may seek to explore everything around you, you may push to the farthest limits of human knowledge, but in the end you will always strike upon something that is unfathomable. It is called life. And this mystery is so inexplicable that it renders the difference between knowledge and ignorance completely relative.

What difference is there between the scholar who observes the smallest and least expected signs of life under a microscope and the old peasant, who can scarcely read and write, when he stands in his garden in the spring and contemplates the blossoms bursting open on the branches of his tree? Both are confronted with the riddle of life! The one can describe it more thoroughly than the other, but for both it is equally inscrutable. All knowledge is finally knowledge of life. All realization is astonishment at this riddle of life—*reverence for life* in its infinite, yet ever new, manifestations. For what does it mean for something to come into being, live, and pass away? How amazing that it renews itself in other existences, passes away again, comes into being once more, and so on and so forth, from infinity to infinity? We can do all things and we can do nothing, for in all our wisdom we are not able to create life. Rather, what we create is dead!

Life means strength, will coming from the abyss and sinking into it again. Life means feeling, sensitivity, suffering. And if you are absorbed in life, if you see with perceptive eyes into this enormous animated chaos of creation, it suddenly seizes you with vertigo. In everything you recognize yourself again. The beetle that lies dead in your path—it was something that lived, that struggled for its existence like you, that rejoiced in the sun like you, that knew anxiety and pain like you. And now it is nothing more than decomposing material—as you, too, shall be sooner or later.

You walk outside and it is snowing. Carelessly you shake the snow from your sleeves. It attracts your attention: a snowflake glistens on your hand. You cannot help looking at it, whether you wish to or not. It glistens in its wonderful design; then it quivers, and the delicate needles of which it consists contract. It is no more; it has melted, dead in your hand. The flake, which fell upon your hand from infinite space, which glistened there, quivered, and died—that is you. Wherever you see life—that is you!

What is this recognition, this knowledge apprehended by the most learned and the most childlike alike? It is reverence for life, reverence for the impenetrable mystery that meets us in our universe, an existence different from ourselves in external appearance, yet inwardly of the same character with us, terribly similar, awesomely related. *The dissimilarity, the strangeness*, between us and other creatures is *here removed.*

Reverence before the infinity of life means the removal of the strangeness, the restoration of shared experiences and of compassion and sympathy. And thus the final result of knowledge is the same, in principle, as that which the commandment to love requires of us. Heart and reason agree together when we desire and dare to be men who attempt to fathom the depths of things.

Rafael Campo

LIKE A PRAYER

Recalling his time as an exhausted intern working through a last, long, in-patient rotation among homeless men with AIDS, physician, poet, and essayist Rafael Campo tells of a harrowing experience on the ward. That experience allows him to realize his capacity for great empathy toward the least among us, while also providing readers with a meditation on the origins of altruism under the most trying of circumstances.

RAFAEL CAMPO, both a teacher and a doctor, works at Harvard Medical School and Boston's Beth Israel Hospital. He has published two books of poetry, *The Other Man Was Me* and *What the Body Told*, and a collection of essays, *The Poetry of Healing*, from which this selection is taken.

As I went about inattentively jotting down his vital signs, and then taking a perfunctory listen to his heart, he entreated me with a voice so raspy from disuse it was almost gentle: "Hey, doc, when you get to church this morning, pray for me." A few soundless moments passed. After I had said nothing in response, he added with the same hoarseness that at higher volume became a surprisingly vicious snarl, "Yeah, you must be a real good fucking Catholic, with a name like that." Now I was annoyed, to have been startled out of my dim reverie, and by such a crass slur. Was he referring to the Latinovoweled surname blazoned on my plastic ID tag, I wondered—or perhaps, I thought with rising contempt, he was familiar with the lesser-known archangel Rafael?

I had simply been trying to get through my tedious daily morning work rounds without a hitch, the hypnotic lines of Madonna's latest hit song, which I had blasted on my car stereo on the way to the county hospital, still pulsing suggestively over and over again in my head: "*Just like a prayer / your voice can take me there / just like a muse to me / you are a mystery . . .*" For the whole of the twenty-minute drive in to work that day, I had kept my car's front windows rolled all the way down to let the bracing wind and all of frivolously sun-drenched San Francisco pour unimpeded into me as I sped down Potrero. But the deepening poverty was too obvious to ignore, the Mission district looking more and more like a destitute Latin American country with each passing block. As a last resort, I tried to make myself admire a few colorfully attired hookers still working their street corners at 6 A.M., the dawn for them meaning not the beginning but the end of yet another day. Anything to bring me outside of myself to some kind of an awakening, to shock me into feeling more a part of the kingdom of the not dying.

I had not even realized that the gorgeous day I wanted so desperately to relish was a Sunday. For me, a dysfunctional intern stumbling through my last in-patient rotation with only randomly and infrequently scheduled days off, each day had grown monotonously more and more indistinguishable from the one before it. Death was inevitable and omnipresent; resurrection was not only impossible but ludicrous. The hushed and somber hospital, whose hermetically sealed neighborhoods of illness and contagion went in house staff parlance by various quasi-celestial nicknames—the busy cancer unit was sarcastically referred to as the Death Star, and the grim and even more crowded AIDS ward was known as the Temple of Doom—had long been my exclusive place of dark worship and forced atonement. If I would have preferred to be in church, it was only because I so despised the hospital.

His nurse entered with a gelatinously floppy bag of IV fluid to hang. According to her, my patient had been babbling incoherently off and on for much of the night, yet I felt how unmistakably and clearly these last few words of his pierced me. *Pray for him?* This patient was a filthy junkie who had bitten another nurse in a squabble over his regular methadone dose; numerous times, I had been paged in the middle of the night and awakened from a precious hour or two of sleep to respond to his incessant demands for other narcotic drugs to treat his "pain," always to arrive to find him resting in apparent comfort amid half-emptied take-out cartons of Chinese food brought in by his rowdy, ponytailed friends. If I could have hoped or prayed for anything, it would have been that he'd be stone-cold dead when I next returned to the ward.

Instead, to my chagrin, each morning he was still there, very much alive and moaning and urinating in his bed, or hurling the occasional intelligible and angry epithet at me. Though nothing was likely to salvage him at this point in his illness, with his terminally low T-cell count of 2, a long history of violence and intravenous drug use, and widespread aggressive lymphoma involving his central nervous system, I was still leery of trying anything new at all—even a begrudged prayer—that might prolong his misery, and thus my own. He was little more than a disgusting chore to me, something akin to mopping up a stubbornly grimy floor. In my view, each new hospitalization he had required, thickening his chart as if only to make it heavier for me to lug back and forth from medical records, was a waste of already scarce public health dollars. This latest crude remark of his was the last straw. I stormed out of his room without even bothering to finish examining him.

By simply going elsewhere in the hospital, however, I could not escape him. I saw versions of him shadily averting their eyes in the elevator, hungrily consuming free food provided by the methadone clinic in the cafeteria, and wildly quarreling in the outdoors smoking area off one of the hospital's main hallways. Wherever I looked, his blunt plea would flood back to me, only to elicit the same reflexive rage. Though one of my intern's strategies for conserving energy was to minimize thinking whenever possible, I found myself obsessively wondering whether I walked around stooped by the heavy burden of some unresolved religious guilt, so that even my most ostensibly faithless and disoriented patients could tell that I was once a Catholic. My hip Ray-Ban sunglasses, my pumping Madonna CDs, my chilling surliness, even my Gay Pride T-shirts worn secretly underneath my scrubs all failed to secularize me sufficiently in the discerning eyes of others. Even through the thick fog of his delirium, somehow he had alighted upon my name.

My name. I locked myself in a windowless staff bathroom, the only place I could think of where I could be completely alone, if the pungent presence of ammonia were ignored. I wondered: What secrets did a name betray? I regarded it from a distance as if for the first time, quietly pronouncing it over and over to myself; undeniably, "Rafael Campo" was as generically Latino as a colorful street festival for a local miracle-working Virgin, but my actual relationship to the Catholic Church was much cooler than my stereotypically churchgoing family's. I was a hard-core outcast for my supposedly sinful life, and no longer even considered myself a member of any faith. It amazed me that a low-life like this patient, who probably had stolen stereos from cars in the hospital staff's parking lot to pay for the heroin he was known to shoot directly into his IVs, could still consider himself among God's children, worthy of a saving prayer. . . .

When that dispicable AIDS patient finally did die, seizing intractably and without my prayers, I was glad, and relished his death over an unappetizing late-night meal with a few of my colleagues in the nearly deserted cafeteria. Still, I knew he would only be succeeded by others.

Sure enough, late one night on call a few days later, I was paged to place an IV in yet another patient with AIDS, one who belonged to an intern for whom I was cross-covering. He was an emaciated young man who had been receiving wide-open fluid resuscitation for dehydration, until he pulled out his first catheter; his veins stood out beneath his yellow skin so clearly that they seemed to beckon me to enter them, so plump that my mouth even watered a little. I prided myself on my ability to obtain intravenous access, so at first I was only mildly annoyed that the nurse had called me to perform what appeared to be so easy a stick. She was probably overworked herself, though when I had arrived an hour or two after her page she seemed to be on a break, and this was one task that could be unquestioningly relegated to a defenseless intern, with the automatic, well-rehearsed apology: "I've tried three times, and I just can't get it."

In a few moments, I had gathered together the necessary supplies in a small heap at the side of his bed: a drape, some sterile gauze, a small syringe filled with saline, a bottle of iodine, a liter bag of normal saline and some clear coiled tubing, a few strips of tape, a rubber tourniquet, the flimsy but requisite pair of latex gloves, and a 16-gauge Angiocath. I had selected such a big needle partly to underscore to his coffee-sipping nurse, without having to say a word, how effortless the job would be for someone competent. The patient remained asleep while I set everything up, the arm I had selected dangling lifelessly off the side of the bed. When I tried to awaken him to explain what I was doing, before I said more than a few words he mumbled, "Just get it over with and get the hell out of my room." Unfazed, I accepted his gruff statement as informed consent and decided by way of retribution not to bother with lidocaine to numb the area. I positioned the gleaming needle at the bifurcation of an especially large vein, which was swollen nicely under the pressure of the tourniquet I had tightened while he still dozed.

As I applied traction with my other gloved hand above the puncture site, I watched intently as the needle pierced the skin delectably, anticipating with confidence the bright flash of red blood in the needle's small reservoir that would indicate that the lumen of the catheter was inside the vein. I marveled at the permission I had to inflict pain, to assault another person with a sharp object under the pretense that I was actually helping him, but knowing that he would be dead soon, just like the rest. I was more surprised than annoyed when no flash occurred, I was perfectly positioned, and the vein was huge. I withdrew and made a second attempt, again with no success. Sweat began to trickle down my brow, and I had to hold his arm down forcefully with the same hand I was using to apply traction to the vein; he was moaning more and more loudly now. A purple hematoma was growing slowly under his skin where I must have nicked the vein, further unpleasant evidence that this was a sentient, living being I was working on, not just the cadaver I foresaw he would become. On the third pass, with my hands visibly trembling, I finally nailed it and, feeling more than a bit relieved, looked away for a moment. I needed to find the syringe I would use to withdraw blood and then flush in a small amount of saline to confirm the patency of my line.

Perhaps it was the strange violation, the unwanted communication of the outside world with so intimate an interior space that aroused him; perhaps it was the pain I knew I caused, but which I so callously, even sadistically, ignored as I focused on my task, that prompted him to react. Before I knew what had happened, he was sitting bolt upright, screaming at the top of his lungs and flailing his arms out in front of him, scattering my neat pile of materials across the floor. I tried to stop him. When the same needle pierced my own skin, my first thought was to deny the literal connection between us, one that emotionally I had been for so long incapable of accepting but that was suddenly as lasting as metal, as pointed as agony. Blood poured out of the hole in his skin so profusely that in seconds the left leg of my scrubs was soaked in it, and I felt the cool slickness against my thigh, perplexed that it did not feel warmer as it was absorbed. I finally came enough to my senses to call out for help and staggered to the door of his room, leaving sticky, bloody sneaker prints behind me, my path in life momentarily made visible by another's suffering.

The look of horror on the nurse's face pulled me across the remaining dimensions through which I had begun to drift, back into the real world. After we had together restrained him enough to apply pressure to the vein and control the bleeding, I went directly to the sink. Both gloves I wore were covered with quickly drying blood, and when I peeled them off, I noticed stonily that the one on my left hand had been pierced through. I washed my hands before looking at them and felt the sting of the antiseptic soap in the middle of the palm of my left hand, the same sinister hand I had used to hold down his arm, the awful hand that had felt the strain of his weakened muscles against me and then the needle's terrible bite. Still afraid to inspect the sore spot, I took my time patting my hands dry and unwillingly noticed flecks of blood on the crumpled white paper as I tossed the used towels in the trash. So I knew. My left hand balled in a fist, I calmly announced to the nurse that I was fine and that I needed to get changed into some clean scrubs, before I exited the room on wobbly legs; she seemed to hover above the dark pool of blood, plump and white and dumb as a dove, and the fact that she said nothing to me made me wonder if she suspected the truth.

The rent in my skin was only two or three millimeters in size, though the small amount of blood that had fanned out in the subcutaneous tissue made a dusky red spot that was alarmingly much bigger, maybe a centimeter or so. I squeezed out whatever blood I could, not knowing whether the drop or two I was able to express was mine or his, or mine mixed with his. I changed my scrub pants in one of the deserted hallways of the labyrinthine OR, the dried blood that had soaked in pulling at the hair on my thigh as I shucked them off, not caring if a stray orderly or scrub nurse happened to spy me undressed: I finally knew how human I was, I was made acutely aware in one terrible moment that all any of us has in the world is the same body. I wanted to pray that I had not been infected, I wanted to believe that a god, any god, had protected me. After I was changed, I found an open utility closet and shut myself in it with the syringes and plastic emesis basins and face masks and blue gauzy hairnets close around me. I stared into the wound in my palm beneath the dim yellow light from a bare bulb, my forsaken faith even more dim; I found that I kept thinking of Christ, with the incongruous and gruesome fact dancing in my mind that in Roman crucifixions the nails were driven not through the palms, as seen in conventional depictions of Christ on the cross, but through the wrists.

I recalled that I had once stuck myself with a needle a few years before, as an inexperienced medical student attempting to draw blood from another patient with AIDS, but that incident had left no mark in my skin, and I had found no hole in the gloves I was wearing. Still, I had been unable to sleep for weeks, and it was several more months before I could even talk about it with anyone. In contrast, what was happening to me in the utility closet felt like an opening, a revelation, a chance for survival; though I certainly would not report to the Needlestick Hotline what had happened to me, perhaps there would be someone else, some higher authority, who would listen to me. Perhaps in the mixing of my blood with another person's, I could learn the true meaning of forgiveness, I could understand human failings, I could begin to fathom how we all share original sin. Perhaps in the possibility of dying of AIDS myself, I could realize finally and fully my capacity for empathy. Perhaps in a prayer, in a poem, in an embrace and a kiss, I could speak again to God.

These days, my version of the physician's "God complex" is to pray secretly at the bedsides of my patients, sometimes thinking myself silly for doing it, but finding it impossible not to do so. Whatever my religion might be—Catholic or Doctor Not of Theology, Queer Sister of Perpetual Indulgence or Undecided—I understand now that one's faith is intensely personal, in the same way each individual has his own hopes and dreams, and that it can be shared not only within the thick walls of churches but also in the open wards of a hospital. In my visions now, the patients who are dying, or who are getting well, all have a place to go; each holds inside and is held by the beating heart and the feverish closeness of his loved ones. Even the most despised and isolated of patients has someone to whom he can turn, one who truly does have the power to heal, a hope that is the source of all poems. The terrifying needlestick is just a reminder, the bearded chaplain on his rounds exudes a kind of comfort, the hideous skin lesion becomes the glorious impact of God's touch. Today I see that the handsome nurse carrying away feces in a bedpan is an angel; the quiet glance we exchange is the meaning of life.

Cortney Davis

THE BODY FLUTE

Throughout the centuries, it has been the nurse's role to attend to the dying and prepare their bodies for the hospital morgue. Sometimes alone, often with families in attendance, the nurse has the opportunity to glimpse the secret moments just before and just after death, moments eloquently detailed in this poem, moments that underscore the need for acting "with integrity, honesty, . . . and respect for the dignity of patients as persons."

CORTNEY DAVIS is a nurse practitioner. Her poems have been published in *Calyx, Hudson Review, Ms., Crazyhorse,* the *Journal of the American Medical Association*, and *Literature and Medicine.* She is the recipient of a 1994 National Endowment for the Arts Fellowship in poetry and two poetry grants from the Connecticut Commission on the Arts. She is co-editor, with Judy Schaefer, of *Between the Heartbeats: Poetry and Prose by Nurses*, from which this poem is taken.

I go on loving the flesh
after you die.
I close your eyes
bathe your bruised limbs
press down the edges of tape
sealing your dry wounds.

I walk with you to the morgue
and pillow your head
against the metal drawer. To me
this is your final resting place.
Your time with me
is the sum of your life.

I have met your husbands and wives
but I know who loved you most,
who owned the sum
of your visible parts.
The doctor and his theory
never owned you.

Nor did "medicine" or "hospital"
ever own you.
Couldn't you, didn't you
refuse tests, refuse to take your medicine?
But I am the nurse
of childhood's sounds in the night,

nurse of the washrag's sting
nurse of needle and sleep
nurse of lotion and hands on skin
nurse of sheets and nightmares
nurse of the flashlight beam at 3 A.M.

I know the privacy of vagina and rectum
I slip catheters into openings
I clean you like a mother does.

That which you allow no one,
you allow me.

Who sat with you that night?
Your doctor was asleep,

your husband was driving in.
Your wife took a few things

home to wash, poor timing,
but she had been by your side for days.

Your kids? They could be anywhere,
even out with the vending machines

working out just how much
you did or didn't do for them.

You waited
until you were alone
with me. You trusted

that I could wait and not be
frightened away.
That I would not expect

anything of you—
not bravery or anger, not even
a good fight.

At death
you become wholly mine.

Your last glance, your last
sensation of touch,
your breath

I inhale, incorporating you
into memory.
Your body

silvery and still on the bed
your lips fluttering into blue.
I pull your hand away from mine.

My other hand lingers, traces
your finger from the knucklebone
to the sheets

into which your body sinks,
my lips over yours,
my cheek near the blue

absence of your breath,
my hands closing
the silver stops of your eyelids.

Jerome Lowenstein

CAN YOU TEACH COMPASSION?

Reflecting on his medical education, the intern in this essay bitterly notes, "I don't know if you can teach compassion, but you surely can teach the opposite!" Jerome Lowenstein's eloquent essay answers the question posed by its title in the affirmative, explaining the importance of "a dedicated, self-conscious effort" on the part of medical educators to nurture humanistic qualities that "cannot be achieved by a chance remark on rounds or even by role modeling."

JEROME LOWENSTEIN is a professor of medicine and co-director of the hypertension and renal disease section at New York University Medical Center. This essay comes from his collection titled *The Midnight Meal.*

In one of our Humanistic Medicine seminars, the small group of medical students, interns, and residents was challenged to respond to the question, Do you think we can teach you compassion? After an uncomfortably long pause, an intern said in a voice that seemed to convey both anger and shame, "I don't know if you can teach compassion, but you surely can teach the opposite!" He was referring to a phenomenon that is well known in the development of medical students and house staff. At a minimum, it might be termed "hardening," a *learned* insensitivity to the pain and suffering and the needs of patients. At its worst it is seen as a dehumanization of patients who are referred to, in order of decreasing humanity, as "MIs," "hits," "crocks," "gomers," and "shpozes." This process, which Robert Jay Lifton has described as "psychic numbing," occurs with remarkable speed, often within the first one or two years of clinical training. The regularity with which this desensitization occurs challenges the notion, which I have often heard expressed, that one cannot change the behavior and attitudes of young men and women already in their middle twenties.

The question is not whether we *can* teach compassion but rather whether we will teach compassion or its opposite. I have heard students being taught the opposite of compassion. Some house staff caution naive medical students against "becoming too involved" with certain patients or counsel that "time spent with the books" will get them further than learning more about any single patient. Academic success and recognition seem to go to the stronger and faster. Early in their training, medical students are troubled by the realization that many of the angry and embittered physicians they see as house staff or attending physicians on the hospital wards stood in their places only a few years earlier.

Why are we faced, at this time, with these questions about teaching compassion? Compassion, empathy, respect for the uniqueness of others are behaviors and values that have always been regarded as the very qualities that lead young men and women to enter the field of medicine. They were never taught, as such, but rather were nurtured and reinforced by prolonged contact with teachers who served as role models, and with patients. As the pace of medicine has accelerated in the second half of the twentieth century, the slow educational process by which physicians "learned compassion" suffered. Physicians today, in their roles as teachers, complain that they feel overburdened by their responsibilities for the care of patients whose illnesses are complex and often require the expertise of teams of specialists. Many physicians are intimidated by the very large body of knowledge they must master and transmit to students and house officers. One way of coping with these very understandable feelings is to narrow one's focus, to deal with only that part of the disease one knows best and leave the rest to others with different areas of expertise. This does not work well in the care of patients, nor does it make for good teaching or role modeling. To focus on a specific problem, no matter how important or interesting, it is usually necessary to direct attention away from the patient, where all problems intersect.

If it be granted that it is possible and necessary to teach compassion, where is the time and where is the place? My response is a personal and perhaps idiosyncratic one. It requires some explanation. For many years I have taken pride in my ability to teach students and house staff. I try to approach clinical problems from the point of understanding the underlying pathophysiology; I feel that pathophysiology provides a solid underpinning for differential diagnosis, provides a sound direction for treatment, and is instructive for students and house staff. In recent years, on a busy teaching service, I found little time to explore with students or house staff issues related to the lives of patients that were presented to me on daily rounds. Patients' understanding of their illnesses or their responses rarely found a place in my daily teaching rounds. Was this because I felt these issues were unimportant or unrelated to the care of patients? Certainly not. I felt that I was coping as well as I could with the time pressures of teaching on an active medical service. Looking back on this time, however, I now recognize that another subliminal factor was responsible for my ordering of priorities. I recall that, as a student and house officer, my role models among attending physicians were familiar with all the recent medical literature; they challenged us to understand complex pathophysiology. The attending physicians whom I and my peers tried to avoid, if any excuse could be found, tended to fill our teaching sessions or rounds with anecdotes and platitudes about patients. I will never be able to accurately reconstruct what they were trying to teach, but I realize now that when I became an attending physician I felt a deep discomfort, during my rounds, whenever I heard myself deviating from the image of one of my rigorous scientific role models.

I was keenly aware that an important element of medical education was not being addressed, by me or by many of my colleagues. I found myself quite comfortable discussing with students and house staff their experiences and responses to patients as well as my own observations, feelings, pleasures, and discomforts in physician-patient interactions in our weekly Humanistic Medicine small-group meetings with medical students and house staff. Yet despite my involvement in the Humanistic Medicine Program, it was rare that I would raise one of these issues on daily morning rounds. I restricted these discussions to our afternoon small-group meetings, although the meetings were with the same group of students and house staff! Two or three years ago, as an experiment, I decided to integrate my "afternoon" style into my morning attending rounds. This was not exactly a planned or deliberate step. I found myself increasingly uncomfortable with the manner in which our students and house staff glossed over critical information in their daily morning case presentations. Patients were described, in a word, as "homeless," "undomiciled," "an IVDA," or "a shooter." The traditional presentation of the patient's social history was frequently no more than a recitation of how much the patient smoked and whether the patient used drugs or alcohol and in which form. The most streamlined case presentations boiled this information down to a simple formula, "*x* pack-years, *y* bags, and *z* quarts daily." I remember vividly the first morning when I interrupted an intern in the middle of his opening sentence, "This is the first hospital admission of this thirty-five-year-old IVDA . . ." I asked, "Would our thinking or care be different if you began your history by telling us that this is a thirty-five-year-old Marine veteran who has been addicted to drugs since he served, with valor, in Vietnam?" There was an embarrassed hush. As I left the ward later that morning, I reflected that the few minutes taken up by my question might have been my most important contribution of the day, possibly more instructive than my comments about pneumocystis pneumonia, arterial oxygen saturation, or respiratory alkalosis. I have continued to insist that patients be "personalized" in case presentations and find that I have been able to integrate details about patients' perceptions, responses, and needs without sacrificing attention to other aspects of clinical medicine. I am no less rigorous in my analysis of clinical data, nor has my interest in pathophysiology waned. The response of students and house staff reassure me that I have not crossed over to "anecdotes and platitudes." I have come to believe that the time and place to teach compassion are the time and place in which all of the rest of medicine is taught.

If we are to preserve and nourish humanistic values in medicine, if we are to teach compassion, it would seem to me that the process must begin with a clear recognition that this is the responsibility of the faculty who teach medical students and young physicians. It would be tragic if humanistic medicine were to become "alternative medicine" or a subject—worse yet, an elective subject—in the curriculum. The presentation of courses on the history of medicine and on humanism in literature has provided a forum for emphasizing the importance of the patient's narrative and for examining characters presented by

Thomas Mann, Lev Tolstoy, and Aleksandr Solzhenitsyn, patients described by Oliver Sachs, and the ways in which illness transforms people's lives. These courses engage ethicists, sociologists, and talented educators from other fields in teaching medicine, but the presentation of such important concepts as "small museum pieces," to my mind, falls short of the real need in medicine today. If "teaching compassion" is a part of teaching medicine, it should be the responsibility of all those who teach clinical medicine. I am sure that there are faculty who would reject the notion that "teaching compassion" is their responsibility. I would view them in the same way I view a teacher of medicine who rejects the idea of teaching physical diagnosis or pathophysiology. This person might be a gifted and valuable teacher, but this outlook is a distinct limitation. As Hashim Khan, a legendary squash player and teacher, wrote, "I once knew a man who played the piano with gloves. He played well, for a man with gloves on."

Kirsten Emmott

1852: J. MARION SIMS PERFECTS A REPAIR FOR VESICOVAGINAL FISTULA

A procedure is perfected and quality of life is improved. The inventor is celebrated, but is the victory worth its price? While documenting a period when surgery was a crude art at best, this historically accurate piece challenges readers to see a side of advancement in medicine often ignored. Kirsten Emmott's poem raises the question of means and ends, and underscores the vital importance of three words in the definition for altruism offered in this anthology: "at *all* times."

KIRSTEN EMMOTT is a general practitioner in British Columbia. This poem is from her collection of poetry *How Do You Feel?* Another poem from her collection, titled "Unwed," appears later in this anthology.

We're slaves, the three of us,
useless now to Master since our troubles;
he gave us to Doctor to try to fix us.

When I lay in labor so long,
I cried to the midwife, save my baby,
just one to keep, so many sold away from me—
but baby he died anyway
after being held fast inside so long.
Doctor said his head wore through my passage
into my water passage.
That's why I drip all day long
out my woman passage—
like a baby, I wear clouts,
I stink, no man want me.
Master say get out the house,
stay in the yard, the field—

Anarcha and Lucy the same,
hurt having Master's babies,
the babies die and they torn for life.
Our cabin stink of piss, our clouts hang to dry
all over the place.

Doctor cut us so many times,
sew us this way, sew us that way,
but the stitches don't take.
Three days later the water and blood
drip out together.
We still torn, we still drip.
Doctor cut Anarcha thirteen times and she still drip.

Maybe all this cuttin' help somebody some day.
I don't know, I got no say.

He gets four strong field hands
to hold me down, kneeling.
He don't say nothin' to me.
I hear him behind me, I hear the knives.
Ain't no use to scream or fight,
"Shut up, gal," and a hand over the mouth—
he puts those spoon things in me,
then he cuts me inside—I feel the blood
runnin' down my legs to the floor—
then he picks up the curved needles—
and it goes on and on
till I pass out.

Fever's right bad the next day always
but we got to sit up and sew.
We too useless for other work.

We sleep side by side on the cabin floor—
no sense wastin' straw on us, we'd need
new pallets every day.
We be better off dead, I cry.
Lucy say no, pray to Jesus and we be healed,
but what Jesus ever done for me?
Anarcha say she cry every time Doctor say to her,
get ready, tomorrow.
He got an idea to sew her up with silver wire,
say this time it work for sure.

Jesus, you a man,
you never said woman made for this,
a field to be sowed with wire
over and over until she bears.
Ain't we done enough bearing?
Jesus?

Robert Jay Lifton
from THE NAZI DOCTORS

This selection exemplifies the horrific antithesis of altruism. Psychiatrist Robert Jay Lifton methodically traces the chilling development of a particular "logic" during the early years of the Third Reich, one that eclipsed "ethical and beneficent medical care" by designating some human beings as "life unworthy of life," burdens on the state, and "human ballast," subject to systematic destruction under the watchful eyes of the German medical community and Adolf Hitler himself. The development of "mercy killing" in Nazi Germany serves as indisputable evidence for insistence that physicians be altruistic "at all times."

Lest the need for such persistent vigilance be questioned, an item in the *New York Times* dated August 26, 2001, noted that Johns Hopkins University was under federal investigation for its oversight of a "study" using "healthy children to test different methods of lead abatement in cheap inner-city rental housing." The *Times* noted that the Maryland Court of Appeals "compared the research to Nazi medical experimentation and the infamous Tuskegee syphilis study."

"The fact that there could be relatively ordinary doctors who killed," Lifton notes, "tells us much about the broad susceptibility of unremarkable men to become killers."

ROBERT JAY LIFTON is Distinguished Professor of Psychiatry and Psychology at John Jay College and the Graduate Center of the City University of New York. He received the National Book Award for his book *Death in Life*.

Hitler had an intense interest in direct medical killing. His first known expression of intention to eliminate the "incurably ill" was made to Dr. Gerhard Wagner at the Nuremberg Party rally of 1935. Karl Brandt, who overhead that remark, later testified that Hitler thought that the demands and upheavals of war would mute expected religious opposition and enable such a project to be implemented smoothly. Hitler was also said to have stated that a war effort requires a very healthy people, and that the generally diminished sense of the value of human life during war made it "the best time for the elimination of the incurably ill." And he was reportedly affected by the burden imposed by the mentally ill not only on relatives and the general population but on the medical profession. In 1936, Wagner held discussions with "a small circle of friends" (specifically, high-ranking officials, some of them doctors) about killing "idiotic children" and "mentally ill" people, and making films in "asylums and idiot homes" to demonstrate the misery of their lives. This theoretical and tactical linking of war to direct medical killing was maintained throughout.[1]

By 1938, the process had gone much further. Discussions moved beyond high-level political circles; and at a national meeting of leading government psychiatrists and administrators, an SS officer gave a talk in which he stated that "the solution of the problem of the mentally ill becomes easy if one eliminates these people."[2]

Toward the end of 1938, the Nazi regime was receiving requests from relatives of newborns or very young infants with severe deformities and brain damage for the granting of a mercy killing.[3] These requests had obviously been encouraged, and were channeled directly to the Chancellery—that is, to Hitler's personal office. Whatever the plans for using war as a cover, the program for killing children was well under way by the time the war began. And from the beginning, this program circumvented ordinary administrative channels and was associated directly with Hitler himself.

The occasion for initiating the actual killing of children, and of the entire "euthanasia" project, was the petition for the "mercy killing" (*Gnadentod*, really "mercy death") of an infant named Knauer, born blind, with one leg and part of one arm missing, and apparently an "idiot." Subsequent recollections varied concerning who had made the petition and the extent of the deformity, as the case quickly became mythologized.*

In the late 1938 or early 1939, Hitler ordered Karl Brandt, his personal physician and close confidant, to go to the clinic at the University of Leipzig, where the child was hospitalized, in order to determine whether the information submitted was accurate and to consult with physicians there: "If the facts given by the father were correct, I was to inform the physicians in [Hitler's] name that they could carry out euthanasia." Brandt was also empowered to tell those physicians that any legal proceedings against them would be quashed by order of Hitler.[4]

Brandt reported that the doctors were of the opinion "that there was no justification for keeping [such a child] alive"; and he added (in his testimony at the Nuremberg Medical Trial) that "it was pointed out [presumably by the doctors he spoke to] that in maternity wards in some circumstances it is quite natural for the doctors themselves to perform euthanasia in such a case without anything further being said about it." The doctor with whom he mainly consulted was Professor Werner Catel, head of the Leipzig pediatrics clinic and a man who was soon to assume a leading role in the project. All was to be understood as a responsible medical process, so that—as Brandt claimed was Hitler's concern—"the parents should not have the impression that they themselves were responsible for the death of this child."[5] On returning to Berlin, Brandt was authorized by Hitler, who did not want to be publicly identified with the project, to proceed in the same way in similar cases: that is, to formalize a program with the help of the high-ranking Reich leader Philip Bouhler, chief of Hitler's Chancellery. This "test case" was pivotal for the two killing programs—of children and of adults. . . .

---

*Hans Hefelmann, chief of the responsible Chancellery office, remembered that the child lacked three limbs and that its grandmother made the request. Brandt made the father the petitioner.

It seemed easier—perhaps more "natural" and at least less "unnatural"—to begin with the very young: first, newborns; then, children up to three and four; then older ones. Similarly, the authorization—at first, oral and secret and to be "kept in a very narrow scope, and cover only the most serious cases"—was later to become loose, extensive, and increasingly known. A small group of doctors and Chancellery officials held discussions in which they laid out some of the ground rules for the project. Then a group of medical consultants known to have a "positive" attitude to the project was assembled, including administrators, pediatricians, and psychiatrists.[6]. . .

Falsification, then was in the service of medical claim. Everyone proceeded *as if* these children were to receive the blessings of medical science, were to be healed rather than killed. The falsification was clearly intended to deceive—the children's families, the children themselves when old enough, and the general public. But it also served psychological needs of the killers in literally expressing the Nazi reversal of healing and killing. For example, a doctor could tell a parent that "it might be necessary to perform a surgical operation that could possibly have an unfavorable result," or explain that "the ordinary therapy employed until now could no longer help their child so that extraordinary therapeutic measures have to be taken." Dr. Heinze, who used such phrases with parents, explained in court testimony that there had been truth to what he said: "A very excitable child . . . completely idiotic . . . could not be kept quiet with the normal dose of sedatives," so that "an overdose . . . had to be used in order to . . . avoid endangering itself through its own restlessness." At the same time, "we physicians know that such an overdose of a sedative, for children usually luminal . . . could cause pneumonia, . . . and that this is virtually incurable."[7] It is quite possible that Dr. Heinze not *only* was consciously lying, but was enabled by the medicalization of the murders partly to deceive himself: to come to believe, at least at moments, that the children were being given some form of therapy, and that their deaths were due to their own abnormality.

In the same spirit, the policy was to gain "consent" from the parents for the transfer. Those who showed reluctance to give that consent received letters emphasizing the seriousness and permanence of their child's disability, telling them that they "should be grateful" that there were available for children thus affected by fate facilities where "the best and most efficacious treatment is available," and then declaring that "neither a delay nor a cancellation of the transfer is possible." Should the parents continue to oppose it, "further steps, such as withdrawal of your guardianship, will have to be taken."[8] This threat to take away legal guardianship usually sufficed, but if it did not there could be the further threat of calling a parent up for special labor duty. The coercion here was in the service not only of the killing policy itself but also of maintaining its medical structure.

That structure served to diffuse individual responsibility. In the entire sequence—from the reporting of cases by midwives or doctors, to the supervision of such reporting by institutional heads, to expert opinions rendered by central consultants, to coordination of the marked forms by Health Ministry officials, to the appearance of the child at the Reich Committee institution for killing—there was at no point a sense of personal responsibility for, or even involvement in, the murder of another human being. Each participant could feel like no more than a small cog in a vast, officially sanctioned, medical machine.

Before being killed, children were generally kept for a few weeks in the institution in order to convey the impression that they were being given some form of medical therapy. The killing was usually arranged by the director of the institution or by the another doctor working under him, frequently by innuendo rather than specific order. It was generally done by means of luminal tables dissolved in liquid, such as tea, given to the child to drink. This sedative was given repeatedly—often in the morning and at night—over two or three days, until the child lapsed into continuous sleep. The luminal dose could be increased until the child went into coma and died. For children who had difficulty drinking, luminal was sometimes injected. If the luminal did not kill the child quickly enough—as happened with excitable children who developed considerable tolerance for the drug because of having been given so much of it—a fatal morphine-scopolamine injection was given. The cause of death was listed as a more or less ordinary disease such as pneumonia, which could even have the kind of kernel of truth we have noted.[9]

The institutional doctor, then, was at the killing edge of the medical structure, whatever the regime's assurance that the state took full responsibility. Yet he developed—in fact, cultivated—the sense that, as an agent of the state, he was powerless: from his vantage point, as one such doctor reported, "these children were already marked for killing on their transfer reports," so that "I did not even bother to examine them." Indeed, whatever examination he performed was no more than a formality, since he did not have the authority to question the definitive judgment of the three-man panel of experts.

Yet later, program administrators countered with the insistence that "the if, when, and how of carrying out a mercy death is up to the judgment of the doctor in charge, who voluntarily and out of conviction agrees to euthanasia and its implementation. It is a 'can' and not a 'must' order."[10] They even claimed that, in some situations, there were no expert opinions at all and the decision about whether to kill a child was left to the discretion of the institutional doctor. To be sure, this kind of later legal testimony was put forward by the program's organizers in order to deny or minimize their own responsibility. But that evasion of responsibility from the top can be said to have been built into the project: the institutional doctor's role as triggerman was a way of investing the actual killing with a "medical responsibility" that was at least partially his. And the contradictory legal status of the "euthanasia" program—a *de facto* law that was not a law—added to the confusion and contradiction surrounding the question of anyone's responsibility.

Inevitably, there was great slippage in whatever discipline originally prevailed—broadening the killing net and fulfilling the regime's ultimate purposes. As the age limit of children included moved upward, it came to include a large of older children and adolescents and even at times overlapped with the adult killing project. Conditions considered a basis for killing also expanded and came to include mongolism (not listed at the beginning) as well as various borderline or limited impairments in children of different ages, culminating in the killing of those designated as juvenile delinquents. Jewish children could be placed in the net primarily because they were Jewish; and at one of the institutions, a special department was set up for "minor Jewish-Aryan half-breeds (*Mischlinge*).

After 1941, the year Hitler officially ordered the general "euthanasia" project terminated, the killing of children continued, indeed probably increased, and was conducted still more haphazardly. It is estimated that five thousand children were killed—but the total was probably much higher if we include the "wild euthanasia" period.[11]

The resistance to children's euthanasia came mostly from families of children killed or threatened with death, later from Catholic and Protestant clergy, and to a lesser extent from within certain medical circles. Certain forms of resistance from within the children's project are worth mentioning here, if only because they were so limited. There were many attempts—it is hard to say how many—on the part of doctors either to avoid diagnoses on children that they knew would lead directly to death, or to arrange to release children from institutions before they were swallowed up by the killing machinery. A Dr. Möckel at Wiesloch is reported to have refused an appointment as chief of a children's section because he claimed to be "too weak" for the implementation of the Reich Committee's program. And there were other reports of high-ranking doctors in certain areas responsible for appointments to these institutions holding back on those appointments because of the claim that candidates were too young and inexperienced. One doctor who had been extremely active as an expert consultant in the adult program refused to kill nine of the twelve children sent to the children's unit he became chief of because, as he put it, "a therapeutic and nursing institution is not the right place for such measures." And there is a report of a nurse who refused to take part in killings of children because she felt herself becoming "hysterical" from the "mental strain."[12] In general, there was probably considerably less medical resistance to the killing of children than to the killing of adults.

NOTES

1. Testimony of Professor Böhm, 12 July 1961. Heyde Trial, pp. 41–42. Also named in the 1936 discussions were Dr. Walter Gross of the Office of Racial Politics and Minister-Director Walter Schultze.
2. Testimony of Otto Mauthe, 20 December 1961, Heyde Trial, pp. 42–43.
3. Brandt testimony, 4 February 1947, *Nuremberg Medical Case*, transcript, pp. 2409–10, and vol. I. p. 894; also in Heyde Trial, pp. 51–52. See also Lothar Gruchmann, "Euthanasie und Justiz im Dritten Reich," *Vierteljahrshefte für Zeitgeschichte* 20 (1972): 238–39, on general euthanasia requests involving the incurably ill during 1938–39; in the absence of a law they were directed to Hitler's Chancellery.
4. Brandt testimony, *Nuremberg Medical Case,* transcript. See also Hans Hefelmann's account, 31 August and 7–14 November 1960, Heyde Trial, pp. 48–51, 53–54; and Gruchmann, "Euthanasie und Justiz," pp. 240–41.
5. Brandt transcript, *Nuremberg Medical Case,* transcript, p. 2410.
6. Heyde Trial pp. 53–54.
7. Heinze testimony, 27 September 1961, Heyde Trial, pp. 150–51.

8. Sample letter to parents, 30 September 1941, Heyde Trial, p. 111; see pp. 100–16.
9. Testimony of Dr. Valentin Faltlhauser, 22–23 April 1948; and Nurse Mina Wörle, 7 May 1948 (Kaufbeuren asylum), Heyde Trial, pp. 143–47.
10. Hefelmann testimony, 7–14 November 1960, Heyde Trial, p. 123.
11. On the broadening of categories, see Heyde Trial, pp. 82–90, 131–34.
12. Ibid., pp. 165–72.

Lawrence Grouse

THE LIE

Today we are far removed from the days when doctors and families colluded to keep diagnoses from patients. Yet, in everyday practice, those in the health care professions are presented with numerous occasions to turn from the direct question, to keep doubts to oneself, or to ponder the odd lab result without mention to the patient. What does it mean to give patients or families information that might corrode hope when hope is all that they have? Are honesty and integrity absolutes? "The Lie" examines these questions and others, not offering answers but revealing the complexity involved in acting with honesty and integrity.

LAWRENCE GROUSE created the *Journal of the American Medical Association*'s (*JAMA*) column "A Piece of My Mind" in 1979, and originally wrote this piece for it. Today he is in the departments of medicine and neurology at the University of Washington School of Medicine.

Annie is from New Hampshire and came here to the foothills of the Blue Ridge Mountains for the horse show. The nurses and I carry her from the car into the emergency room and gently place her on the gurney. She was kicked in the abdomen by her horse and lay in a field for over an hour until friends found her and brought her to the hospital. Even though I am working in the emergency room of a small hospital, I am confident. The nurses know their jobs. Faced with a serious surgical problem, we work well together.

Within a few minutes we have inserted two IV's, one in a forearm vein, another in the external jugular; her blood pressure, however, remains marginal. The fluid from the abdominal tap is grossly bloody and so is her urine. Annie remains calm. Her serious eyes are piercing; I hold her hand to reassure her, but also to take her pulse. She is bleeding very rapidly into her abdomen. Nothing I do seems to help, and I am scared. She is in shock, yet she converses politely and inquires about her condition.

"Thank you for helping me," she says. "Really, it wasn't the horse's fault!"

"We're not worried about the horse, Annie," I say. "The horse is fine."

"Is it a serious injury?" She pauses. "Will I live?"

"Everything will work out, Annie," I tell her. "It may be a little rough for a bit, but it will work out."

"Are you sure?" she asks, gazing steadily at me. "Please, tell me honestly."

I don't answer for a moment. I look at her. I am already fond of her and I do not want to lie. I squeeze her hand and smile. I am unsure how she will do, but I say, "Yes, I'm sure."

After a third IV is in place, her blood pressure stabilizes. The general surgeon and the urologist arrive and plan their emergency workup and exploratory surgery. I breathe a sign of relief as they take charge of her care. Suddenly, we find that the door to the surgical suite in the emergency room has been inadvertently locked and the head nurse's key won't open it. Annie and a nurse are locked inside. There is a great deal of key rattling and doorknob shaking. The pitch of people's voices starts to rise. I break into a sweat. The head nurse yells orders into the telephone and almost immediately three burly maintenance men with crowbars appear.

"Get rid of that door! Now!" the head nurse bellows.

The door is splintered in twenty seconds. Annie is laughing, tells us not to worry, tells us that she is fine. She thinks it is the funniest scene ever.

At surgery, we find that Annie has a severely lacerated liver and a ruptured kidney. The liver is repaired; the kidney is removed, but when I wake up the next morning and look in on Annie, disseminated intravascular coagulation has developed and she is receiving heparin. Four nurses and two physicians have already given blood for her. The intensive care unit hosts a steady stream of staff who have helped Annie and who come by with a few encouraging words. Her parents have arrived. Annie's father is a college professor: a tall, angular man, feeling frightened and out of place. Annie's mother is a small woman with delicate features. The surgeon's wife accompanies them. By the following day, when I leave the hospital after my weekend shift, several of the staff, including the head nurse, have each given two units of blood for Annie.

Two weeks later—during my next shift—I am waylaid and hugged by a happy and ambulatory Annie.

"Everyone here has been so good to me," Annie beams.

As we sit over a cup of coffee, her parents timidly inquire whether Annie might have been close to death on her arrival at the hospital. I can't help bragging about treating Annie in the emergency room. As I launch into the story, I find that Annie remembers it all, and she chimes in with an exact rendition of our entire conversation on the day of the accident. I am amazed! She was in shock, and still she remembers every word I said. I finish my story with a flourish. "When I found that you had abdominal bleeding and I still couldn't bring up your blood pressure with two IV's, I have to admit that I thought you were a goner."

Annie seems shocked to hear this. She looks at me angrily and says, "Don't you remember? You said you were sure I would live. I remembered that promise all the time! I put a great deal of weight on what you said, and you . . ." Suddenly, for the first time since the accident, and to everyone's surprise, tears are in her eyes and she is weeping; she is inconsolable because I lied to her.

Walt Whitman

THE WOUND DRESSER

from Leaves of Grass

At the outbreak of the Civil War, the distinguished American poet Walt Whitman was writing freelance journalism and visiting the wounded in New York–area hospitals. In December 1862 he traveled to Washington, D.C., to take care of his brother, who had been wounded in the war. In Washington, Whitman was overwhelmed by the suffering of so many young men; he decided to stay and attend the wounded and dying.

Through he first brought out his collection of poems, titled *Leaves of Grass*, in 1855, Whitman continued to revise it, adding poems across a span of more than thirty years. This section, taken from the book's final edition of 1891–92, describes the wounds Whitman dresses and the suffering he sees as he threads his way through the hospitals, trying to "pacify with soothing hand" the many men mortally wounded in the Civil War.

WALT WHITMAN (1819–1892) published at least six editions of *Leaves of Grass* between 1855 and 1891.

1

An old man bending I come among new faces,
Years looking backward resuming in answer to children,
Come tell us old man, as from young men and maidens that love me,
(Arous'd and angry, I'd thought to bear the alarum, and urge relentless war,
But soon my fingers fail'd me, my face droop'd and I resign'd myself,
To sit by the wounded and soothe them, or silently watch the dead;)
Years hence of these scenes, of these furious passions, these chances,
Of unsurpass'd heroes, (was one side so brave? the other was equally brave;)
Now be witness again, paint the mightiest armies of earth,
Of those armies so rapid so wondrous what saw you to tell us?
What stays with you latest and deepest? of curious panics,
Of hard-fought engagements or sieges tremendous what deepest remains?

2

O maidens and young men I love and that love me,
What you ask of my days those the strangest and sudden your talking
recalls,
Soldier alert I arrive after a long march cover'd with sweat and dust,
In the nick of time I come, plunge in the fight, loudly shout in the rush of
successful charge,
Enter the captur'd works—yet lo, like a swift-running river they fade,
Pass and are gone they fade—I dwell not on soldiers' perils or soldier's
joys,
(Both I remember well—many the hardships, few the joys, yet I was
content.)

But in silence, in dreams' projections,
While the world of gain and appearance and mirth goes on,
So soon what is over forgotten, and waves wash the imprints off the sand,
With hinged knees returning I enter the doors, (while for you up there,
Whoever you are, follow without noise and be of strong heart.)

Bearing the bandages, water and sponge,
Straight and swift to my wounded I go,

Where they lie on the ground after the battle brought in,
Where their priceless blood reddens the grass the ground,
Or to the rows of the hospital tent, or under the roof'd hospital,
To the long rows of cots up and down each side I return,
To each and all one after another I draw near, not one do I miss,
An attendant follows holding a tray, he carries a refuse pail,
Soon to be fill'd with clotted rags and blood, emptied, and fill'd again.

I onward go, I stop,
With hinged knees and steady hand to dress wounds,
I am firm with each, the pangs are sharp yet unavoidable,
One turns to me his appealing eyes—poor boy! I never knew you,
Yet I think I could not refuse this moment to die for you, if that would
save you.

3

On, on I go, (open doors of time! open hospital doors!)
The crush'd head I dress, (poor crazed hand tear not the bandage away,)
The neck of the cavalry-man with the bullet through and through I
examine,
Hard the breathing rattles, quite glazed already the eye, yet life struggles
hard,
(Come sweet death! be persuaded O beautiful death!
In mercy come quickly.)

From the stump of the arm, the amputated hand,
I undo the clotted lint, remove the slough, wash off the matter and blood,
Back on his pillow the soldier bends with curv'd neck and side-falling head,
His eyes are closed, his face is pale, he dares not look on the bloody stump,
And has not yet look'd on it.

I dress a wound in the side, deep, deep,
But a day or two more, for see the frame all wasted and sinking,
And the yellow-blue countenance see.

I dress the perforated shoulder, the foot with the bullet-wound,
Cleanse the one with a gnawing and putrid gangrene, so sickening, so
offensive,
While the attendant stands behind aside me holding the tray and pail.

I am faithful, I do not give out,
The fractur'd thigh, the knee, the wound in the abdomen,
These and more I dress with impassive hand, (yet deep in my breast a fire,
a burning flame.)

4

Thus in silence in dreams' projections,
Returning, resuming, I thread my way through the hospitals,
The hurt and wounded I pacify with soothing hand,
I sit by the restless all the dark night, some are so young,
Some suffer so much, I recall the experience sweet and sad,
(Many a soldier's loving arms about this neck have cross'd and rested,
Many a soldier's kiss dwells on these bearded lips.)

Susan Onthank Mates

THE GOOD DOCTOR

Helen van Horne is the essence of what it means to be a good doctor and a doctor who is good. Chairperson of Medicine at City Hospital in the Bronx, she is on the ward at 5 A.M. and at 11 P.M., helping and overseeing everywhere, dedicating herself to patients and students alike.

What unfolds in this story, then, is all the more shocking—and instructive—as readers are asked to ponder how such a good doctor could go so terribly awry. Susan Onthank Mates's complex, disturbing story offers a rich exploration of basic human need, lofty altruism, and the double standard that lies just beneath the surface within the patriarchal culture of medicine.

SUSAN ONTHANK MATES, a former concert violinist, is now a practicing physician and writer living in Barrington, Rhode Island. "The Good Doctor" was the winner of the 1994 John Simmons Short Fiction Award.

Some years ago, during a winter that drove even the thieves and addicts indoors, Helen van Horne arrived to run the medicine department at City Hospital. Born in Wisconsin and just returned from Africa, she expected to feel at home in the South Bronx.

"Why," she asked Diana, as they rounded on the men's ward after a meeting of the community board, "do they hate me, so soon?"

"You look very clean," said Diana kindly. "Your blouses are always white." She didn't add, you are so pale, your blue eyes so light they seem a disfigurement. Diana Figueroa was the medical chief resident for the year.

"Are you married?" asked Helen, noticing the gold band on Diana's smooth brown finger.

"Yes," said Diana, and Helen imagined a home, two children, and a swing set. When Helen chose medical school, the act implied spinsterhood. Aware of her attractiveness, she tried but found herself unable to offer the standard plea for forgiveness: my patients, my students will be my children. Instead, she swept behind the patients who disapproved, the wedded college classmates, the condescending but lecherous professors, in the dust of her flight to Africa.

"What does your husband do?" she asked Diana.

"He said he wanted to be a lawyer." Diana finished writing in a chart, signed her name, and handed it to Helen.

"Oh," said Helen. "I suppose one of you might have to work part time." She tried to imagine herself, when she was a young doctor, coming home at eight or nine in the evening, on her day off call, to talk to a child instead of throwing herself into bed.

"One of us does work part time," said Diana. "When he works at all." She laughed. "Men," she said.

Helen began reading the chart. "I suppose that's fine, then," she said. She countersigned Diana's note, which was incisive and succinct. I will help this chief resident, she thought. She is smart, like I was, and young enough to be my daughter. It pleased Helen to think of a daughter, married and a doctor.

In Tanzania, Helen ran a dispensary, single-handed, far into the bush. She operated by automobile headlight, diagnosed by her senses alone, tended the roses next to her well, and learned the language of solitude. "A good summer," she wrote to her sisters. "Not too much malaria, I've got the women to allow tetanus vaccination, now if only the generator doesn't break down again." She had two brief love affairs, otherwise the years passed from grassy summer to muddy winter to grassy summer like figures of a dance.

She slipped into relationship with the Masai and the earth: she cleaned the clinic each sunrise, ordered seasonal supplies with the solstice, and stopped numbering days entirely. She menstruated on the full moon, and the villagers came when they came, appearing unexpectedly on the horizon, carrying their sick in hammocks slung horizontally between tall men. After fifteen years, Helen described Tanzanian mountain fever in a clear and intelligent communication to the British journal *Lancet*, and because the virus was isolated from her specimens, and because it was interesting in its mode of replication and transmission, Helen's name became known.

On the day she received the letter from City Hospital, Helen folded it carefully into her skirt pocket, slung the rusted clinic shotgun on her back, and took the long path over the ridge. When she had first set up, the missionary nuns who preceded her said to always take the jeep. Lions, they warned earnestly, shaking their heads. Elephants. Rhinoceros.

Helen sat on a rock and watched a pair of gazelles leaping across the bleached grass on the other side of the ridge. In the distance, a giraffe swayed against the trees. I live in a Garden of Eden, she thought, why would I ever want to leave? She looked down the way she had come, to the tin roof of her clinic. It was such an insignificant mark on the land, so easily removed. She traced the varicosities on her leg and felt suddenly afraid.

And so Diana became the guide of her return, pointing out the snow that bent the branches of the blue spruce whose roots cracked through the concrete of the long-abandoned formal entry to City Hospital. "I grew up on Willis Avenue," Diana told her as they sat in the cafeteria.

"I grew up on a farm near Madison," Helen replied, "but my parents are dead. There's no one who knows me there now."

They sat for a moment, surveying the crowd of people, the yellowed linoleum, and the sturdy wooden tables. "Three types of students rotate here: do-gooders, voyeurs, and dropouts sent by the dean," said Diana. She nodded down the table and Helen saw an extraordinary beautiful young man with smooth, almost hairless golden skin, laughing and tossing his head. Like the African sun, thought Helen. Like sex.

"Mike Smith," said Diana. "A real goof-off. Kicked out everywhere else, the patients complained." Helen looked down at her lunch, conscious of her gray hair and how long it had been since she'd worked with men. She stared at the boiled tongue and sauerkraut.

"You'll get used to it," said Diana. "Some of the cooks are Puerto Rican, some are from the South."

Helen took a bite of the meat. "I'll write a letter to the dean," she said, "about that boy. These patients deserve consideration, too. A failing student should be failed."

"It won't," said Diana, "do any good."

Helen studied Diana's smooth face, her soft black eyebrows, and her neatly organized list of patients dipped to the board next to her lunch. "I hope you have enough time with your husband," said Helen. "I hope you decide to have children, soon, before you get too old."

In the afternoon of the day she came, Helen carried her two suitcases up to the staff quarters and sat on the narrow bed. There was a single bureau in the room, battered but solid oak, standing at a slight tilt on the warped linoleum. In the top drawer she found a tourniquet, a pen, index cards, and several unused needles. She picked them out carefully and dropped them into the garbage, then lined the drawer with paper towels from the sink. Folding her skirts into the bottom drawer, she found a package of condoms tucked into the back right corner.

The window stuck several times before it finally creaked all the way up. Car horns, salsa music from the local bar, sirens, the sooty yearnings of urban life blasted into the room. Helen wrapped her arms around herself and stood, considering. She looked across at the decaying curve of the expressway, traffic crowded like wildebeest during mating season in the Serengeti. Then, turning back to the task of unpacking, she noticed faint fingernail scratches, hieroglyphics of passion, etched on the green wall at the head of the bed.

Over the next few months, Dr. Helen van Horne took charge of the department. She reviewed charts, observed procedures, met everyone including housekeepers and orderlies. "What disinfectant do you use?" she asked. "Why is this man waiting so long at X-ray?" She was on the wards at five in the morning and eleven at night, her faded hair pulled into a ponytail, starting an intravenous at a cardiac arrest, checking the diabetics' drawers for candy. Sometimes, standing in front of a washbasin, or sitting at a deserted nursing station at the change of shift, she would suddenly find herself watching the papery skin on the backs of her hands. What do I have to show for the years? she asked herself, but then a young woman gasping from rheumatic heart disease, or an old man bent with cancerous metastases passed by her, and she told herself: it doesn't matter. And she got back to work.

"What are they doing?" she asked Diana as they passed a window looking toward the inner courtyard of the hospital. Michael Smith, the contours of his back glistening in the heat, kicked a ball toward some other students, boys and girls, who were encouraging several small children to kick it back.

"Oh," laughed Diana, "he's too much, isn't he?"

"The children will pull out their IVs," said Helen.

Diana walked around to the door. "Mr. Smith," she called, "the children will pull out their IVs."

"*Anything* you say Dr. Figueroa," said the boy.

"He played football for Harvard," said Diana, apologetically, when she came back inside.

"When you are a teacher," said Helen, looking back to check on the children but involuntarily glancing at Michael Smith's tight buttocks, "you must be careful about personal relationships. There is the issue of abuse of power." She looked away quickly, and with humiliation.

"Yes," said Diana. "But," she added, "the men do it all the time."

After that, Helen gave the teaching of the students over to Diana. She herself spent even more hours attending research meetings at the medical school and supervising the medical service. She set up studies and chaired meetings. She read textbooks of molecular biology. "We are beginning to see a new syndrome of infections in IV drug users," she said in conference, and felt her power as the other doctors listened, because she was the Helen van Horne of Tanzanian mountain fever. She was senior and spoke with authority of microbial isolation and immune alterations. She submitted scholarly articles, and her roots spread into this identity, Chairman of Medicine at City Hospital. She stood taller, her walk grew firmer.

Once, she brought Diana with her to the medical school, to listen to her lecture. Afterwards, the men in the audience, who were division chiefs but not department chairmen, spoke to her carefully and politely. The dean, who was the same age as Helen, came up to tease her about her theories, and Helen, who had, despite herself, imagined the touch of his hands and the feel of his skin, caught each barb and sent it back, leaning against the podium and laughing. But when she introduced Diana to him, he widened his stance. When Diana said how much she admired his research, he put his arm around her and introduced her to the other men, who, one after another, smiled with authority and watched her smooth brown cheeks.

Helen threw herself into work. "Examine these patients and report to me," she told the students. "Tell me if they are rude," she told the patients, "tell me if you think they will make good doctors," and the women always remarked on Michael Smith. Oh, they said, his hair, his eyes, his body. "He's careless," snapped Helen to Diana, "missed diagnoses, wrong medications." But when the boy stood to be rebuked, Helen felt the speculation in his eyes. She tightened her lips. "If you don't work, I will fail you, don't think I won't," she told him. But he glanced at her breasts and her nipples hardened.

"I don't want to be any superdoctor," he said, looking at her seriously. "I want to enjoy my life, you know what I mean?"

She laughed, because she had felt that way, too, then walked away. You are a fifty-year-old woman, she told herself. You are inappropriate. You are disgusting.

Later, on the wards, she rounded with Diana and set stern rules. "No more than six units of blood *per* bleeder," Helen said, after she watched an intern run ten units into a cirrhotic.

"But he's a young man," said Diana.

"He'll vomit up twice as much tomorrow," said Helen. "We don't have enough blood." She felt a pleasure in teaching this resident, after all the years of solitude. The girl would be a good doctor, she thought, but she needed disappointment.

"City Hospital," read the dean's reply, "has always been an albatross to the Medical School." It was spring now, and Helen watched the cornflowers pushing up through the cobbled ramp leading to the ambulance bay. She wondered if the dean had ever seen an albatross. Wingspan as wide as a man's arms, Daedalus, Icarus, she thought, and remembered the bird that followed them all the way from Dar es Salaam to Madagascar. Her lover was Indian, son of the supply ship's owner, a merchant in Dar. "Look," he said to her as they were making love. His gold neckchain lay fallen in a spray of sweat from his dark chest onto hers, looped around one pink nipple. "You belong to me," he said. That was when her skin was smooth and firm, her hair a pale sheet of gold. She had wished, suddenly and just for a moment, that a child, his child, would seed and grow in her womb. A year later, he was gone.

Helen fell into the rhythms of the Bronx. She met with Diana each morning and each evening. "The students," said Diana, "are improving."

"They need to be taught to do good," said Helen. "You are teaching them by example." She surprised herself. She had avoided a moral vocabulary. These had been the words of distance between herself and her parents: duty, family, obligation.

But Diana smiled and slicked back her hair. She had begun to wear it in a ponytail, too, a thick curly fall to complement Helen's thin fair one.

"Stick in the mud," Michael Smith teased her. "Dr. van Horne, Jr." He'd become friendly with the head of housekeeping, a middle-aged black man from Yonkers, and the two of them sat on the steps outside the emergency room talking football and joking, catcalling women as they walked by.

Diana stopped in front of him. "You left a patient in the hall last night and went off without signing him out. When I *just happened* to come by, he was already going into diabetic coma."

Michael Smith paled. "I'm sorry," he said.

"Tell it to the patient," said Diana, and left.

"But is he okay?" called Smith. She didn't answer.

Everyone in the hospital knew and respected Helen now. "Good morning, doctor," she was greeted by the man who ladled out the scrambled eggs. "Good evening," by the woman mopping the women's ward. Sometimes the Spanish workers slipped and called her "sister" when they stopped to thank her for taking care of a relative. Helen would glance at her own upright reflection in the glass doors, curious to see how she might be mistaken for a nun.

She became convinced that this was how the people of the hospital saw her, as a nun, a medical missionary to the South Bronx. Bride of Christ, she taunted herself, standing in her room one night as the moonlight spread across the floor and crept up her ankles. Spinster Mother of City Hospital. How had this happened to her? That night she plaited her sheets into dreams: her nails became claws; her arms, wings of a nun's habit; and she felt the spring air rustle her belly as she swooped on a creature, garbage rat, skittering city mouse, swallowing its body with one snap while its head lay severed and bleeding on the ground.

Yes, she told herself, waking the next morning. The meaning of her years in Africa came to her suddenly as if in revelation. Apprenticeship. Learning to subjugate her will. She would dedicate herself to the patients and the students of City Hospital. Her face took on a pregnant glow, and she felt more content than she could remember in her life.

Because the dean would not remove Michael Smith, Helen decided she would make him into a doctor. She gave most of the teaching duties to Diana, but she no longer avoided the boy. To Diana she said, "You must think of how you will fit your practice around your family, and how you will choose a job where your husband can find work too." Diana smiled but said nothing. To Michael Smith, whom she caught leaving the hospital at five, with a blood sugar left unchecked, she said, "You must do whatever is necessary for the patients' good, even if it means you don't eat, don't sleep, or don't leave the hospital."

Smith flushed slightly, then looked over her left shoulder at a flurry of young nurses who were leaving, too, and said, "I'm going into radiology."

"Good," said Helen. "You'll make money. But first, you must pass your medicine rotation." As she walked away, she felt his eyes on the sway of her hips. Students, she told herself, become infatuated with the power of their teachers. Later that night, sitting at the bedside of a dying man, a drug addict infected on a hole he had eroded in his heart, Helen felt herself strengthen and harden in conviction. None of the private hospitals taught the concept of service. It was here the boy would learn to be a doctor, and it was her responsibility to teach him.

The third week of May began the wave of deaths. Death was of course a familiar presence at City Hospital, but like a wild tide, people began dying in unprecedented numbers. First, it was several cardiac failures on the men's wards, then a medication allergy on the women's ward, then one of the drug rehabilitation doctors fell out of a closet one morning, curled in the fetal position with a needle in his arm and stone-cold dead.

Helen called a meeting of the hospital's physicians. "I can't find a pattern," she said, "but I feel a connection, somewhere underneath." She didn't add, and I feel somehow responsible.

The next day staphylococcus broke out in the neonatal nursery, crops of pustules erupted on even the heartiest of infants. Helen stood outside the plate glass of the babies' ward and watched the nurses wrap a tiny corpse, folding the blanket around the child, a flannel shroud. Why, she asked herself, because even Africa had not prepared her for the speed and the sweep of these deaths. Overcome, she paced the streets outside the hospital, walking blindly past the rubble, the garbage, and the deserted streets, in the long twilights of the late spring.

But the final straw was Henry, the chief of maintenance, who sat, sighed, and fell over one day at dinner. It was Michael Smith who leapt on his chest and screamed, "Help," because he'd been sitting with Henry, once again playing poker when he should have been drawing the evening bloods on the men's ward. They all came, residents, students, Helen, Diana. They ran a code in the cafeteria just as they would have in the emergency room: hooked up the EKG machine, pumped the chest, breathed in the slack mouth, started several large-bore IVs, and called to each other pulse, medication, paddles, step back, shock. But it was different, thought Helen, as she pierced the skin over his clavicle for a central line and glanced at his waxy face. It was Henry. She slipped and hit the artery. A geyser of blood sprayed her, Michael Smith, and the girl who was ventilating with the ambu-bag. When she got the vein, on the third try, she pushed it forward, but his blood clotted even as she pushed it in. "What the hell," she shouted, and there was a pause because they realized, inescapably, after fifteen minutes of flopping his flaccid blue arms, cracking his posthumous ribs, and watching the cardiogram read off an unremittingly straight line, that they were working on a dead man.

"Enough," said Helen. "Get a clean sheet. Wipe up this blood. Get these people out of here."

Michael Smith stood behind her, shaking and weeping, staring at Henry's still face. "His wife," he said, "his children."

"I'm sorry," said Helen.

The narrow hall that led to her room seemed longer than usual and peculiarly dry. She licked her lips, but her tongue stuck to the faint moisture on the roof of her mouth. She thought of calling Henry's wife, getting back to the wards, a memorial service, but the image of a corpse she had once found intruded. It was out in the bush at the end of the dry season, a young boy mauled by a lion so that one arm lay at an unnatural angle, connected only by a tendon that had hardened into rawhide. She stood at her door, looking straight ahead at the eroded slats.

The student, Michael Smith, came up behind her quietly. "Please," he said, touching her arm. She turned slowly and noticed that he was taller than she, how young he was, that his cheeks and nose were freckled with blood, and that he was still weeping.

"What do you want?" she asked him gently, but he just stared at her, moving his hand along her arm. "No," she said, seeing her pale face reflected in his eyes. He reached around her with his other arm and opened the door, pressing against her so she could feel the heat of his body radiating into her own. "Smith," she started, as he bent to kiss her neck. She felt revolted by her wave of desire, sick, like she might vomit. "Go away," she said, "now, before I have to report you to the dean." But when he looked up, his eyes wide and unfocused like a sleepwalker's, she pulled him to her breast and slowly licked the sweat that beaded across his face. "I'm sorry," she whispered. Afterwards, as he lay across her, naked and exhausted, she murmured it again, tracing his lips, "I'm sorry."

"I love you," Smith said, rolling over and going back to sleep, curling defenselessly. Helen stared at him, then got up and showered, letting the water run for hours down her face, between her legs. Then she chose her whitest blouse and went out onto the wards.

"Look," she said to the men's ward secretary. "Has the ward been repainted?"

"No," said the woman.

"But," Helen said in the nursery, "the babies are all so plump and healthy."

"Yes," said the practical nurse who was bathing a new arrival.

Helen walked a long path through the hospital. The women's ward had a new but familiar smell: dust soaked into earth, the beginning of the rainy season.

When she found Diana, she was going over cardiograms with Michael Smith in the emergency room.

"I called Henry's wife," said Diana.

"Yes," said Helen, taking the cardiogram from her. "What's wrong with this patient?"

"Thirty-year-old man with chest pain," began Diana, glancing over at Helen. Michael Smith was looking over Helen's shoulder at the strip of paper. Diana frowned. "Came in this morning," she went on. Michael ran his hand slowly up Helen's thigh. Diana stopped and stared at Helen, at her grey hair, at her grooved cheeks. Helen examined the cardiogram as though nothing had happened.

Diana cleared her throat, her face mottled scarlet. "I understand, Dr. van Horne," she said, "that you've told Mr. Smith he will pass his medicine rotation?"

Helen didn't answer for a moment. "Will you take a fellowship next year?" she asked. "Of course, it is easier to adjust around a husband and children if you work in the emergency room."

"I left my husband," said Diana. "I wanted to be like you."

Helen looked down again at the cardiogram, but her hand began to shake. After a few minutes she said, "And do you think Mr. Smith should pass?"

"No," said Diana.

"Then fail him," said Helen.

"Christ," said Smith to Helen, "that's unfair." When she didn't answer, he looked wounded for a moment, then slammed out of the cubicle.

Diana stared at Helen, embarrassed. "He'll go to the dean," she started.

"Yes," said Helen, "he would be right to do that." She folded the cardiogram carefully back into the chart. She thought of Henry's dead body lying on the gurney waiting for his wife. His lips had turned a particular shade of blue, like the dusky sapplure of Lake Tanganyika at the last moment before the fall of night. It was the most beautiful color she had ever seen.

Helen sat on the bed in her room. "I regret to inform you," she wrote to the dean. She stopped and got up, staring at her face in the mirror, overcome with self-disgust. She seemed to herself grotesque, an old woman, a sexual vampire. "Is there ever any justification," she wrote on the wall beside the mirror, "for a teacher—" And yet, the deaths had stopped. She started again, "If A is a middle-aged woman, and B is a young male student, and insects grow, *must* grow in the rotted womb of fallen trees," but she lost interest and turned to the window. Cars honked and revved their engines, beasts of the Serengeti growled and spoke to her. She walked to the window and threw it open, as far as it would go. "It's the rainy season," she shouted to them, "order up the antibiotics, sow the crops." She saw them crowded on the expressway, antelope, giraffe, lions, surrounded by fields of ripened corn. "Yes," she whispered, because she felt at home. She heard the cry of the ambulances, the voices swelling from the emergency room, the beat of the hospital as it trembled with its load of humanity, and for her children, the patients and the students, she obeyed. She spread her arms Daedalus, Icarus, straight at the hot sun of the South Bronx, and hesitated.

Helen climbed down from the windowsill and sat at her desk. "The men," she said firmly, to herself, "do it all the time." She listened for a moment, for a rebuttal. Then she pulled on a white coat, to cover herself, and went out onto the wards.

Hart Crane

EPISODE OF HANDS

The act of treating another human being, of holding another's hand, becomes an act of supplication and healing in this eloquent expression of what can lie unexpressed between doctor and patient and the power of the most basic of human responses.

HART CRANE, born in 1899, published his first poem as a seventeen-year-old boy. His first book, *White Buildings*, was published a decade later. His masterpiece *The Bridge* was published in 1930. Hart Crane committed suicide in 1932 at the age of thirty-three.

The unexpected interest made him flush.
Suddenly he seemed to forget the pain,—
Consented,—and held out
One finger from the others.

The gash was bleeding, and a shaft of sun
That glittered in and out among the wheels,
Fell lightly, warmly, down into the wound.

And as the fingers of the factory owner's son,
That knew a grip for books and tennis
As well as one for iron and leather,—
As his taut, spare fingers wound the gauze
Around the thick bed of the wound,
His own hands seemed to him
Like wings of butterflies
Flickering in sunlight over summer fields.

The knots and notches—many in the wide
Deep hand that lay in his,—seemed beautiful.
They were like the marks of wild ponies' play,—
Bunches of new green breaking a hard turf.

And factory sounds and factory thoughts
Were banished from him by that larger, quieter hand
That lay in his with the sun upon it.
And as the bandage knot was tightened
The two men smiled into each other's eyes.

Shusaku Endo

from DEEP RIVER

This excerpt tells the story of Kiguchi's World War II military comrade, Tsukada. As Kiguchi looks out the windows of the plane bearing him toward India many years later, he recalls the terrible wartime events he and Tsukada endured in Burma—past events now at the heart of Tsukada's present-day illness. As Kiguchi remembers the hospital doctors' efforts on Tsukada's behalf, he concludes that neither the attending physician "nor any of the doctors in the psychotherapy ward of [the] hospital could comprehend Tsukada's suffering." Endo's novel shows that continued care "for dying patients even when the disease-specific therapy is no longer available or desired" may be an instructive irony, both medical and moral.

SHUSAKU ENDO is considered one of Japan's greatest contemporary writers, known for his searing examinations of moral and religious issues. Besides *Deep River*, he is best known for his novel *Silence* and his biographical meditation titled *A Life of Jesus*.

That evening Tsukada passed a bloody stool. With blood appearing, it was now clear that he was hemorrhaging from somewhere in his esophagus or stomach.

He was given an endoscope examination several days later. Tsukada's wife telephoned Kiguchi with the disheartening results. "They . . . they don't know where the hemorrhaging is coming from. The doctors are at a loss."

The bleeding, though intermittent, continued. Kiguchi felt as though his own demands for a confession from Tsukada had been the cause, and he found as many free moments from work as he could to visit the hospital.

Often the foreign volunteer Gaston would be sitting at Tsukada's bedside.

"Mr. Tsukada, tell me about rock," Gaston gleefully announced one day.

"About rock?"

"Mr. Tsukada go to river and look for rock. Rock shaped like Fujisan."

"I told him about landscape rocks. Although I don't suppose there's any way a foreigner can understand something as cultured as landscape rocks."

Kiguchi was relieved at Tsukada's answer, for he seemed not to feel uneasy about his own condition. In any case, at some point in time Tsukada and this horse-faced foreigner had become fast friends.

"But there's one thing about this young fellow I really can't stand." Tsukada harangued Gaston in his typically haughty tone. "He says he honestly believes there's a God."

"Yes."

"Where is he, then? If he's there, show him to me."

"Ye-es. Inside Mr. Tsukada."

"In my heart, you mean?"

"Ye-es."

"I don't get it. How can anybody today claim anything so foolish? Why, we've got rockets flying to the moon!"

Gaston shrugged his shoulders and smiled. He seemed to have realized, from the kind of food he was delivering on the trays, that Tsukada's condition was not good. His meals, which had been moving toward normal food for a time, had changed back to a liquid diet again. Kiguchi sensed that Gaston, mocked and made a fool of as he was, brought a meager sort of comfort to the patients. About the degree of comfort afforded by the wan winter sun trickling through the clouds. Still, each day Gaston brought temporary diversion to the many suffering patients here. At this hospital, he performed the role of the Pierrot in a circus.

Tsukada finally stopped hemorrhaging, and the worried faces around him relaxed. Kiguchi confided only a portion of Tsukada's confession to the doctor in charge. He did not mention Minamikawa's name, and hinted only vaguely that Tsukada had eaten the flesh of an enemy soldier.

"I see. So you were in Burma with Mr. Tsukada, were you? It must have been terrible. I was just a child evacuated to the provinces at the time, but even in Japan we had a shortage of food."

"That doesn't even begin to compare with what we went through!" Kiguchi retorted with unintentional anger. He had heard from family members, and experienced them himself after repatriation, of the desperate shortages of food in Japan, but these bore no comparison to those of the Japanese soldiers who had wandered along the Highway of Death like sleepwalkers, drenched by the rain. Their starvation, after they had eaten tree bark and insects dug from the ground, after they had eaten everything, was of a totally different realm from those who received a ration, however paltry, of rice.

Keenly aware of the difference between his own generation and that of this doctor, Kiguchi concluded that neither this man nor any of the doctors in the psychotherapy ward of this hospital could comprehend Tsukada's suffering.

"I think it would be best if we didn't provoke Tsukada any more."

"What do you mean, provoke?"

"I don't think it's good to make him talk about the secrets he's buried in his heart. I think it's what caused him to hemorrhage this last time."

"That may be true. We'll just have to watch him and see how he does for a while."

"Since he's not drinking while he's here, I think all you have to do is turn that into a good habit for him."

The doctor, twirling his ballpoint pen between his fingers, nodded as if he understood. Esophageal varices were, after all, a disease for which there was no treatment.

The event they feared finally occurred. It was Saturday when Tsukada coughed up a huge amount of blood for the second time. When Kiguchi got the urgent message and raced to the hospital, the doctors had stopped his vomiting and moved him from the ward to a private room. Nurses busily scurried in and out of the room, and the atmosphere was taut as a bowstring all the way out into the hallway.

A balloonlike tube had been inserted into his throat, and he moaned in pain. Stains from the blood he had regurgitated still splotched the floor here and there.

"Gaston's the one who picked him up. There was blood all over Gaston's clothes. Gaston . . ." In her state of distress, Tsukada's wife kept repeating trivial information to Kiguchi.

"He's stabilized for now," the head doctor, who stood wearily at the door of the room, whispered to Kiguchi. "But this is the crisis point."

Five days later the bleeding was finally stanched and the balloon tube was removed from his throat.

Tsukada seemed to sense the approach of death.

"I've really done nothing but cause you one headache after another," he said with more feeling than he had previously displayed. "I'm so sorry."

He said some things privately to his wife. Kiguchi could hear her whimpering as he stood in the hallway. Patients passing Tsukada's room on their way to the bathroom glared uneasily at the hypodermic syringes and the oxygen tank.

"My husband wants you to send for Gaston," his wife told Kiguchi when she emerged from the room with a tearstained faced. "He keeps asking for him."

"For Gaston?"

"Yes."

Evidently Gaston was teaching a class at the Berlitz Language School that day, since he had not appeared at the hospital.

"Where's Gaston?" Tsukada repeatedly asked Kiguchi. "I want to ask Gaston something."

It was past six, after the patients had finished eating their supper, when Gaston finally got the message and appeared. An air of tension still filled the room and the hallway. Gaston got permission from the nurses' station and hesitantly opened the door to Tsukada's room.

"Mr. Tsukada. I pray. I pray."

"Gaston. I . . . during the war . . . I did something horrible. It hurts me to remember it. Very much."

"Is OK. OK."

"No matter how horrible?"

"Ye-es."

"Gaston. I . . . during the war . . ." Tsukada gasped for breath, and in a strained voice he continued, ". . . in Burma, I ate the flesh of a dead soldier. There was nothing to eat. I had to do it to stay alive. Someone who's fallen that far into the hell of starvation—would your God forgive even someone like that?"

Tsukada's wife, who had been staring at the floor as she listened to her husband's confession, said softly, "Darling. Darling . . . you've suffered for so long." She already knew her husband's secret.

Gaston closed his eyes and said nothing. He looked almost like a monk engaged in solitary prayer. When he opened his eyes again, there was a stern look on his comical face that Kiguchi had never seen before.

"Mr. Tsukada. You are not only one to eat human flesh."

Kiguchi and Tsukada's wife listened in astonishment to the stumbling Japanese words that came from Gaston's mouth.

"Mr. Tsukada. Four years, maybe five years ago, did you hear news that an airplane is broken and falls into Andes Mountains? Airplane hit mountain, and many people hurt. Andes Mountains is cold. On sixth day before help comes, nothing is left to eat."

Kiguchi remembered seeing in a newspaper or on television that an Argentine plane had crashed in the Andes four or five years earlier. He had seen a photograph of the search party beside a form that resembled an aircraft but so blurred it looked like a reflection in a pool of water, along with several men and women who had survived the crash.

"A man was in that airplane. Like you, he very much likes to drink, and in plane he only gets drunk and sleeps. When plane has accident in Andes Mountains, drunk man hits back and chest, is much badly hurt."

In his broken Japanese, Gaston related the following story.

The drunken man said to the survivors who had cared for him over the course of three days: "You have nothing left to eat, do you? After I die, you must eat the flesh of my body. You must eat it whether you want to or not. Help will surely come."

Kiguchi vaguely remembered this part of the story as well. The survivors, who were rescued on the seventy-second day, openly confessed what they had done. They had miraculously survived because they had consumed the flesh of those who had already died.

"Those who passed away encouraged us to do so," one of the survivors related. This news had struck Kiguchi, who had roamed and fled through the jungles of Burma, so close at hand and so vividly that it remained in the depths of his consciousness even now.

"When these people come back from Andes alive, everyone very happy. Families of dead people also very happy. No one angry with them for eating people's flesh. The wife of drunk man say, he did a good thing for first time. People from his town always say bad things about him, but they stop saying. They believe he has gone to heaven."

Gaston exhausted every word he knew in Japanese to comfort Tsukada. He came to Tsukada's room every day after that and held the dying man's hands between his own palms, talked to him and encouraged him. Kiguchi could not tell whether such comfort eased Tsukada's pain. But the figure of Gaston kneeling beside his bed looked like a bent nail, and the bent nail struggled to become one with the contortions of Tsukada's mind, and to suffer along with Tsukada.

Two days later, Tsukada died. His face was more at peace than anyone had imagined it could be, but a look of peace always comes at last to the dying. "He looks like he's sleeping," Tsukada's wife mumbled, but Kiguchi couldn't help but feel that this peaceful death-mask had been made possible because Gaston had soaked up all the anguish in Tsukada's heart.

Gaston was nowhere to be found when Tsukada died. The nurses had no idea where he had gone.

PART TWO

Physicians Must Be Knowledgeable

PHYSICIANS must understand the scientific basis of medicine and be able to apply that understanding to the practice of medicine. They must have sufficient knowledge of the structure and function of the body (as an intact organism) and its major organ systems and of the molecular, cellular, and biochemical mechanisms that maintain the body's homeostasis in order to comprehend disease and to incorporate wisely modern diagnostic and therapeutic modalities in their practice. They must engage in lifelong learning to remain current in their understanding of the scientific basis of medicine.

Alice Jones
THE CADAVER

The exploration of cadavers has guided the beginning study of medicine for centuries. Cadavers have been the means by which students have acquired "sufficient knowledge of the structure . . . of the body," and anatomy itself has come to symbolize a critical rite of passage for medical students. For many students, it is the first time they don the garb of their profession, learn to work with its tools, speak its language—and touch death.

In this poem, physician Alice Jones writes of the process of dissection and the complexity of both the process and the feelings that accompany the weeks spent exploring the body of another human being.

ALICE JONES is a graduate of Goddard College and New York Medical College. After several years of practice in internal medicine, she completed a second residency in psychiatry, which she now practices. Her poems have appeared in *Poetry*, the *New England Review*, the *Gettysburg Review*, and the *Kenyon Review*. This poem is taken from her collection of poems titled *The Knot*.

I

Overwhelmed by smell, warned
by this ancient sense, you approach
the body, cool and supine
on the chrome table. This rubbery
thing will show you the mysteries
as you open his insides,
expose them to fluorescent light
and the lab's cold air. Sick
of looking, hating the slippery
touch that pickles your fingertips
into ridges, as if you'd been in the tub
all day, you fly out through the double
doors to pace the hard linoleum,
breathe air free of formaldehyde,
feel your separateness in the swing
of your legs, your bladder fullness,
and blood-pumped warmth. You list
your differences from the inert man
who teaches you the body's form and names,
who teaches you the body's death.

II

On your schedule, it says Gross Anatomy Lab
so you're all on time, cluster
around the doorway to be outside
of the odor and at some distance
from the silent shapes on the tables.
A white-coated instructor appears,
with the look of a dapper marine,
calls out names from his list by fours.
You're bunched with three other J's,
white males, who check out each others'
equipment—the blue plastic boxes
of scalpels and probes, the atlas
in paper or hardback, opaque latex gloves.

They notice your metzenbaum scissors
stolen from a summertime lab job.
While the text begins with the chest
and you read in advance, he says start
with the forearms and places two of you
on each side of the damp sheet
that covers something. While you wait
for your first look at death, the level
of laughter rises, as among soldiers
nearing the enemy front.
Later, you walked to the car,
a collection of fragments,
disarticulated bones, muscle spindles,
vessels and nerves, you wondered
what held you together. At home
the cats wouldn't come near you
even after a shower. And you thought
you'd never be a whole animal again.

III

Older than your father,
with trim beard, wry facial lines
and dilated pupils, you imagine the name
Joseph for him, not thinking then
of the father who had so little to do
in the old story, who after the annunciation
only sheltered the divine parasite,
like a bewildered bird
constantly feeding the fat cuckoo
placed in his small nest.
In this way the cadaver fathered
knowledge, provided no live seed,
but gave the place for learning,
its food and shelter. You explored
the deep nest of the thorax, held
by the springy bows of the ribs,

the deep gutters linked
to the paraspinal troughs, that emptied
into the dark hole of the pelvis.
You knew these hollows like home,
almost comfortable there
once you'd cleaned out the matted meat
of the right upper lobe
that was once aerated lung,
before the cancer ate it.
You wondered who this was,
who would make the sacrifice
and freely give that which
used to be stolen from graves.
Didn't they imagine their bodies
picked over by cannibals, hungry
for learning, who would expose
their insides, take parts away
in avid hands, to consume
each shred of flesh?
Didn't they know there'd be jokes—
the young husband leaving his
cadaver-mate wife a Valentine's note
tucked inside the left ventricle?
Who would choose this way
to stretch their time above ground?
Would they have thought only
of the slow gestation, embedded
in some student's cortex, to form
a lifetime's template for all
future bodies—patients and lovers?

IV

There weren't enough corpses
to go around, so several students
shared, each played out some
internal drama on the body

of the dead father, and like unruly
children growing self-assured, quarreled
often. You fought over who would expose
the optic nerve, who severed the trochlear.
One morning you arrived
to find that the obsessive lab partner
had wrestled the cadaver
into lithotomy position to dissect
the pelvic floor, had started at 6 A.M.
and finished before you arrived.
So you probed and learned the places,
all the cutting being done.
In the territorial battles over forearms
and hearts, the things with many segments
to learn, or intricate nerve ramifications
and muscle insertions, for these
there was an aluminum bin of parts.
You could sit on high wooden stools
around the table and examine spare limbs,
pull each tendon, watch which finger rose,
make disembodied fuck-you signs
at each other's backs.

V

The instructor shows a tape
of highlights, before doing
the pelvis. The actor playing
doctor says "First eviscerate
the abdomen" and you clench
your teeth as they show
someone scooping out the guts.
Then, "The best approach
to the pelvic viscera
is the sagittal section."
And they show someone
pretend to cut (it had been done

in advance) down the midline
and lift away the whole leg
and groin and half the pelvis,
separate it from the body
en bloc, then zoom
to the remaining half a uterus,
one ovary and fallopian tube.
It was that silent lifting away
one quarter of the body
leaving clean-cut edges,
that, more than any battle film,
had the cool and precise quality
of a recurrent nightmare's inevitable end.

VI

A dream full of walking corpses
came in the second week. You grew
uncertain in the days, worried
about your skin and thought
what a huge burden to hold in
all that is in there—
the glistening viscera packed
under a clear omentum. You remember
in grade school the day
they showed an anatomical picture,
it was the moment you realized
that the tube that led
from your mouth did not open up
on an empty black vault,
but that the insides were full
of colors and bulges, large
purple shapes, and were pleased
to find yourself so rich
and well housed; but scared
that the thinness of walls
would burst from the pulsing

pressure of all those organs,
those nameless things—all that
just to take peas and carrots
and bread and grind it up
into shit. You knew then
there were things that no one
had told you, grew alarmed
to find your safe shelter
part of the secret. And this
terror surfaced in nightmares—
the basement full of dead bodies
that sit up when you enter, roll
their eyes, stand on detachable legs,
wave their own and others' hands
as they perform some tribal dance
that you are part of.
You watch as one lies down, uses
the saw to split her own thorax,
opens her heart to the air.

VII

Field guides taught those who learned
each coastal shrub and bird,
who needed to know the word
for each tree to hold off darkness
in the woods. Or, it was their way
to love the world, to recite
the names for things that grow,
our sibling creatures. We each
tame wilderness by naming it.
You wanted to find your way
in the world of flesh, surprised
to find yourself embodied so,
born out of the unyielding place
where you swam, a small fish
sealed in shiny membranes, bound

within muscular layers, suspended
by the round ligaments, until expelled,
a piece of earth's strange biology.
You remember as a child finding places
which no one would say aloud,
their functions or their pleasures.
These things with weight and texture
could be felt by your palpating fingers,
their details encompassed by the eye.
You believe the knowledge
and its recitation can almost
hold off death. When your tongue pronounces:
intertrochanteric fossa, greater and
lesser omentum, orbicularis oculi,
splanchnic bed, pubic symphysis,
hallucis longus, ciliate ganglion,
you think this lore will keep
the body warm and whole,
so sensation won't dissolve the walls.
Like a child says prayers in the dark
in a language she doesn't know,
or an infant in the crib rubs
her mouth, tastes her fingers,
for the soothing friction of flesh,
and to know that hand and lips are there,
or thrashes to know what arms contain her,
you name the parts to know the edges hold,
will keep inside the disparate forces
that push in their own directions,
threaten to burst the boundaries,
flood the surface, annihilate you.

VIII

As you worked on the thigh, bisected
the long strap of the sartorius, admired
the pinnate shape of the rectus femoris,

separated the pectineus, adductor longus,
gracilis, followed the great saphenous vein
into the pocket of the femoral canal
in its row of nerve, artery, vein and ligament,
someone walked in carrying a radio,
and you heard them announce the fall
of Saigon, the end of the war, and then
went back to removing pads of dense
yellow fat to carve out muscles,
trace them from origin to insertion,
so they look like sculpture
more than the dissection of death.
You return to your small quiet war
where you're willing to pay the blood price
to master the body, its frailties,
to prove yourself armored, able,
untouched by scenes of carnage.
They were like the images left
from the summer's job, where you prepped
dogs for the heart surgeons to practice
transplant techniques. That meant
walk to the 17th floor to fetch
a lab dog, wild and unused to humans,
lead it down to the concrete-floored room,
bind its muzzle with a slipknot,
shave the forepaw, inject the nembutal IV,
quickly intubate, then tie the heavy thing,
spread-eagled, to the metal table,
do cut downs for arterial lines
in the soft folds of the groin,
then with the cautery, open the skin,
a smell of burnt fur and fried fat,
then take the bone saw to crack the sternum,
wedge it apart with the retractors'
metal jaws, cover the rib ends with paraffin
to keep the field dry, slice open

the pericardium, tie it like a sling,
cradling the still beating red heart,
wired now to monitors, then mop up the blood,
stand aside to play scrub nurse
and watch the real surgeons begin.

IX

Gauze towels swathe the head,
resembling some bedouin's
or mummy's, and all of you
choose to keep the covers on
after that one first look
at this most human of parts
with its soft bony planes,
places you know have been stroked,
kissed, the flare of nostrils,
the frail curve of eyelid,
the glimpse of pink tongue.
Your group stands and looks, uncertain
in their own bodies, so you volunteer
and make the tentative first cuts
across the scalp, then finding it tough
and thick as grapefruit rind,
cut more deeply, down to the fibrous layers.
You quarter it, slide the blade's
handle end in to separate the fascia
attachments, making a velcro-like sound.
You bare the rounded bones, peel
the edges of scalp down past the eyebrows,
with relief, you cover the eyes,
and wait for the diener to come
with his bone saw, which in its noisy
harmlessness stops at flesh
and only cuts denser stuff.
You watch him prop the head
to saw the horizontal circle,

making a smell of burned bone,
then take his chisel, whack it
for the final pop, like the sound
of a coconut cracked open,
and on this last hinge, lift
the shallow ivory bowl to expose
the familiar convolutions
of grey matter that your brain
will begin to examine.

X

Valhalla of cadavers, where
hospital-slain heroes will themselves
into your inexperienced hands, here
you learn the labels for all
the structures of your mute
first patient. He didn't quicken
under your omnipotent touch.
He did not wake, speak or
rise from the dead. Instead,
his useful death fed you. His meat,
preserved above ground, formed a feast,
served on a silver table. Just as
your father filled you with knowledge,
to make you like him, not her,
the body's names formed a knife edge
that cleaved you two. He lifted
you out of her confining lap,
out of the glacier where you and she
were frozen, where the skin surfaces
stuck like a tongue to iced metal.
He ripped you loose, left you still feeling
the red rawness of your attachment.
Then he gave you words to seal the surface,
to heal you, make you whole.
At night you feel disloyal

as you nestle your bony head
on the bowed twigs of someone's ribs,
listen to the regular clicks
as his heart's valvular leaflets
open and close. You consider
the cusps' clock-like rhythm,
remember their texture, these
small invisible pocketed flaps.
You start naming the shapes
that lie under your hand, within
this mortal body you've clung to
after leaving the others, after
moving away from the too small
nest of the father's chest, of
the mother's arms, having
with knives, delivered yourself.

XI

So how do they dispose of the bodies,
you asked, rinsing scraps off your hands,
down the drain of the stainless-steel sink,
where you'd washed the sludge out
of the large bowel so you could examine
haustral markings and the cecal valve.
They said all the parts
are saved for burial or cremation
and you wondered how they know
who's who, if all these people
commingle in death, fill
each other's graves. You imagine
the burning bodies looking
like those from the dog lab
after you dumped them into
the hospital's main incinerator—
the sudden brushfire of fur
and skin, the flames folding

into the dark evacuated cavities
to be extinguished there
or at high heat eat through
the smooth-surfaced walls,
leaving ignited patches of bone.
You want to utter some blessing
when you pull up the sheet the last time,
over his familiar body. You wonder
if you'll think of him, your model
of death, when you fold mottled hands
across your chest as it ceases to rise
and fall, as you exhale from the bottom
of your lungs and the air grows still
in the small caverns of your nostrils,
as heartbeats dissolve into fibrillation,
muscle fibers lock, all sphincters
give way and you drop to room temperature,
your dilated eyes gazing at nothing.

XII

Having fed like a worm on the bones of the dead
or like a bird, on the body's worms,
you grow large and leave home
prepared for your adult life
of minding the sick, performing
technical procedures on the dying.
You know where you are
when, after your young patient dies,
you go to the morgue, see them place
her on the elevated metal table,
hear the dozens of aluminum-tipped ends
of her cornrowed braids clatter
as they fall away limply
from her blue-lipped face. You watch
her resilient skin give way
under the bright blade as they open

the large flaps of her body's walls,
sever the great vessels, lift out
her heart and lungs in one piece,
hung from the cartilage handle
of her trachea. You recite the branches
as they trace her pulmonary arteries
searching for the clot that killed her.
On the hospital wards, there are moments
that remind you of the lab, when you tell
the old man to turn his head, so you can
insert the needle in his jugular, enter beside
the belly of the sternocleidomastoid.
You know how it wraps its tendon
along the clavicle, feel the vein's
sheath give, watch the paper drape
over his breathing face lift for a second,
then you forget again that this meat
you dig in is warm and pulsing,
as you aim your precise hand
at the visible landmarks of the unseen world
whose map now lies in your mind.

Anton Chekhov

ANYUTA

Stepan Klochkov, a medical student in his third year, struggles hard to understand the structure of the ribs and the lungs. In the process of such intense study, he completely overlooks the human predicament of the woman standing before him whose ribs he studies. This short, ironic piece from 1886 is by one of the world's master storytellers.

ANTON CHEKHOV (1860–1909), physician, playwright, and short-story writer, is considered one of Russia's greatest writers. A number of his stories and plays feature doctors, in all their greatness and infamy.

In the cheapest room of a big block of furnished apartments, Stepan Klochkov, a medical student in his third year, was walking to and fro, zealously cramming anatomy. His mouth was dry and his forehead perspiring from the unceasing effort to learn it by heart.

In the window, covered by patterns of frost, sat on a stool the girl who shared his room—Anyuta, a thin little brunette of five and twenty, very pale, with mild gray eyes. Sitting with bent back she was busy embroidering with red thread the collar of a man's shirt. She was working against time. . . . The clock in the passage struck two drowsily, yet the little room had not been put to rights for the morning. Crumpled bedclothes, pillows thrown about, books, clothes, a big filthy stop-pail filled with soapsuds in which cigarette ends were swimming, and the litter on the floor—all seemed as though purposely jumbled together in one confusion. . . .

"The right lung consists of three parts . . . ," Klochkov repeated. "Boundaries! Upper part on anterior wall of thorax reaches the fourth or fifth rib, on the lateral surface, the fourth rib . . . behind to the *spina scapulæ* . . ."

Klochkov raised his eyes to the ceiling, striving to visualize what he had just read. Unable to form a clear picture of it, he began feeling his upper ribs through his waistcoat.

"These ribs are like the keys of a piano," he said. "One must familiarize oneself with them somehow, if one is not to get muddled over them. One must study them in the skeleton and the living body. . . . I say, Anyuta, let me pick them out."

Anyuta put down her sewing, took off her blouse, and straightened herself up. Klochkov sat down facing her, frowned, and began counting her ribs.

"H'm! . . . One can't feel the first rib; it's behind the shoulder blade. . . . This must be the second rib. . . . Yes . . . this is the third . . . this is the fourth. H'm! . . . yes. . . . Why are you wriggling?"

"Your fingers are cold!"

"Come, come . . . it won't kill you. Don't twist about. That must be the third rib, then . . . this is the fourth. . . . You look such a skinny thing, and yet one can hardly feel your ribs. That's the second . . . that's the third. . . . Oh, this is muddling, and one can't see it clearly. . . . I must draw it. . . . Where's my crayon?"

Klochkov took his crayon and drew on Anyuta's chest several parallel lines corresponding with the ribs.

"First-rate. That's all straightforward. . . . Well, now I can sound you. Stand up!"

Anyuta stood up and raised her chin. Klochkov began sounding her, and was so absorbed in this occupation that he did not notice how Anyuta's lips, nose, and fingers turned blue with cold. Anyuta shivered, and was afraid the student, noticing it, would stop drawing and sounding her, and then, perhaps, might fail in his exam.

"Now it's all clear," said Klochkov when he had finished. "You sit like that and don't rub off the crayon, and meanwhile I'll learn up a little more."

And the student again began walking to and fro, repeating to himself. Anyuta, with black stripes across her chest, looking as though she had been tattooed, sat thinking, huddled up and shivering with cold. She said very little as a rule; she was always silent, thinking and thinking. . . .

In the six or seven years of her wanderings from one furnished room to another, she had known five students like Klochkov. Now they had all finished their studies, had gone out into the world, and, of course, like respectable people, had long ago forgotten her. One of them was living in Paris, two were doctors, the fourth was an artist, and the fifth was said to be already a professor. Klochkov was the sixth. . . . Soon he, too, would finish his studies and go out into the world. There was a fine future before him, no doubt, and Klochkov probably would become a great man, but the present was anything but bright; Klochkov had no tobacco and no tea, and there were only four lumps of sugar left. She must make haste and finish her embroidery, take it to the woman who had ordered it, and with the quarter ruble she would get for it, buy tea and tobacco.

"Can I come in?" asked a voice at the door.

Anyuta quickly threw a woollen shawl over her shoulders. Fetbov the artist, walked in.

"I have come to ask you a favor," he began, addressing Klochkov and glaring like a wild beast from under the long locks that hung over his brow. "Do me a favor; lend me your young lady just for a couple of hours! I'm painting a picture, you see, and I can't get on without a model."

"Oh, with pleasure," Klochkov agreed. "Go along, Anyuta."

"The things I've had to put up with there," Anyuta murmured softly.

"Rubbish! The man's asking you for the sake of art, and not for any sort of nonsense. Why not help him if you can?"

Anyuta began dressing.

"And what are you painting?" asked Klochkov.

"Psyche; it's a fine subject. But it won't go, somehow. I have to keep painting from different models. Yesterday I was painting one with blue legs. 'Why are your legs blue?' I asked her. 'It's my stockings stain them,' she said. And you're still cramming! Lucky fellow! You have patience."

"Medicine's a job one can't get on with without grinding."

"H'm! . . . Excuse me, Klochkov, but you do live like a pig! It's awful the way you live!"

"How do you mean! I can't help it. . . . I only get twelve rubles a month from my father, and it's hard to live decently on that."

"Yes . . . yes . . . ," said the artist, frowning with an air of disgust; "but, still, you might live better. . . . An educated man is in duty bound to have taste, isn't he? And goodness knows what it's like here! The bed not made, the slops, the dirt . . . yesterday's porridge in the plates. . . . Tfoo!"

"That's true," said the student in confusion, "but Anyuta has had no time today to tidy up; she's been busy all the while."

When Anyuta and the artist had gone out Klochkov lay down on the sofa and began learning, lying down; then he accidentally dropped asleep, and waking up an hour later, propped his head on his fists and sank into gloomy reflection. He recalled the artist's words that an educated man was in duty bound to have taste, and his surroundings actually struck him now as loathsome and revolting. He saw, as it were in his mind's eye, his own future, when he would see his patients in his consulting room, drink tea in a large dining room in the company of his wife, a real lady. And now that slop-pail in which the cigarette ends were swimming looked incredibly disgusting. Anyuta, too, rose before his imagination—a plain, slovenly, pitiful figure . . . and he made up his mind to part with her at once, at all costs.

When, in coming back from the artist's, she took off her coat, he got up and said to her seriously:

"Look here, my good girl . . . sit down and listen. We must part! The fact is, I don't want to live with you any longer."

Anyuta had come back from the artist's worn out and exhausted. Standing so long as a model had made her face look thin and sunken, and her chin sharper than ever. She said nothing in answer to the student's words, only her lips began to tremble.

"You know we should have to part sooner or later, anyway," said the student. "You're a nice, good girl, and not a fool; you'll understand. . . ."

Anyuta put on her coat again, in silence wrapped up her embroidery in paper, gathered together her needles and thread: she found the screw of paper with the four lumps of sugar in the window, and laid it on the table by the books.

"That's . . . your sugar . . . ," she said softly, and turned away to conceal her tears.

"Why are you crying?" asked Klochkov.

He walked about the room in confusion, and said:

"You are a strange girl, really. . . . Why, you know we shall have to part. We can't stay together forever."

She had gathered together all her belongings, and turned to say good-bye to him, and he felt sorry for her.

"Shall I let her stay on here another week?" he thought. "She really may as well stay, and I'll tell her to go in a week"; and, vexed at his own weakness, he shouted to her roughly:

"Come, why are you standing there? If you are going, go; and if you don't want to, take off your coat and stay! You can stay!"

Anyuta took off her coat, silently, stealthily, then blew her nose also stealthily, sighed, and noiselessly returned to her invariable position on her stool by the window.

The student drew his textbook to him and began again pacing from corner to corner. "The right lung consists of three parts," he repeated; "the upper part, on anterior wall of thorax, reaches the fourth or fifth rib. . . ."

In the passage some one shouted at the top of his voice: "Grigory! The samovar!"

Jack Coulehan

THE MAN WITH STARS INSIDE HIM

A doctor's attempt to diagnose and comprehend his patient Antonio's pneumonia becomes an occasion for wonder at the body's structure and functioning. This poem is a tribute to the body's unique sounds and secrets—even in the midst of life-threatening disease.

JACK COULEHAN is a professor of medicine and preventative medicine, and co-director of the Medicine in Contemporary Society Program at Stony Brook Health Sciences Center. This selection is taken from his collection of poems titled *The Knitted Glove.*

Deep in this old man's chest,
a shadow of pneumonia grows,
I watch Antonio shake
with a cough that traveled here
from the beginning of life.
As he pulls my hand to his lips
and kisses my hand,
Antonio tells me
for a man whose death
is gnawing at his spine,
pneumonia is a welcome friend,
a friend who reaches
deep between his ribs without a sound
and puff! a cloud begins to squeeze
so delicately
the great white image of his heart.

The shadow on his X-ray grows
each time Antonio moves,
each time a nurse
smoothes lotion on his back
or puts a fleece between his limbs.
Each time he takes a sip of ice
and his moist cheek shakes with cough,
the shadow grows.

In that delicate shadow
is a cloud of gas
at the galaxy's center,
a cloud of cold stunned nuclei
beginning to spin,
spinning and shooting
a hundred thousand embryos of stars.
I listen to Antonio's chest

where stars crackle from the past,
and hear the boom
of blue giants, newly caught,
and the snap of white dwarfs
coughing, spinning.

The second time
Antonio kisses my hand
I feel his dusky lips
reach out from everywhere in space.
I look at the place
his body was,
and see inside, the stars.

Rachel Naomi Remen

FROM THE HEART

A second-year medical student at the beginning of her study of pathology examines a human heart with a congenitally malformed anterior coronary artery. Rachel Naomi Remen makes this examination the basis of her cautionary story about the balance between scientific objectivity and responding "from the heart."

RACHEL NAOMI REMEN is the co-founder and medical director of the Commonweal Cancer Help Program in Bolinas, California, and is currently a clinical professor of family and community medicine at San Francisco School of Medicine. She is the author of *My Grandfather's Blessings*, from which this essay is taken, and the best-selling book *Kitchen Table Wisdom*.

Almost fifty-eight years ago, I attended preschool in the little park around the corner from our apartment in upper Manhattan. As the shy and timid only child of older parents it had taken me a long time to feel safe in the company of other children, and my mother or my nana often sat on a bench within eyesight to give me the courage to remain in the group.

Eventually I was able to stay there alone. One day close to Halloween, my nana left me at the park, and I spent the morning with the other four-year-olds making masks. Close to noon the teachers threaded string through our creations and helped us to put them on. I had never worn a mask and I was entranced.

About this time, mothers began arriving to pick up their children, and as soon as I saw my own mother walking toward the class I stood and waved to her. She did not respond in any way. She stopped just inside the door, her eyes searching the room. Suddenly I realized that she did not know who I was and I began to cry, terrified. All her efforts to soothe me and explain why she had not recognized me failed to comfort me. I simply could not understand why she had not known me. I knew who I was with my mask on. Why didn't she? I never went back to the nursery school again. I felt too invisible, too alone, too vulnerable.

Most of us wear masks. We may have worn them so long that we have forgotten we have put them on. Sometimes our culture may even demand we wear them.

A young woman named LaVera told me of something that happened when she was a first-year medical student. Those were anxious times, and it was not uncommon for people to work and study eighteen hours a day for weeks on end. In the evening, members of her class were in the habit of releasing the day's tension by playing basketball on the court in the basement of the medical students' residence. No one kept score, and people would drop in and out of the game for fifteen minutes or a half hour—however long it was before their anxiety about needing to study took them back upstairs to their desks. Often the game went on for hours, and the two teams that called it quits had no players in common with the teams that had started the game.

About four months into the year, in the midst of one of these games, one of her classmates had suddenly collapsed and died surrounded by other freshman students who had no idea how to help him. He was twenty-one years old.

Although many of the students were deeply shaken by the event, nothing further was said about the matter. The school made no opportunity to acknowledge either the tragedy of the death or the feelings of the class. The young man's belongings had been packed up and sent to his parents who lived in another state. No one from his class or from the school had attended his funeral, which was held near his home.

The pace of the first year was intense and the competition fierce. Despite their shock and distress, the members of the class simply went on. Few talked about their classmate even at first, and by the spring of the year, the incident seemed almost forgotten.

At the beginning of their second year, the class began the study of pathology. In one of the laboratory sessions on congenital anomalies the instructor began passing around trays, each holding a preserved human specimen that demonstrated a specific birth defect. Wearing gloves, the students examined each specimen and then passed it on.

One of these specimens was a heart with a congenitally malformed anterior coronary artery. As it was being passed hand to hand through the class, the instructor commented in a casual way that it was the heart of the young man who had died the year before.

Without lifting her head, LaVera looked out of the corner of her eye. No one around her seemed to react. All her classmates wore expressions of detached scientific interest. A wave of panic rose up in her until she realized that she, too, was wearing a mask of professional detachment. No one could possibly know the terrible distress she was feeling. She was flooded with relief. She remembers thinking that she was going to be able to DO this. She was going to be able to become a real physician.

LaVera closed her eyes as she finished her story and sat in silence for a moment. She rocked back and forth slightly and began to cry.

After more than thirty-five years as a physician, I have found at last that it is possible to be a professional and live from the heart. This was not something that I learned in medical school.

Medical training instills a certain scientific objectivity or distance. Other perspectives may become suspect. In particular, the perspective of the heart is seen as unprofessional or even dangerous. The heart with its capacity to connect us to others may somehow mar our judgment and make us incompetent. Such training changes us. We may need to heal from it. It has taken me years to realize that being a human being is not unprofessional.

My training encouraged me to give away vital parts of myself in the belief that this would make me of greater service to others. In the end I found that abandoning my humanity in order to become of service made me vulnerable to burnout, cynicism, numbness, loneliness, and depression. Abandoning the heart weakens us.

The heart has the power to transform experience. No matter what we do, finding fulfillment may require learning to cultivate the heart and its capacity for meaning in the same way that we are now taught to pursue knowledge or expertise. We will need to connect intimately to the life around us. Knowledge alone will not help us to live well or serve well. We will need to take off our masks in order to do that.

Jeffrey R. Botkin

THE SEDUCTIVE BEAUTY OF PHYSIOLOGY

In this piece, Jeffrey R. Botkin suggests that physiology provides the organizing structure for the study of medicine. This structure, he contends, helps mitigate the uncertainties of clinical medicine, thereby providing a measure of comfort for the medical student—a false comfort if the student does not recognize that the complexities and uncertainties of clinical medicine are not so easily pigeonholed. Rather, it is the study of cultures, behavioral sciences, ethics, anthropology, and health care systems that, taken together, contribute to the student's understanding of the context of illness and provide a necessary addition to the structure of the basic sciences.

JEFFREY R. BOTKIN is an associate professor in the Department of Pediatrics of the University of Utah, Salt Lake City.

Physiology has become the leading intellectual interest in clinical medicine. The influence physiology has in contemporary medicine stems, in part, from the power afforded by knowledge, but also by the process of contemporary medical education. Bright students adept at biology and organic chemistry are self-selected to pursue the profession of medicine. The formal introduction to medicine then proceeds through a flood of factual detail channelled through discrete scientific disciplines. These basic sciences are intended to be the fundamental building blocks of the medical mind. A few cross threads connecting these disciplines may be apparent to the perceptive student, but, as a rule, the effort is one of accumulating raw materials for later development.

It is physiology that provides the grand design for these disparate elements. The pieces begin to form relation to one another as the fascinating processes of life become increasingly apparent from the dissections, the Giemsa-stained tissues, and the detailed biochemical pathways. There is a compelling beauty to the flow and regulation of life processes—the maintenance of sodium balance, the homeostasis of blood glucose, the response to novel invaders, and so forth. Yet these processes are not mystical in their beauty; when adequately understood they are logical and elegant. With the fundamental building blocks in place, physiology makes sense. The development of this conceptual structure can be intellectually exciting, like the thrill of the scientist when the pieces suddenly fit—a quiet "Eureka!" on a grand scale. Rational rules appear to govern organic function.

But the contrasting realities of clinical medicine soon become apparent to the young physician as he or she is first challenged by patients. Students are (or should be) struck by the pervasive uncertainty in clinical medicine. The anxiety produced by this uncertainty is intense. There are two types of uncertainty that must be distinguished: the uncertainty of the physician's individual knowledge of medicine and the uncertainty of our collective knowledge.[1] The first is a reflection of individual limitations; we simply cannot remember everything we have been taught, and we cannot digest the mass of information that overwhelms us daily. However, we may believe that the brighter we are, the harder we work, and the more experience we have, the more this uncertainty will diminish. In truth, experience and hard work may also serve to clarify the limits of our uncertainty and lead to a wiser use of our limited knowledge. But if this route to wisdom escapes the physician, it may become increasingly difficult with time to admit uncertainty to patients or to colleagues. This uncertainty may be seen as an embarrassing admission of modest intellectual powers, inadequate study, and/or insufficient experience. It is when physicians conceal their uncertainty, whether consciously or unconsciously, that they become a significant threat to the welfare of patients.

The uncertainty created by our human limitations must be contrasted with the intrinsic uncertainty of science and medicine. This latter type of uncertainty is composed of two related components. The first is simply our current state of knowledge: there is a vast body of knowledge to be acquired and a vast body of knowledge to be revised. We shall not see the end of this process. Second, there is the problem of applying our knowledge to the individual patient. The clues of the careful history, the basics and the subtleties of the physical exam, the use of technical tests and probes, and a comprehensive knowledge of physiology and pathology may not tell us why *this* patient is ill. Katz has observed that physicians will readily admit this type of uncertainty to one another,[2] but that we are frequently reluctant to reveal uncertainty to patients. Socrates took a certain pride in proclaiming his ignorance, but most of us do not. We are perhaps afraid that such honesty will diminish our power with patients, and indeed it might. Our traditional reluctance to admit our ignorance and the popular glorification of "medical miracles" lead some patients to confuse the origins of uncertainty. Patients may search in vain for a "better doctor" to provide them information that simply cannot be provided.

These pervasive uncertainties are intellectual irritants. In the midst of this uncertainty remains a solid core of practical knowledge—the rational rules of the human organism. Herein lies the seductive power of physiology. Knowledge of physiologic rules provides the ability to control physiologic processes. There is that psychological surge of power when the blood gases normalize from our astute manipulations of the ventilator, or when the heart's erratic rhythm smooths to a sinus beat. The power is afforded not only from our capabilities, but through a perceived understanding of our capabilities. We know what should work and why it should work—physiology is in our hands. The profound satisfaction this produces is compelling and provides safe refuge from pervasive uncertainties. This leads not so much to a "technological imperative"—the need to use technology for its own sake—but to a "physiologic imperative"—the desire to take control over those life processes susceptible to our technology. As residents, when death for our patients seemed inevitable, we strove for what we termed a "Harvard Death"—in which the body's electrolytes remained in balance. This was a pointless exercise of power from the perspective of the patient, but a satisfying exercise for those of us unable to deal with death on other terms.

The pursuit of normal physiology defines much of modern clinical medicine. Obviously this is good and right in the majority of clinical circumstances where normal physiology serves the interest of the patient. But reestablishing normal physiologic processes is obviously a narrow goal—a goal that serves only the portion of the human organism amenable to physiologic description and control. Despite the advances afforded by experimental medicine, humans have yet to be explained or understood in the vocabulary of physiology. This ignorance of ourselves and our mutual unpredictability is a fundamental element of self-perception and social relations. At the present time, at least, we can continue to believe that we, as individuals, are more than the sum total of our physiologic processes. Whether this is due to a soul or is only biology at a higher order of complexity remains to be determined.

When an individual is in good health, organic function is only background noise. For an individual in poor health, organic function becomes relevant in two ways. One is the intrinsic value of normal function, apparent when disease causes pain or suffering. The second is the instrumental value of health. Normal or adequate organic function is a primary good through which we pursue our other goals.[3] If medicine is to serve us as individuals, it must address organic function on both levels.

As the science of organic function, physiology must be seen as the servant of our other goals and thus of the human values that determine those goals. For better or worse, human values often lie well within the realm of uncertainty. Even our own personal values may be frequently uncertain—at least in the context of illness, where complex choices may be layered on pain and fear. The values of our patients are all the more remote from our grasp. It is little wonder that physicians may seek refuge in the science of the organism, and that our patients are often eager followers of our firm—but perhaps misguided—lead on technical adventures.

But safe refuge from uncertainty is not our destination. Patients understand this when the tests and technology multiply, but no advantage is gained either for the instrumental value of organic function or for its intrinsic value. The physiologic knowledge gained may simply have no use. Physicians understand this when they lament what they have done to patients in "the unit," but they do not know what else to do. Of course, the rational science of the organism may seem enough when it is sufficient to restore organic function. I do not wish to minimize the very real value of this aspect of modern medicine. But when this rational science falls short, the refuge it provides offers cold comfort.

How should we respond to this seduction by physiology? One response would be to denigrate the role of the basic sciences in medicine. Few within medicine or society would welcome such a direction. Rational science has produced extraordinary benefits, and the yield from medical science is only beginning. The detailed analysis of the human genome, as well as the DNA of other life forms, is only one example of pursuits that will transform medicine, presumably for our benefit. It is not knowledge *per se* that should be suspect.

A second response to the power of physiology could be the further subspecialization of medicine. Those intellectually oriented toward the rational science of the organism could be encouraged to focus on these skills at the exclusion of others. Those more adept at developing relationships with patients and weighing the uncertainties of human values could be encouraged to foster these skills. With appropriate collaboration, perhaps the team approach to illness will serve all a patient's needs. To a significant extent, this is the developing nature of medical care in U.S. teaching hospitals. Intensivists, consultants, and house staff often thrive on the technical analysis and control of physiology. To attend to the other aspects of patient welfare, nurses, chaplains, social workers, and—occasionally—medical ethicists are functioning like additional consultants.

But subspecialization is doomed to failure from the patient's perspective. Patients certainly want physicians to be technically knowledgeable and adept, but this is not all they want.[4] Patients want someone to care for them and someone to trust and confide in, and they want this most when the rational science of the organism offers the least. These two desires for competence and care cannot be compartmentalized and attended to by teams. Similarly, the physician who only enjoys the thrill of technical analysis and control will never be satisfied in routine clinical practice. There are simply not enough technical challenges, and the human demands of patients will soon overwhelm those with little interest in this fundamental aspect of medicine. The wealth of technical thrills evaporates after residency for those who are not subspecialists.

Perhaps a better approach is to embrace complexity and uncertainty. Physiology and the rational science of the organism must be aggressively pursued, but it is crucial that science be placed in a broader perspective for physicians in training.[5] Competency in the basic sciences provides the tools for care, but it cannot be synonymous with care. Months of biochemistry, histology, and microbiology in the medical school curriculum are clearly excessive and beyond the needs of the vast majority of physicians. In addition, this concentration on scientific disciplines gives a false impression of the capabilities necessary for clinical competence. Those who wish to pursue basic science in greater detail should have the opportunity to do so, but this flood of information should not be foisted on all students with the assumption that it will contribute significantly to patient care.

The marginal value of detailed (and fleeting) knowledge of the basic sciences does not justify the cost—the lack of time to study the nature of illness (not disease) in all its diversity. An understanding of the history and the philosophy of medicine is essential to placing our work in proper perspective, as is the study of the differing cultural, ethnic, and religious views of illness and disease. Medical schools need to address basic questions: What are the goals of medicine? What are the legitimate powers of the physician in the relationship with patients, and in the promotion of social welfare? Legal issues relevant to medicine must be presented in the curriculum, and medical schools should introduce the newer disciplines of medical anthropology, risk analysis, decision theory, and health-care economics. The goal of a basic medical education must be to understand organic dysfunction in its physical, personal, and social context. This does not constitute a denigration of the traditional science curriculum, only the attempt to place it in balance with the other skills necessary for adequate patient care.

Would such a curriculum change the nature of medicine practiced by its students? Should we make physiology less seductive, or should we seek students more immune to seduction? With some notable exceptions,[6] we have been tinkering around the edges of medical education with efforts in both of these directions attempting to squeeze a few hours of "bioethics" into the curriculum and by marketing medicine to more students with majors in literature, music, and philosophy. This is progress to be sure, but incremental progress, the results of which will be impossible to measure. Bolder experiments are necessary in order to promote fundamental changes in the nature of medical education. . . .

Integral to this broader study of medicine is the recognition of uncertainty—the uncertainty of medical knowledge, the uncertainty of personal limitations, and the uncertainty of human values.[7] The resolution of these uncertainties is not imminent, so they must be recognized and embraced as reality and as a fundamental component of our work. Uncertainty must remain an intellectual irritant if medicine is to progress. It is the flight from uncertainty to false idols—the rational science of the organism—that risks the integrity of our profession and our true value as physicians.

NOTES

1. R. Fox, "Training for Uncertainty," in *The Student Physician*, ed. R. Merton, G. Reader, and P. Kendall (Cambridge, MA: Harvard University Press, 1957), 207–41.
2. J. Katz, *The Silent World of Doctor and Patient* (New York: Free Press, 1984), 165–206.
3. N. Daniels, *Just Health Care* (New York: Cambridge University Press, 1985), 32–35.
4. R. E. Murphy, "First Day," *Journal of the American Medical Association* 261 (1989): 1509.
5. D. C. Tosteson, "New Pathways in General Medical Education," *New England Journal of Medicine* 322 (1990): 234–38; D. Bok, "Needed: A New Way to Train Doctors," *Harvard Magazine* (May–June 1984): 32–43; S. H. Miles, L. W. Lane, J. Bickel et al., "Medical Ethics Education: Coming of Age," *Academic Medicine* 64 (1989): 705–14; E. Pelligrino, "Educating the Humanist Physician: An Ancient Ideal Reconsidered," *Journal of the American Medical Association* 227 (1974): 1288–94.
6. Bok, "Needed"; E. G. Dimond, "The UMKC Medical Education Experiment: An Alternative Pathway to Physicianhood," *Journal of the American Medical Association* 260 (1988): 956–58.
7. L. Thomas, *Late Night Thoughts on Listening to Mahler's Ninth Symphony* (New York: Bantam Books, 1984), 143–55.

Lorrie Moore

from PEOPLE LIKE THAT ARE THE ONLY PEOPLE HERE: CANONICAL BABBLING IN PEED ONK

In this brief, powerful scene, a mother whose baby has been diagnosed with cancer struggles to comprehend the disease's implications as she visits the Pediatric Oncology ("Peed Onk") ward for the first time. The scene illuminates what people undergo in trying to become knowledgeable about incomprehensible, catastrophic illness when it affects a child.

LORRIE MOORE is a professor of English at the University of Wisconsin, Madison. Her work has appeared in the *New Yorker*, the *Paris Review*, the *New York Times*, and *Harper's*. She is the author of *Self-Help, Anagrams, Like Life*, and *Who Will Run the Frog Hospital?* This story is from a collection of short stories titled *Birds of America*.

Take Notes. In the end, you suffer alone. But at the beginning you suffer with a whole lot of others. When your child has cancer, you are instantly whisked away to another planet: one of bald-headed little boys. Pediatric Oncology. Peed Onk. You wash your hands for thirty seconds in antibacterial soap before you are allowed to enter through the swinging doors. You put paper slippers on your shoes. You keep your voice down. A whole place has been designed and decorated for your nightmare. Here is where your nightmare will occur. We've got a room all ready for you. We have cots. We have refrigerators. "The children are almost entirely boys," says one of the nurses. "No one knows why. It's been documented, but a lot of people out there still don't realize it." The little boys are all from sweet-sounding places—Janesville and Appleton—little heartland towns with giant landfills, agricultural runoff, paper factories, Joe McCarthy's grave (alone a site of great toxicity, thinks the Mother. The soil should be tested).

All the bald little boys look like brothers. They wheel their IVs up and down the single corridor of Peed Onk. Some of the lively ones, feeling good for a day, ride the lower bars of the IV while their large, cheerful mothers whiz them along the halls. *Wheee!*

Theodore Deppe
ADMISSION, CHILDREN'S UNIT

Faced with the disturbing task of admitting into the children's unit a boy whose back has been repeatedly and intentionally burned with a lit cigarette, a nurse contemplates the legend of Saint Lawrence teaching his disciples to recognize "the smell of sin." This poem cautions us about having "sufficient knowledge" to glean a moral diagnosis as well as a medical one—in this case, about a way of life.

THEODORE DEPPE works on a psychiatric unit for children; he is also a creative writing teacher in a high school for the arts and the author of *Children of the Air*. His work has appeared in *Crazyhorse*, the *Kenyon Review*, and other publications. Deppe received an NEA Fellowship in poetry and a poetry grant from the Connecticut Commission on the Arts.

Later, I'd look up the story a friend told me years ago,
how St. Lawrence taught his disciples to recognize the smell
of sin, how they'd set off in pairs through the Roman Empire,
separating good from evil, hoping to speed the Lord's return.
It must have been this scrap of legend, half-remembered,
that moved in me last week when I stopped suddenly and,

trying nor to stare at the woman, drew my breath in and smelled
her, catching a scent that was there and then not there.
She was telling me how her son set fire to his own room,
how she'd found him fanning the flames with a pile of comics,
and what could she do with such a child? Her hair
was pulled back in a ponytail, her face shining and suffering,

and what she had done, it turns out, was hold her son down
so her boyfriend could burn him with cigarettes.
The details didn't, of course, come out at first, but I sensed them.
The boy's refusal to take off his shirt. His letting me, finally, lift
it to his shoulders, examine the six wounds arranged in a cross,
raised, ashy, second or third degree, I don't know which.

Silence in the room, and then the mother blaming
the boyfriend, blaming the boy himself.
I kept talking to her in a calming voice, straining for something
I thought I smelled beneath her cheap perfume—a scent
maddening, of course, because nameless, little top note
of thrill followed by something—how can I describe this?

a bass note after, or under, the other smells, as if something
not physical had begun to rot.
I'd like to say all this happened when I first started
to work as a nurse, before I'd learned not to judge the parents,
but this was last week, the mother was crying,
I thought of handing her a box of tissues, and didn't.

When the Romans crucified Lawrence, according to the story
even the church won't stand behind anymore, he asked Jesus
to forgive him for judging others when his own sin was so large.
He wept on the cross because he smelled his own soul
and knew he was lost. Only when the soldiers lifted him down
did they find rose petals, clutched in his fists,

a new species exuding a fragrance never before smelled on earth.
The boy got up, sullen, wordless, brought his mother
Kleenex from my desk, pressed his head into her side.
Bunched the bottom of her sweatshirt in both hands
as if anchoring himself to her. Glared at me.
It took four of us to pry the boy from his mother's arms.

Terry Tempest Williams

THE VILLAGE WATCHMAN

As she tells the story of her institutionalized Uncle Alan, Terry Tempest Williams reflects on being knowledgeable about the multidimensional nature of a word often used in medicine: "normal." Alan's surprising answer to Williams's question, "What is it really like to be inside your body?" highlights the revelatory power of engagement.

TERRY TEMPEST WILLIAMS writes about the natural landscape and her Mormon faith. She is the author of *An Unspoken Hunger*, from which this essay is taken; *Refuge*, the story of her mother's battle with ovarian cancer; and, most recently, *Leap*. The recipient of a Lannan Literary Fellowship and a Guggenheim Fellowship, she lives with her husband, Brooke Williams, in Grand County, Utah.

Stories carved in cedar rise from the deep woods of Sitka. These totem poles are foreign to me, this vertical lineage of clans; Eagle, Raven, Wolf, and Salmon. The Tlingit craftsmen create a genealogy of the earth, a reminder of mentors, that we come into this world in need of proper instruction. I sit on the soft floor of this Alaskan forest and feel the presence of Other.

The totem before me is called "Wolf Pole" by locals. The Village Watchman sits on top of Wolf's head with his knees drawn to his chest, his hands holding them tight against his body. He wears a red-and-black-striped hat. His eyes are direct, deep-set, painted blue. The expression on his face reminds me of a man I loved, a man who was born into this world feet first.

"Breech—" my mother told me of her brother's birth. "Alan was born feet first. As a result, his brain was denied oxygen. He is special."

As a child, this information impressed me. I remember thinking fish live underwater. Maybe Alan had gills, maybe he didn't need a face-first gulp of air like the rest of us. His sweet breath of initiation came in time, slowly moving up through the soles of his tiny webbed feet. The amniotic sea he had floated in for nine months delivered him with a fluid memory. He knew something. Other.

Wolf, who resides in the center of this totem, holds the tail of Salmon with his feet. The tongue of Wolf hangs down, blood-red, as do his front paws, black. Salmon, a sockeye, is poised downriver—a swish of a tail and he could be gone, but the clasp of Wolf is strong.

There is a story of a boy who was kidnapped from his village by the Salmon People. He was taken from his family to learn the ways of water. When he returned many years later to his home, he was recognized by his own as a Holy Man privy to the mysteries of the unseen world. Twenty years after my uncle's death, I wonder if Alan could have been that boy.

But our culture tells a different story, more alien than those of Tlingit or Haida. My culture calls people of sole-births retarded, handicapped, mentally disabled or challenged. We see them for who they are not, rather than for who they are.

My grandmother, Lettie Romney Dixon, wrote in her journal, "It wasn't until Alan was sixteen months old that a busy doctor cruelly broke the news to us. Others may have suspected our son's limitations, but to those of us who loved him so unquestionably, lightning struck without warning. I hugged my sorrow to myself. I felt abandoned and lost. I wouldn't accept the verdict. Then we started the trips to a multitude of doctors. Most of them were kind and explained that our child was like a car without brakes, like an electric wire without insulation. They gave us no hope for a normal life."

Normal. Latin: *normalis; norma,* a rule; conforming with or constituting an accepted standard, model, or pattern, especially corresponding to the median or average of a large group in type, appearance, achievement, function, or development.

Alan was not normal. He was unique; one and only; single; sole; unusual; extraordinary; rare. His emotions were not measured, his curiosity not bridled. In a sense, he was wild like a mustang in the desert and, like most wild horses, he was eventually rounded up.

He was unpredictable. He created his own rules, and they changed from moment to moment. Alan was twelve years old, hyperactive, mischievous, easily frustrated, and unable to learn in traditional ways. The situation was intensified by his seizures. Suddenly, without warning, he would stiffen like a rake, fall forward and crash to the ground, hitting his head. My grandparents could not keep him home any longer. They needed professional guidance and help. In 1957 they reluctantly placed their youngest child in an institution for handicapped children called the American Fork Training School. My grandmother's heart broke for the second time.

Once again, from her journal: "Many a night my pillow is wet from tears of sorrow and senseless dreamings of 'if things had only been different,' or wondering if he is tucked in snug and warm, if he is well and happy, if the wind still bothers him. . . ."

The wind may have continued to bother Alan, certainly the conditions he was living under were less than ideal, but as a family there was much about his private life we never knew. What we did know was that Alan had an enormous capacity for adaptation. We had no choice but to follow him.

I followed him for years.

Alan was ten years my senior. In my mind, growing up, he was mythic. Everything I was taught not to do, Alan did. We were taught to be polite, to not express displeasure or anger in public. Alan was sheer, physical expression. Whatever was on his mind was vocalized and usually punctuated with colorful speech. We would go bowling as a family on Sundays. Each of us would take our turn, hold the black ball to our chest, take a few steps, swing our arm back, forward, glide, and release—the ball would roll down the alley, hit a few pins, we would wait for the ball to return, and then take our second run. Little emotion was shown. When it was Alan's turn, it was an event. Nothing subtle. His style was Herculean. Big man. Big ball. Big roll. Big bang. Whether it was a strike or a gutter, he clapped his hands, spun around in the floor, slapped his thighs and cried, "God-damn! Did you see that one? Send me another ball, sweet Jesus!" And the ball was always returned.

I could always count on my uncle for a straight answer. He was my mentor in understanding that one of the remarkable aspects of being human was to hold opposing views in our mind at once.

"How are you doing?" I would ask.

"Ask me how I am feeling?" he answered.

"Okay, how are you feeling?"

"Today? Right now?"

"Yes."

"I am very happy and very sad."

"How can you be both at the same time?" I asked in all seriousness, a girl of nine or ten.

"Because both require each other's company. They live in the same house. Didn't you know?"

We would laugh and then go on to another topic. Talking to my uncle was always like entering a maze of riddles. Ask a question. Answer with a question and see where it leads you.

My younger brother Steve and I spent a lot of time with Alan. He offered us shelter from the conventionality of a Mormon family. At our home during Christmas, he would direct us in his own nativity plays. "More—" he would say to us, making wide gestures with his hands. "Give me more of yourself." He was not like anyone we knew. In a culture where we were taught socially to be seen not heard, Alan was our mirror. We could be different too. His unquestioning belief in us as children, as human beings, was in startling contrast to the way we saw the public react to him. It hurt us. What we could never tell was if it hurt him.

Each week, Steve and I would accompany our grandparents south to visit Alan. It was an hour's drive to the training school from Salt Lake City, mostly through farmlands.

We would enter the grounds, pull into the parking lot of the institution where a playground filled with huge papier-mâché storybook figures stood (a twenty-foot pied piper, a pumpkin carriage with Cinderella inside, the old woman who lived in a shoe), and nine out of ten times, Alan would be standing outside his dormitory waiting for us. We would get out of the car and he would run toward us, throwing his powerful arms around us. His hugs cracked my back and at times I had to fight for my breath. My grandfather would calm him down by simply saying, "We're here, son. You can relax now."

Alan was a formidable man, now in his early twenties, stocky and strong.

His head was large with a protruding forehead that bore many scars, a line-by-line history of seizures. He always had on someone else's clothes—a tweed jacket too small, brown pants too big, a striped golf shirt that didn't match. He showed us appearances didn't matter, personality did. If you didn't know him, he could look frightening. It was an unspoken rule in our family that the character of others was gauged in how they treated him. The only thing consistent about his attire was that he always wore a silver football helmet from Olympus High School where my grandfather was coach. It was a loving, practical solution to protect Alan when he fell. Quite simply, the helmet cradled his head and absorbed the shock of the seizures.

"Part of the team," my grandfather Sanky would say as he slapped him affectionately on the back. "You're a Titan, son, and I love you—you're a real player on our team."

The windows to the dormitory were dark, reflecting Mount Timpanogos to the east. It was hard to see inside, but I knew what the interior held. It looked like an abandoned gymnasium without bleachers, filled with hospital beds. The stained white walls and yellow-waxed floors offered no warmth to its residents. The stench was nauseating, sweat and urine trapped in the oppression of stale air. I recall the dirty sheets, the lack of privacy, and the almond-eyed children who never rose from their beds. And then I would turn around and face Alan's cheerfulness, the open and loving manner in which he would introduce me to his friends, the pride he exhibited as he showed me around his home. I kept thinking, Doesn't he see how bad this is, how poorly they are being treated? His words would return to me, "I am very happy and I am very sad."

For my brother and me, Alan was our guide, our elder. He was fearless. But neither one of us will ever be able to escape the image of Alan kissing his parents good-bye after an afternoon with family and slowly walking back to his dormitory. Before we drove away, he would turn toward us, take off his silver helmet, and wave. The look on his face haunts me still. Alan walked point for all of us.

Alan liked to talk about God. Perhaps it was in these private conversations that our real friendship was forged.

"I know Him," he would say when all the adults were gone.

"You do?" I asked.

"I talk to Him every day."

"How so?"

"I talk to Him in my prayers. I listen and then I hear His voice."

"What does He tell you?"

"He tells me to be patient. He tells me to be kind. He tells me that He loves me."

In Mormon culture, children are baptized a member of the Church of Jesus Christ of Latter-Day Saints when they turn eight years old. Alan had never been baptized because my grandparents believed it should be his choice, not something simply taken for granted. When he turned twenty-two, he expressed a sincere desire to join the Church. A date was set immediately.

The entire Dixon clan convened in the Lehi Chapel, a few miles north of the group home where Alan was now living. We were there to support and witness his conversion. As we walked toward the meetinghouse where this sacred rite was to be performed, Alan had a violent seizure. My grandfather and Uncle Don, Alan's elder brother, dropped down with him, holding his head and body as every muscle thrashed on the pavement like a school of netted fish brought on deck. I didn't want to look, but to walk away would have been worse. We stayed with him, all of us.

"Talk to God," I heard myself saying under my breath. "I love you, Alan."

"Can you hear me, darling?" It was my grandmother's voice, her hand holding her son's hand.

By now, many of us were gathered on our knees around him, our trembling hands on his rigid body.

> And we, who have always thought
> Of happiness as rising, would feel
> The emotion that almost overwhelms us
> Whenever a happy thing falls.
>
> —*Rainer Maria Rilke*

Alan opened his eyes. "I want to be baptized," he said. The men helped him to his feet. The gash on his left temple was deep. Blood dripped down the side of his face. He would forgo stitches once again. My mother had her arm around my grandmother's waist. Shaken, we all followed him inside.

Alan's father and brother ministered to him, stopped the bleeding and bandaged the pressure wound, then helped him change into the designated white garments for baptism. He entered the room with great dignity and sat on the front pew with a dozen or more eight-year-old children seated on either side. Row after row of family sat behind him.

"Alan Romney Dixon." His name was called by the presiding bishop. Alan rose from the pew and met his brother Don, also dressed in white, who took his hand and led him down the blue-tiled stairs into the baptismal font filled with water. They faced the congregation. Don raised his right arm to the square in the gesture of a holy oath as Alan placed his hands on his brother's left forearm. The sacred prayer was offered in the name of the Father, the Son, and the Holy Ghost, after which my uncle put his right hand behind Alan's shoulder and gently lowered him into the water for a complete baptism by immersion.

Alan emerged from the holy waters like an angel.

> The breaking away of childhood
> Left you intact. In a moment,
> You stood there, as if completed
> In a miracle, all at once.
>
> —*Rainer Maria Rilke*

Six years later, I found myself sitting in a chair across from my uncle at the University Hospital, where he was being treated for a severe ear infection. I was eighteen. He was twenty-eight.

"Alan," I asked. "What is it really like to be inside your body?"

He crossed his legs and placed both hands on the arms of the chair. His brown eyes were piercing.

"I can't tell you what it's like except to say I feel pain for not being seen as the person I am."

A few days later, Alan died alone; unique; one and only; single; in American Fork, Utah.

The Village Watchman sits on top of his totem with Wolf and Salmon—it is beginning to rain in the forest. I find it curious that this spot in southeast Alaska has brought me back into relations with my uncle, this man of sole-birth who came into the world feet first. He reminds me of what it means to live and love with a broken heart; how nothing is sacred, how everything is sacred. He was a weather vane—a storm and a clearing at once.

Shortly after his death, Alan appeared to me in a dream. We were standing in my grandmother's kitchen. He was leaning against the white stove with his arms folded.

"Look at me now, Terry," he said smiling. "I'm normal—perfectly normal." And then he laughed. We both laughed.

He handed me his silver football helmet that was resting on the counter, kissed me, and opened the back door.

"Do you recognize who I am?"

On this day in Sitka, I remember.

Bernard Pomerance

from THE ELEPHANT MAN: A PLAY

The Elephant Man is based on the life of Joseph "John" Merrick, who lived in London in the late nineteenth century. Suffering from an extreme case of neurofibromastosis, Merrick was born severely deformed, and people ran down the street screaming in horror and disgust at the sight of him. Merrick was rescued from circus freak shows and public humiliation by a physician named Frederick Treves. Treves discovered that Merrick was a highly intelligent, deeply sensitive, and refined man—one who became something of a celebrity among London society.

The play explores the relationship between doctor and patient—in particular, the knowledge doctor and patient have of one another and how they "diagnose" one another in the course of medical treatment. In the first of two scenes reprinted here, Dr. Treves lectures a group of doctors about Merrick's condition in painstaking detail. In the second scene, it is Merrick's turn to lecture a group of "pinheads" about Dr. Treves's condition as he sees it.

BERNARD POMERANCE is an American playwright living in London. He is best known for *The Elephant Man*.

SCENE III: WHO HAS SEEN THE LIKE OF THIS?

TREVES *lectures.* MERRICK *contorts himself to approximate projected slides of the real Merrick.*

TREVES: The most striking feature about him was his enormous head. Its circumference was about that of a man's waist. From the brow there projected a huge bony mass like a loaf, while from the back of his head hung a bag of spongy fungous-looking skin, the surface of which was comparable to brown cauliflower. On the top of the skull were a few long lank hairs. The osseous growth on the forehead, at this stage about the size of a tangerine, almost occluded one eye. From the upper jaw there projected another mass of bone. It protruded from the mouth like a pink stump, turning the upper lip inside out, and making the mouth a wide slobbering aperture. The nose was merely a lump of flesh, only recognizable as a nose from its position. The deformities rendered the face utterly incapable of the expression of any emotion whatsoever. The back was horrible because from it hung, as far down as the middle of the thigh, huge sacklike masses of flesh covered by the same loathsome cauliflower stain. The right arm was of enormous size and shapeless. It suggested but was not elephantiasis, and was overgrown also with pendant masses of the same cauliflower-like skin. The right hand was large and clumsy—a fin or paddle rather than a hand. No distinction existed between the palm and back, the thumb was like a radish, the fingers like thick tuberous roots. As a limb it was useless. The other arm was remarkable by contrast. It was not only normal, but was moreover a delicately shaped limb covered with a fine skin and provided with a beautiful hand which any woman might have envied. From the chest hung a bag of the same repulsive flesh. It was like a dewlap suspended from the neck of a lizard. The lower limbs had the characters of the deformed arm. They were unwieldy, dropsical-looking, and grossly misshapen. There arose from the fungous skin growths a very sickening stench which was hard to tolerate. To add a further burden to his trouble, the wretched man when a boy developed hip disease which left him permanently lame, so that he could only walk with a stick. (*To* MERRICK) Please. (MERRICK *walks.*) He was thus denied all means of escape from his tormentors.

VOICE: Mr. Treves, you have shown a profound and unknown disorder to us. You have said when he leaves here it is for his exhibition again. I do not think it ought to be permitted. It is a disgrace. It is a pity and a disgrace. It is an indecency in fact. It may be a danger in ways we do not know. Something ought to be done about it.

TREVES: I am a doctor. What would you have me do?

VOICE: Well, I know what to do. *I* know.

Silence. A policeman enters as lights fade out.

SCENE XVIII: WE ARE DEALING WITH AN EPIDEMIC

TREVES *asleep.* MERRICK *at lecturn.*

MERRICK: The most striking thing about him, note, is the terrifyingly normal head. This allowed him to lie down normally, and therefore to dream in the exclusive personal manner, without the weight of others' dreams accumulating to break his neck. From the brow projected a normal vision of benevolent enlightenment, what we believe to be a kind of self-mesmerized state. The mouth, deformed by satisfaction at being the hub of the best of existent worlds, was rendered therefore utterly incapable of self-critical speech, thus of the ability to change. The heart showed signs of worry at this unchanging yet untenable state. The back was horribly stiff from being kept against a wall to face the discontent of a world ordered for his convenience. The surgeon's hands were well-developed and strong, capable of the most delicate carvings-up, for others' own good. Due also to the normal head, the right arm was of enormous power; but, so incapable of the distinction between the assertion of authority and the charitable act of giving, that it was often to be found disgustingly beating others—for their own good. The left arm was slighter and fairer, and may be seen in typical position, hand covering the genitals, which were treated as a sullen colony in constant need of restriction, governance, punishment. For their own good. To add a further burden to his trouble, the wretched man when a boy developed a disabling spiritual duality, therefore was unable to feel what others feel, nor reach harmony with them. Please. (TREVES *shrugs.*) He would thus be denied all means of escape from those he had tormented.

PINS *enter.*

FIRST PIN: Mr. Merrick. You have shown a profound and unknown disorder to us. You have said when he leaves here, it is for his prior life again. I do not think it ought to be permitted. It is a disgrace. It is a pity and a disgrace.

It is an indecency in fact. It may be a danger in ways we do not know. Something ought to be done about it.

MERRICK: We hope in twenty years we will understand enough to put an end to this affliction.

FIRST PIN: Twenty years! Sir, that is unacceptable!

MERRICK: Had we caught it early, it might have been different. But his condition has already spread both east and west. The truth is, I am afraid, we are dealing with an epidemic.

Lewis Thomas

LEECH, LEECH, ET CETERA

In this lively discussion of medicine and what it has meant to be a doctor during the course of history, Lewis Thomas begins with an exercise in comparative philology, an examination of the origins of words. Why, Thomas wonders, was the word "leech" used for a doctor and at the same time for the worm for many centuries? Or, as Thomas puts it, "Which came first, leech the doctor or leech the worm?"

In posing and answering this question, Thomas models the importance of the practice of invigorating scientific knowledge as the basis for medicine.

LEWIS THOMAS (1914–1994) a physician, teacher, and essayist, was probably best known for his writing on a variety of subjects. He was a former dean of New York University Medical School and president of the Memorial Sloan Kettering Cancer Center. Thomas's first book, *The Lives of a Cell*, a collection of twenty-nine essays first written for the *New England Journal of Medicine*, won the National Book Award. His other books include *The Medusa and the Snail* and *The Youngest Science*, from which this essay was taken.

A few years ago, I blundered into the fringes of a marvelous field of scholarship, comparative philology. I wondered—I forget the occasion—why leech was the word for the doctor and at the same time for the worm used by the doctor for so many centuries. Which came first, leech the doctor or leech the worm?

The lovely *American Heritage Dictionary* has a fifty-page appendix of Indo-European roots, based in large part on *Pokorny's Dictionary of Indo-European Languages*. My wife searched New York's bookstores and found a copy of *Pokorny* in a rare-book store for my birthday, and I have never since looked back.

The evolution of language can be compared to the biological evolution of species, depending on how far you are willing to stretch analogies. The first and deepest question is open and unanswerable in both cases: how did life start up at its very beginning? What was the very first human speech like?

Fossils exist for both, making it possible to track back to somewhere near the beginning. The earliest forms of life were the prokaryotes, organisms of the same shape and size as bacteria; chains of cocci and bacilli left unmistakable imprints within rocks dating back as far as 3.5 billion years. Similar microorganisms comprised the total life of the planet for the next 2.5 billion years, living free or, more often, gathered together as immense colonies in "algal mats," which later on fossilized into the formidable geological structures known as stromatolites. It was only recently, perhaps a billion years ago, that the prokaryotic algae had pumped enough oxygen into the earth's atmosphere so that nucleated cells could be formed. The mitochondria, which provide oxidative energy for all nucleated cells, and the chloroplasts of plant cells, which engage the sun's energy for producing the planet's food and oxygen, are the lineal descendants of bacteria and blue-green algae, and have lived as symbionts with the rest of us for a billion years.

The fossils of human language are much more recent, of course, and can only be scrutinized by the indirect methods of comparative philology, but they are certainly there. The most familiar ones are the Indo-European roots, prokaryote equivalents, the ancestors of most of the Western and some of the Eastern languages: Sanskrit, Greek, Latin, all the Slavic and Germanic tongues, Hittite, Tocharian, Iranian, Indic, some others, all originating in a common speech more than 20,000 years ago at a very rough guess. The original words from which the languages evolved were probably, at the outset, expressions of simple, non-nucleated ideas, unambiguous etymons.

The two leeches are an example of biological mimicry at work in language. The root for leech the doctor goes back to the start of language: *leg* was a word meaning "to collect, with derivatives meaning to speak" and carried somehow the implication of knowledge and wisdom. It became *laece* in Old English, *lake* in Middle Dutch, with the meaning of doctor. Along the way, in early Germanic, it yielded *lekjaz*, a word meaning "an enchanter, speaking magic words," which would fit well with the duties of early physicians. The doctor was called the leech in English for many centuries, and a Danish doctor is still known as *Laege*, a Swedish one as *Lakere.*

Leg gave spawn to other progeny, different from the doctor but with related meanings. Lecture, logic, and logos are examples to flatter medicine's heart.

Leech the worm is harder to trace. The *OED* has it in tenth-century records as *lyce*, later *laece*, and then the two leeches became, for all practical purposes, the same general idea. Leech the doctor made his living by the use of leech the worm; leech the worm was believed (wrongly, I think) to have had restorative, health-giving gifts and was therefore, in its way, a sort of doctor. The technical term "assimilation" is used for this fusion of words with two different meanings into a single word carrying both. The idea of collecting has perhaps sustained the fusion, persisting inside each usage: blood for the leech, fees (and blood as well) for the doctor. Tax collectors were once called leeches, for the worm meaning, of course.

The word doctor came from *dek*, meaning something proper and acceptable, useful. It became *docere* in Latin, to teach, also *discere*, to learn, hence disciple. In Greek it was understood to mean an acceptable kind of teaching, thus dogma and orthodox. Decorum and decency are cognate words.

Medicine itself emerged from root *med*, which meant something like measuring out, or taking appropriate measures. Latin used *med* to make *mederi*, to look after, to heal. The English words moderate and modest are also descendants of *med*, carrying instructions for medicine long since forgotten; medical students ought to mediate (another cognate) from time to time about these etymological cousins.

The physician came from a wonderful word, one of the master roots in the old language, *bheu*, meaning nature itself, being, existence. *Phusis* was made from this root in Greek, on its way to the English word physic, used for medicine in general, and physics, meaning the study of nature.

Doctor, medicine, and physician, taken together with the cognate words that grew up around them, tell us a great deal about society's ancient expectations from the profession, hard to live up to. Of all the list, moderate and modest seem to me the ones most in need of remembering. The root *med* has tucked itself inside these words, living as a successful symbiont, and its similar existence all these years inside medicine should be a steady message for the teacher, the healer, the collector of science, the old leech.

Medicine was once the most respected of all the professions. Today, when it possesses an array of technologies for treating (or curing) diseases which were simply beyond comprehension a few years ago, medicine is under attack for all sorts of reasons. Doctors, the critics say, are applied scientists, concerned only with the disease at hand but never with the patient as an individual, whole person. They do not really listen. They are unwilling or incapable of explaining things to sick people or their families. They make mistakes in their risky technologies; hence the rapidly escalating cost of malpractice insurance. They are accessible only in their offices in huge, alarming clinics or within the walls of terrifying hospitals. The word "dehumanizing" is used as an epithet for the way they are trained, and for the way they practice. The old art of medicine has been lost, forgotten.

The American medical schools are under pressure from all sides to bring back the family doctor—the sagacious, avuncular physician who used to make house calls, look after the illnesses of every member of the family, was even able to call the family dog by name. Whole new academic departments have been installed—some of them, in the state-run medical schools, actually legislated into existence—called, in the official catalogues, *Family Practice, Primary Health Care, Preventive Medicine, Primary Medicine.* The avowed intention is to turn out more general practitioners of the type that everyone remembers from childhood or from one's parents' or grandparents' childhood, or from books, movies, and television.

What is it that people have always expected from the doctor? How, indeed, has the profession of medicine survived for so much of human history? Doctors as a class have always been criticized for their deficiencies. Montaigne in his time, Molière in his, and Shaw had less regard for doctors and their medicine than today's critics. What on earth were the patients of physicians in the nineteenth century and the centuries before, all the way back to my professional ancestors, the shamans of prehistory, hoping for when they called for the doctor? In the years of the great plagues, when carts came through the town streets each night to pick up the dead and carry them off for burial, what was the function of the doctor? Bubonic plague, typhus, tuberculosis, and syphilis were representative examples of a great number of rapidly progressive and usually lethal infections, killing off most of the victims no matter what was done by the doctor. What did the man do, when called out at night to visit the sick for whom he had nothing to offer for palliation, much less cure?

Well, one thing he did, early on in history, was plainly magic. The shaman learned his profession the hardest way: he was compelled to go through something like a version of death itself, personally, and when he emerged he was considered qualified to deal with patients. He had epileptic fits, saw visions, and heard voices, lost himself in the wilderness for weeks on end, fell into long stretches of coma, and when he came back to life he was licensed to practice, dancing around the bedside, making smoke, chanting incomprehensibilities, and *touching* the patient everywhere. The touching was the real professional secret, never acknowledged as the central, essential skill, always obscured by the dancing and the chanting, but always busily there, the laying on of hands.

There, I think, is the oldest and most effective act of doctors, the touching. Some people don't like being handled by others, but not, or almost never, sick people. They *need* being touched, and part of the dismay in being very sick is the lack of close human contact. Ordinary people, even close friends, even family members, tend to stay away from the very sick, touching them as infrequently as possible for fear of interfering, or catching the illness, or just for fear of bad luck. The doctor's oldest skill in trade was to place his hands on the patient.

Over the centuries, the skill became more specialized and refined, the hands learned other things to do beyond mere contact. They probed to feel the pulse at the wrist, the tip of the spleen, or the edge of the liver, thumped to elicit resonant or dull sounds over the lungs, spread ointments over the skin, nicked veins for bleeding, but the same time touched, caressed, and at the end held on to the patient's fingers.

Most of the men who practiced this laying on of hands must have possessed, to begin with, the gift of affection. There are, certainly, some people who do not like other people much, and they would have been likely to stay away from an occupation requiring touching. If, by mistake, they found themselves apprenticed for medicine, they probably backed off or, if not, turned into unsuccessful doctors.

Touching with the naked ear was one of the great advances in the history of medicine. Once it was learned that the heart and lungs made sounds of their own, and that the sounds were sometimes useful for diagnosis, physicians placed an ear over the heart, and over areas on the front and back of the chest, and listened. It is hard to imagine a friendlier human gesture, a more intimate signal of personal concern and affection, than these close bowed heads affixed to the skin. The stethoscope was invented in the nineteenth century, vastly enhancing the acoustics of the thorax, but removing the physician a certain distance from his patient. It was the earliest device of many still to come, one new technology after another, designed to increase that distance.

Today, the doctor can perform a great many of his most essential tasks from his office in another building without ever seeing the patient. There are even computer programs for the taking of a history: a clerk can ask the questions and check the boxes on a printed form, and the computer will instantly provide a printout of the diagnostic possibilities to be considered and the laboratory procedures to be undertaken. Instead of spending forty-five minutes listening to the chest and palpating the abdomen, the doctor can sign a slip which sends the patient off to the X-ray department for a CT scan, with the expectation of seeing within the hour, in exquisite detail, all the body's internal organs which he formerly had to make guesses about with his fingers and ears. The biochemistry laboratory eliminates the need for pondering and waiting for the appearance of new signs and symptoms. Computerized devices reveal electronic intimacies of the flawed heart or malfunctioning brain with a precision far beyond the touch or reach, or even the imagining, of the physician at the bedside a few generations back.

The doctor can set himself, if he likes, at a distance, remote from the patient and the family, never touching anyone beyond a perfunctory handshake as the first and only contact. Medicine is no longer the laying on of hands, it is more like the reading of signals from machines.

The mechanization of scientific medicine is here to stay. The new medicine works. It is a vastly more complicated profession, with more things to be done on short notice on which issues of life or death depend. The physician has the same obligations that he carried, overworked and often despairingly, fifty years ago, but now with any number of technological maneuvers to be undertaken quickly and with precision. It looks to the patient like a different experience from what his parents told him about, with something important left out. The doctor seems less like the close friend and confidant, less interested in him as a person, wholly concerned with treating the disease. And there is no changing this, no going back; nor, when you think about it, is there really any reason for wanting to go back. If I develop the signs and symptoms of malignant hypertension, or cancer of the colon, or subacute bacterial endocarditis, I want as much comfort and friendship as I can find at hand, but mostly I want to be treated quickly and effectively so as to survive, if that is possible. If I am in bed in a modern hospital, worrying about the cost of that bed as well, I want to get out as fast as possible, whole if possible.

In my father's time, talking with the patient was the biggest part of medicine, for it was almost all there was to do. The doctor-patient relationship was, for better or worse, a long conversation in which the patient was at the epicenter of concern and knew it. When I was an intern and scientific technology was in its earliest stage, the talk was still there, but hurried, often on the run.

Today, with the advance of medicine's various and complicated new technologies, the ward rounds now at the foot of the bed, the drawing of blood samples for automated assessment of every known (or suggested) biochemical abnormality, the rolling of wheelchairs and litters down through the corridors to the X-ray department, there is less time for talking. The longest and most personal conversations held with hospital patients when they come to the hospital are discussions of finances and insurance, engaged in by personnel trained in accountancy, whose scientific instruments are the computers. The hospitalized patient feels, for a time, like a working part of an immense, automated apparatus. He is admitted and discharged by batteries of computers, sometimes without even learning the doctors' names. The difference can be strange and vaguely dismaying for patients. But there is another difference, worth emphasis. Many patients go home speedily, in good health, cured of their diseases. In my father's day this happened much less often, and when it did, it was a matter of good luck or a strong constitution. When it happens today, it is more frequently due to technology.

There are costs to be faced. Not just money, the real and heavy dollar costs. The close-up, reassuring, warm touch of the physician, the comfort and concern, the long, leisurely discussions in which everything including the dog can be worked into the conversation, are disappearing from the practice of medicine, and this may turn out to be too great a loss for the doctor as well as for the patient. This uniquely subtle, personal relationship has roots that go back into the beginnings of medicine's history, and needs preserving. To do it right has never been easy; it takes the best of doctors, the best of friends. Once lost, even for as short a time as one generation, it may be too difficult a task to bring it back again.

If I were a medical student or an intern, just getting ready to begin, I would be more worried about this aspect of my future than anything else. I would be apprehensive that my real job, caring for sick people, might soon be taken away, leaving me with the quite different occupation of looking after machines. I would be trying to figure out ways to keep this from happening.

Mikhail Bulgakov

BAPTISM BY ROTATION

from A Country Doctor's Notebook

After graduating from medical school, Mikhail Bulgakov spent the next eighteen months in an isolated, rural area of Russia. This story reflects the new practitioner's uncertainty and the challenge of moving from book knowledge to practical knowledge. Although he feels isolated and timorous, he has no choice as a doctor but to treat the woman who has been brought to his hospital in the throes of a difficult labor. He takes what is offered by the midwife, then retreats for a hasty consultation with his text. When he completes the procedure (with a positive outcome), he reflects on the need to "engage in lifelong learning."

MIKHAIL BULGAKOV (1891–1940) graduated from medical school at Kiev University in 1916. After practicing for a decade, Bulgakov became a full-time writer. *A Country Doctor's Notebook*, from which this story was taken, was first published in 1925–27. Bulgakov is also the author of the modern masterpiece *The Master and Margarita.*

As time passed in my country hospital, I gradually got used to the new way of life.

They were braking flax in the villages as they had always done, the roads were still impassable, and no more than five patients came to my daily surgery. My evenings were entirely free, and I spent them sorting out the library, reading surgical manuals and spending long hours drinking tea alone with the gently humming samovar.

For whole days and nights it poured with rain, the drops pounded unceasingly on the roof and the water cascaded past my window, swirling along the gutter and into a tub. Outside was slush, darkness and fog, through which the windows of the *feldsher*'s house and the kerosene lantern over the gateway were no more than faint, blurred patches of light.

On one such evening I was sitting in my study with an atlas of topographical anatomy. The absolute silence was only disturbed by the occasional gnawing of mice behind the sideboard in the dining room.

I read until my eyelids grew so heavy that they began to stick together. Finally I yawned, put the atlas aside, and decided to go to bed. I stretched in pleasant anticipation of sleeping soundly to the accompaniment of the noisy pounding of the rain, then went across to my bedroom, undressed, and lay down.

No sooner had my head touched the pillow than there swam hazily before me the face of Anna Prokhorova, a girl of seventeen from the village of Toropovo. She had needed a tooth extracting. Demyan Lukich, the *feldsher*, floated silently past holding a gleaming pair of pincers. Remembering how he always said "suchlike" instead of "such" because he was fond of a highfalutin style, I smiled and fell asleep.

About half an hour later, however, I suddenly woke up as though I had been pinched, sat up, stared fearfully into the darkness and listened.

Someone was drumming loudly and insistently on the outer door and I immediately sensed that those knocks boded no good.

Then came a knock on the door of my quarters.

The noise stopped, there was a grating of bolts, the sound of the cook talking, an indistinct voice in reply, then someone came creaking up the stairs, passed quietly through the study and knocked on my bedroom door.

"Who is it?"

"It's me," came the reply in a respectful whisper. "Me, Aksinya, the nurse."

'What's the matter?'

"Anna Nikolaevna has sent for you. They want you to come to the hospital as quickly as possible."

"What's happened?" I asked, feeling my heart literally miss a beat.

"A woman has been brought in from Dultsevo. She's having a difficult labor."

"Here we go!" I thought to myself, quite unable to get my feet into my slippers. "Hell, the matches won't light. Ah well, it had to happen sooner or later. You can't expect to get nothing but cases of laryngitis or abdominal catarrh all your life."

"All right, go and tell them I'm coming at once!" I shouted as I got out of bed. Aksinya's footsteps shuffled away from the door and the bolt grated again. Sleep vanished in a moment. Hurriedly, with shaking fingers, I lit the lamp and began dressing. Half past eleven . . . What could be wrong with this woman who was having a difficult birth? Malpresentation? Narrow pelvis? Or perhaps something worse. I might even have to use forceps. Should I send her straight into town? Out of the question! A fine doctor he is, they'll all say. In any case, I have no right to do that. No, I really must do it myself. But do what? God alone knows. It would be disastrous if I lost my head—I might disgrace myself in front of the midwives. Anyway, I must have a look first; no point in getting worried prematurely . . .

I dressed, threw an overcoat over my shoulders, and hoping that all would be well, ran to the hospital through the rain across the creaking duckboards. At the entrance I could see a cart in the semi-darkness, the horse pawing at the rotten boards under its hooves.

"Did you bring the woman in labor?" I asked the figure lurking by the horse.

"Yes, that's right . . . we did, sir," a woman's voice replied dolefully.

Despite the hour, the hospital was alive and bustling. A flickering pressure-lamp was burning in the surgery. In the little passage leading to the delivery room Aksinya slipped past me carrying a basin. A faint moan came through the door and died away again. I opened the door and went into the delivery room. The small, whitewashed room was brightly lit by a lamp in the ceiling. On a bed alongside the operating table, covered with a blanket up to her chin, lay a young woman. Her face was contorted in a grimace of pain and wet strands of hair were sticking to her forehead. Holding a large thermometer,

Anna Nikolaevna was preparing a solution in a graduated jug, while Pelagea Ivanovna was getting clean sheets out of the cupboard. The *feldsher* was leaning against the wall in a Napoleonic pose. Seeing me, they all jerked into life. The pregnant woman opened her eyes, wrung her hands and renewed her pathetic, long drawn-out groaning.

"Well now, what seems to be the trouble?" I asked, sounding confident.

"Transverse lie," Anna Nikolaevna answered promptly as she went on pouring water into the solution.

"I see-ee," I drawled, and added, frowning: "Well, let's have a look . . ."

"Aksinya! Wash the doctor's hands!" snapped Anna Nikolaevna. Her expression was solemn and serious.

As the water flowed, rinsing away the lather from my hands, reddened from scrubbing, I asked Anna Nikolaevna a few trivial questions, such as when the woman had been brought in, where she was from . . . Pelagea Ivanovna's hand turned back the blanket, I sat down on the edge of the bed and began gently feeling the swollen belly. The woman groaned, stretched, dug her fingers into her flesh and crumpled the sheet.

"There, there, relax . . . it won't take long," I said as I carefully put my hands to the hot, dry, distended skin.

The fact was that once the experienced Anna Nikolaevna had told me what was wrong, this examination was quite pointless. I could examine the woman as much as I liked, but I would not find out any more than Anna Nikolaevna knew already. Her diagnosis was, of course, correct: transverse lie. It was obvious. Well, what next?

Frowning, I continued palpating the belly on all sides and glanced sidelong at the midwives' faces. Both were watching with intense concentration, and their looks registered approval of what I was doing. But although my movements were confident and correct, I did my best to conceal my unease as thoroughly as possible.

"Very well," I said with a sigh, standing up from the bed, as there was nothing more to be seen from an external examination. "Let's examine her internally."

Another look of approval from Anna Nikolaevna.

"Aksinya!"

More water flowed.

"Oh, if only I could consult Döderlein now!" I thought miserably as I soaped my hands. Alas, this was quite impossible. In any case, how could Döderlein help me at a moment like this? I washed off the thick lather and painted my fingers with iodine. A clean sheet rustled in Pelagea Ivanovna's hands and, bending down over the expectant mother, I began cautiously and timidly to carry out an internal examination. Into my mind came an involuntary recollection of the operating theater in the maternity hospital. Gleaming electric lights in frosted-glass globes, a shining tiled floor, taps and instruments aglitter everywhere. A junior registrar in a snow-white coat is manipulating the woman, surrounded by three intern assistants, probationers, and a crowd of students doing their practicals. Everything bright, well ordered and safe.

And there was I, all on my own, with a woman in agony on my hands and I was responsible for her. I had no idea, however, what I was supposed to do to help her, because I had seen childbirth at close quarters only twice in my life in a hospital, and both occasions were completely normal. The fact that I was conducting an examination was of no value to me or to the woman; I understood absolutely nothing and could feel nothing of what was inside her.

It was time to make some sort of decision.

"Transverse lie . . . since it's a transverse lie I must . . . I must . . ."

"Turn it round by the foot," muttered Anna Nikolaevna as though thinking aloud, unable to restrain herself.

An older, more experienced doctor would have looked askance at her for butting in, but I am not the kind to take offense.

"Yes," I concurred gravely, "a podalic version."

The pages of Döderlein flickered before my eyes. Internal method . . . Combined method . . . External method . . . Page after page, covered in illustrations. A pelvis; twisted, crushed babies with enormous heads . . . a little dangling arm with a loop on it.

Indeed I had read it not long ago and had underlined it, soaking up every word, mentally picturing the interrelationship of every part of the whole and every method. And as I read it I imagined that the entire text was being imprinted on my brain forever.

Yet now only one sentence of it floated back into my memory:

"A transverse lie is a wholly unfavorable position."

Too true. Wholly unfavorable both for the woman and for a doctor who only qualified six months ago.

"Very well, we'll do it," I said as I stood up.

Anna Nikolaevna's expression came to life.

"Demyan Lukich," she turned to the *feldsher*, "get the chloroform ready."

It was a good thing that she had said so, because I was still not certain whether the operation was supposed to be done under anesthesia or not! Of course, under anesthesia—how else?

Still, I must have a look at Döderlein . . .

As I washed my hands I said:

"All right, then . . . prepare her for anesthesia and make her comfortable. I'll be back in a moment; I must just go to my room and fetch some cigarettes."

"Very good, doctor, we'll be ready by the time you come back," replied Anna Nikolaevna.

I dried my hands, the nurse threw my coat over my shoulders, and without putting my arms into the sleeves, I set off for home at a run.

In my study I lit the lamp and, forgetting to take off my cap, rushed straight to the bookcase.

There it was—Döderlein's *Operative Obstetrics*. I began hastily to leaf through the glossy pages.

". . . version is always a dangerous operation for the mother . . ."

A cold shiver ran down my spine.

"The chief danger lies in the possibility of a spontaneous rupture of the uterus . . ."

Spon-tan-e-ous . . .

"If in introducing his hand into the uterus the obstetrician encounters any hindrances to penetrating to the foot, whether from lack of space or as a result of a contraction of the uterine wall, he should refrain from further attempts to carry out the version . . ."

Good. Provided I am able, by some miracle, to recognize these "hindrances" and I refrain from "further attempts," what, might I ask, am I then supposed to do with an anesthetized woman from the village of Dultsevo?

Further:

"It is absolutely impermissible to attempt to reach the feet by penetrating behind the back of the fetus . . ."

Noted.

"It must be regarded as erroneous to grasp the upper leg, as doing so may easily result in the fetus being revolved too far; this can cause the fetus to suffer a severe blow, which can have the most deplorable consequences . . ."

"Deplorable consequences." Rather a vague phrase, but how sinister. What if the husband of the woman from Dultsevo is left a widower? I wiped the sweat from my brow, rallied my strength, and disregarded all the terrible things that could go wrong, trying only to remember the absolute essentials: what I had to do, where and how to put my hands. But as I ran my eye over the lines of black print, I kept encountering new horrors. They leaped out at me from the page.

". . . in view of the extreme danger of rupture . . ."

". . . the internal and combined methods must be classified as among the most dangerous obstetric operations to which a mother can be subjected . . ."

And as a grand finale:

". . . with every hour of delay the danger increases . . ."

That was enough. My reading had borne fruit: my head was in a complete muddle. For a moment I was convinced that I understood nothing, and above all that I had no idea what sort of version I was going to perform: combined, bipolar, internal, external . . .

I abandoned Döderlein and sank into an armchair, struggling to reduce my random thoughts to order. Then I glanced at my watch. Hell! I had already spent twenty minutes in my room, and they were waiting for me.

". . . with every hour of delay . . ."

Hours are made up of minutes, and at times like this the minutes fly past at insane speed. I threw Döderlein aside and ran back to the hospital.

Everything there was ready. The *feldsher* was standing over a little table preparing the anesthetic mask and the chloroform bottle. The expectant mother already lay on the operating table. Her ceaseless moans could be heard all over the hospital.

"There now, be brave," Pelagea Ivanovna muttered consolingly as she bent over the woman, "the doctor will help you in a moment."

"Oh, no! I haven't the strength . . . No . . . I can't stand it!"

"Don't be afraid," whispered the midwife. "You'll stand it. We'll just give you something to sniff, and then you won't feel anything."

Water gushed noisily from the taps as Anna Nikolaevna and I began washing and scrubbing our arms bared to the elbow. Against a background of groans and screams Anna Nikolaevna described to me how my predecessor, an experienced surgeon, had performed versions. I listened avidly to her, trying not to miss a single word. Those ten minutes told me more than everything I had read on obstetrics for my qualifying exams, in which I had actually passed the obstetrics paper "with distinction." From her brief remarks, unfinished sentences and passing hints I learned the essentials which are not to be found in any textbooks. And by the time I had begun to dry the perfect whiteness and cleanliness of my hands with sterile gauze, I was seized with confidence and a firm and absolutely definite plan had formed in my mind. There was simply no need to bother any longer over whether it was to be a combined or bipolar version.

None of these learned words meant anything at that moment. Only one thing mattered: I had to put one hand inside, assist the version with the other hand from outside and without relying on books but on common sense, without which no doctor is any good, carefully but firmly bring one foot downwards and pull the baby after it.

I had to be calm and cautious yet at the same time utterly decisive and unfaltering.

"Right, off you go," I instructed the *feldsher* as I began painting my fingers with iodine.

At once Pelagea Ivanovna folded the woman's arms and the *feldsher* clamped the mask over her agonized face. Chloroform slowly began to drip out of the dark yellow glass bottle, and the room started to fill with the sweet, nauseous odour. The expressions of the *feldsher* and midwives hardened with concentration, as though inspired . . .

"Haaa! Ah!" The woman suddenly shrieked. For a few seconds she writhed convulsively, trying to force away the mask.

"Hold her!"

Pelagea Ivanovna seized her by the arms and lay across her chest. The woman cried out a few more times, jerking her face away from the mask. Her movements slowed down, although she mumbled dully:

"Oh . . . let me go . . . ah . . ."

She grew weaker and weaker. The white room was silent. The translucent drops continued to drip, drip, drip on to the white gauze.

"Pulse, Pelagea Ivanovna?"

"Firm."

Pelagea Ivanovna raised the woman's arm and let it drop: as lifeless as a leather thong, it flopped on to the sheet. Removing the mask, the *feldsher* examined the pupil of her eye.

"She's asleep."

A pool of blood. My arms covered in blood up to the elbows. Bloodstains on the sheets. Red clots and lumps of gauze. Pelagea Ivanovna shaking and slapping the baby, Aksinya rattling buckets as she poured water into basins.

The baby was dipped alternately into cold and hot water. He did not make a sound, his head flopping lifelessly from side to side as though on a thread. Then suddenly there came a noise somewhere between a squeak and a sigh, followed by the first weak, hoarse cry.

"He's alive . . . alive . . . ," mumbled Pelagea Ivanovna as she laid the baby on a pillow.

And the mother was alive. Fortunately nothing had gone wrong. I felt her pulse. Yes, it was firm and steady; the *feldsher* gently shook her by the shoulder as he said:

"Wake up now, my dear."

The bloodstained sheets were thrown aside and the mother hastily covered with a clean one before the *feldsher* and Aksinya wheeled her away to the ward. The swaddled baby was borne away on his pillow, the brown, wrinkled little face staring out from its white wrapping as he cried ceaselessly in a thin, pathetic whimper.

Water gushing from the taps of the sluice. Anna Nikolaevna coughed as she dragged hungrily at a cigarette.

"You did the version well, doctor. You seemed very confident."

Scrubbing furiously at my hands, I glanced sidelong at her: was she being sarcastic? But no, her expression was a sincere one of pride and satisfaction. My heart was brimming with joy. I glanced round at the white and bloodstained disorder, at the red water in the basin and felt that I had won. But somewhere deep down there wriggled a worm of doubt.

"Let's wait and see what happens now," I said.

Anna Nikolaevna turned to look at me in astonishment.

"What can happen? Everything's all right."

I mumbled something vague in reply. What I had meant to say was to wonder whether the mother was really safe and sound, whether I might not have done her some harm during the operation . . . the thought nagged dully at my mind. My knowledge of obstetrics was so vague, so fragmentary and bookish. What about a rupture? How would it show? And when would it show—now or, perhaps, later? Better not talk about that.

"Well, almost anything," I said. "The possibility of infection cannot be ruled out," I added, repeating the first sentence from some textbook that came into my mind.

"Oh, th-at," Anna Nikolaevna drawled complacently. "Well, with luck nothing of that sort will happen. How could it, anyway? Everything here is clean and sterile."

It was after one o'clock when I went back to my room. In a pool of light on the desk in my study lay Döderlein open at the page headed "Dangers of Version." For another hour after that, sipping my cooling tea, I sat over it, turning the pages. And an interesting thing happened: all the previously obscure passages became entirely comprehensible, as though they had been flooded with light; and there, at night, under the lamplight in the depth of the countryside I realized what real knowledge was.

"One can gain a lot of experience in a country practice," I thought as I fell asleep, "but even so one must go on and on reading, reading . . . more and more . . ."

Judy Schaeffer

WHO OWNS THE LIBRETTO?

Patients and their families often deal with health crises by gathering information. Sometimes the information is factual and valuable, sometimes anecdotal, but in the end it provides them with a sense of control over events and often comforts them. In this poem, Judy Schaeffer describes the search by a child's parents for information about their child's illness. Are they searching because the doctors were unable to explain it, because they did not accept what the doctors told them, or because it isn't real to them unless explained in a text?

The surreptitious nature of the search detailed in this poem reflects the feelings of many patients and their families when entering the world of medicine—a world marked by a foreign language, strange powers, forbidding institutions, as well as a knowledge that seems distant and out of reach.

JUDY SCHAEFFER is a registered nurse certified in pediatrics. She is a staff member of the magazines *Wild Onion* and *Mediphors*, and a member of the Kienle Center for Humanistic Medicine. She is also a co-editor, with Cortney Davis, of *Between the Heartbeats: Poetry and Prose by Nurses*, from which this poem is taken.

They browsed quickly through
The medical stacks
Text after text
Pushing page after page
He watched her quick movements
He held her gray coat
To allow her armroom
And give her space to breathe
She pulled from
Shelf after shelf
Bent on her knees
Stretched up her arms
Then leaned back and sat down
Lifted her knees as in
Stirrup for childbirth
Book after hardbound book
Looking for a gush of water
Found one
This one
Splash of a waterfall
Look at this one
Pointed him to it
The illness there
Their respirations now fast
The illness of their child
Described with paragraphical details
Graphs and diagrams
Percentages and prognoses
They looked
Side to side
Held their breath
So as not to be caught
In their act
Not to be scolded
In their act of love

Their moment of near death
The inner sanctum
Stacks on stacks
Of well-worded knowledge
Of medical texts
An act of suspicion
That would confirm or deny
What the doctors told

PART THREE

Physicians Must Be Skillful

PHYSICIANS must be highly skilled in providing care to individual patients. They must be able to obtain from their patients an accurate history that contains all relevant information; to perform in a highly skilled manner a complete and a limited, organ-system-specific, physical examination; to perform skillfully those diagnostic procedures warranted by their patients' conditions and for which they have been trained; to obtain, interpret properly, and manage information about laboratory and radiology studies that relate to the patient's conditions; and to seek consultation from other physicians and other health care professionals when indicated. They must understand the etiology, the pathogenesis, and the clinical, laboratory, roentgenologic, and pathologic manifestations of the diseases or conditions they are likely to confront in their practice of their specialty. They must also understand the scientific basis and evidence of effectiveness for each of the therapeutic options that are available for patients at different times in the course of the patients' conditions, and be prepared to discuss those options with patients in an honest and objective fashion. Physicians must also be able to communicate with patients' families about all their concerns regarding the patients' health and well-being. They must be sufficiently knowledgeable about both traditional and nontraditional modes of care to provide intelligent guidance to their patients.

David Nash

THE TALLIS CASE

What is it like to make house calls on people who are "too poor for a society doctor but too proud for the clinic"? In this essay, David Nash recounts working diligently to provide in a highly skilled manner a physical examination of "an ancient Jew" in his home—and what happens when he tries to offer a therapeutic option he strongly believes may save his elderly patient's life.

The physician in "The Tallis Case" discovers the rewards of treating the patient in his own world.

DAVID NASH, a board certified internist, is the founding director of the Office of Health Policy and Clinical Outcomes at Thomas Jefferson University and an associate professor of medicine at Jefferson Medical College in Philadelphia. "The Tallis Case" appeared in the *JAMA* column "A Piece of My Mind."

I approach my responsibilities of teaching cardiology to medical students and house officers with some ambivalence. Of course, I have always enjoyed and usually learned something from my contacts with these young colleagues, but lately their emphasis seems to be entirely on technical procedures. Few of my charges express an interest in entering full-time solo practice; most are not enthusiastic about honing their skills in bedside physical diagnosis. None believes in house calls.

I can remember making house calls on people who were too poor for a society doctor but too proud for the clinic. My mind can still conjure up the kind of call I'd get, almost always at night.

"Doctor, can you come? Quick! It's Zadhr, he's not feeling too good."

"What seems to be the trouble?"

"How should I know? He just doesn't feel good. Please come."

It was usually more a plea than a command. I'd roll over to the side of the bed and fall into my clothes. Bleary-eyed, I'd stagger to my car and fume because it started so slowly in the cold. Heated garages were an unachieved luxury when I started in practice. Somehow I'd find the address, although more often than not I'd get lost in the process. About the time I was cursing under my breath, I'd spot the telltale light and an anxious kerchief-clad face at the window, one hand pulling the curtains apart for a better view.

"You're the doctor?" would be the greeting, punctuated by lifted eyebrows and a faint grimace of disbelief. I looked young for my age. People trusted older, more experienced doctors in those days.

"I'm Dr. Nash. Where's the patient?" I usually preferred to get right down to business, considering it was the middle of the night.

"What's your hurry? Take off your coat. Zadhr is in the bedroom." The ancient female before me was annoyed. It was obvious to her that youths no longer concerned themselves with manners, and she didn't really approve of young pishers passing themselves off as real doctors, even if one could not pay.

Her eyes spotted my little black bag and she seemed reassured for the moment. She heaved a sigh, somewhere between a grunt and a wheeze, and led the way.

The house was of typical frame construction, two-storied and of pre–World War I vintage. The banisters that led up to the master bedroom were hand carved and glistened with a dark patina of hardwood and years of furniture polish. A threadbare runner led up the stairs. At the top I could hear the sounds of respiratory distress.

The ancient Jew sitting bolt upright in bed against several down pillows looked regal with his white beard and long sideburns. His nightclothes were white, and a small yarmulke adorned his gray, tufted scalp. Dark, bright eyes burned at me through the somber dimness of the room lit by a single 60-watt bulb. He offered no greeting or complaint, just a long soul-piercing stare. I was mesmerized for a moment, and then the noise of his breathing broke through my consciousness and I knew I had my hands full.

My physical examination was brief and confirmatory. The old man was in severe congestive heart failure. He was literally drowning in his own juices.

"Did he eat anything salty?"

"Nothing. A little schmaltz herring; a bowl of chicken soup; he doesn't eat enough."

She could not see me wince. Wisely, I stopped myself from explaining the reality of salt restriction to an old Orthodox matriarch who was salting flesh before I was born.

Well, at least I knew what had to be done.

"He has to go to the hospital. Where's the phone?"

"No!" It was the only word Zadhr had said. It did not brook discussion, but I wasn't quite wise enough to realize that.

"Look," I started, speaking a little louder than necessary to emphasize my conviction and the academic knowledge that my professors had assured me would carry the day once I got into practice. "Look, he's in heart failure. I can treat him better in the hospital. It's important."

"Doctor, you heard my husband. He doesn't want to go. Treat him here."

I knew further negotiations would be fruitless. I gave him digoxin, a diuretic, and a shot of morphine, but he was still working too hard breathing. Then my training finally came in handy. I told the old lady what I needed. With hesitation she went to the kitchen and cut the cord away from the curtains. I arranged the tourniquet around the old man's arms and legs. With the blood trapped in his extremities, he began to breathe better again.

During the next several hours, his congestive heart failure abated. Finally he dozed off, able to lie flat again for the first time in a week.

The old lady had given me several cups of tea during the long night's vigil, so I was wide awake when dawn broke. Convinced that the patient would survive, I turned to go. At the door she pressed something in my hand and murmured an awkward thanks.

As I started the engine, I opened the brown paper wrapper. Inside was a hand-embroidered tallis case, its velvet worn by a lifetime of weekly use.

I wonder how many of my students will feel as rewarded for their efforts.

Abraham Verghese
from MY OWN COUNTRY

In 1985, the first AIDS patient in Johnson City, Tennessee, was rushed into the Johnson City Medical Center intensive care unit to the horror of everyone in this isolated part of the country. This excerpt from Verghese's book *My Own County: A Doctor's Story of a Town and Its People in the Age of AIDS* is a breakneck account of the arrival of a national epidemic in the Smoky Mountains and of the deep suspicion and fear it aroused at a time when the medical community was only dimly aware of acquired immune deficiency syndrome, let alone its etiology or the "effectiveness for each of the therapeutic options that are available for patients" afflicted with AIDS.

As much a vivid, firsthand account of moment-by-moment life in the emergency room as it is a description of a turning point in the history of the AIDS epidemic, this excerpt shows the agonizing limits of doctors' skillfulness in the face of unknown disease, and the fears such lack of skill and knowledge produce in an entire community.

ABRAHAM VERGHESE is a specialist in infectious diseases in El Paso, Texas, where he is a professor of medicine at Texas Tech University. He is the author of *The Tennis Partner*, an excerpt from which appears elsewhere in this anthology.

Summer, 1985. A young man is driving down from New York to visit his parents in Johnson City, Tennessee.

I can hear the radio playing. I can picture his parents waiting, his mother cooking his favorite food, his father pacing. I see the young man in my mind, despite the years that have passed; I can see him driving home along a route that he knows well and that I have traveled many times. He started before dawn. By the time it gets hot, he has reached Pennsylvania. Three hundred or so miles from home, he begins to feel his chest tighten.

He rolls up the windows. Soon, chills shake his body. He turns the heater on full blast; it is hard for him to keep his foot on the accelerator or his hands on the wheel.

By the time he reaches Virginia, the chills give way to a profuse sweat. Now he is burning up and he turns on the air conditioner, but the perspiration still soaks through his shirt and drips off his brow. His lungs feel heavy as if laden with buckshot. His breath is labored, weighted by fear and perhaps by the knowledge of the burden he is bringing to his parents. Maybe he thinks about taking the next exit off Interstate 81 and seeking help. But he knows that no one can help him, and the dread of finding himself sick and alone keeps him going. That and the desire for home.

I know this stretch of highway that cuts through the Virginia mountains; I know how the road rises, sheer rock on one side, how in places the kudzu takes over and seems to hold up a hillside, and how, in the early afternoon, the sun glares directly into the windshield. He would have seen hay rolled into tidy bundles, lined up on the edges of fields. And tobacco plants and sagging sheds with their rusted, corrugated-tin roofs and shutterless side-openings. It would have all been familiar, this country. His own country.

In the early evening of August 11, 1985, he was rolled into the emergency room (ER) of the Johnson City Medical Center—the "Miracle Center," as we referred to it when we were interns. Puffing like an overheated steam engine, he was squeezing in forty-five breaths a minute. Or so Claire Bellamy, the nurse, told me later. It had shocked her to see a thirty-two-year-old man in such severe respiratory distress.

He sat bolt upright on the stretcher, his arms propped behind him like struts that braced his heaving chest. His blond hair was wet and stuck to his forehead; his skin, Claire recalled, was gun-metal gray, his lips and nail beds blue.

She had slapped an oxygen mask on him and hollered for someone to pull the duty physician away from the wound he was suturing. A genuine emergency was at hand, something she realized, even as it overtook her, she was not fully comprehending. She knew what it was not: it was *not* severe asthma, status asthmaticus; it was *not* a heart attack. She could not stop to take it all in. Everything was happening too quickly.

With every breath he sucked in, his nostrils flared. The strap muscles of his neck stood out like cables. He pursed his lips when he exhaled, as if he was loath to let the oxygen go, hanging on to it as long as he could.

Electrodes placed on his chest and hooked to a monitor showed his heart fluttering at a desperate 160 beats per minute.

On his chest x-ray, the lungs that should have been dark as the night were instead whited out by a veritable snowstorm.

My friend Ray, a pulmonary physician, was immediately summoned. While Ray listened to his chest, the phlebotomist drew blood for serum electrolytes and red and white blood cell counts. The respiratory therapist punctured the radial artery at the wrist to measure blood oxygen levels. Claire started an intravenous line. And the young man slumped on the stretcher. He stopped breathing.

Claire punched the "Code Blue" button on the cubicle wall and an operator's voice sounded through the six-story hospital building: "Code Blue, emergency room!"

The code team—an intern, a senior resident, two intensive care unit nurses, a respiratory therapist, a pharmacist—thundered down the hallway.

Patients in their rooms watching TV sat up in their beds; visitors froze in place in the corridors.

More doctors arrived; some came in street clothes, having heard the call as they headed for the parking lot. Others came in scrub suits. Ray was "running" the code; he called for boluses of bicarbonate and epinephrine, for a second intravenous line to be secured, and for Claire to increase the vigor but slow down the rate of her chest compressions.

The code team took their positions. The beefy intern with Nautilus shoulders took off his jacket and climbed onto a step stool. He moved in just as Claire stepped back, picking up the rhythm of chest compression without missing a beat, calling the cadence out loud. With locked elbows, one palm over the back of the other, he squished the heart between breastbone and spine, trying to squirt enough blood out of it to supply the brain.

The ER physician unbuttoned the young man's pants and cut away the underwear, now soiled with urine. His fingers reached for the groin, feeling for the femoral artery to assess the adequacy of the chest compressions.

A "crash cart" stocked with ampules of every variety, its defibrillator paddles charged and ready, stood at the foot of the bed as the pharmacist recorded each medication given and the exact time it was administered.

The clock above the stretcher had been automatically zeroed when the Code Blue was called. A code nurse called out the elapsed time at thirty-second intervals. The resident and another nurse from the code team probed with a needle for a vein to establish the second "line."

Ray "bagged" the patient with a tight-fitting mask and hand-held squeeze bag as the respiratory therapist readied an endotracheal tube and laryngoscope.

At a signal from Ray, the players froze in midair while he bent the young man's head back over the edge of the stretcher. Ray slid the laryngoscope in between tongue and palate and heaved up with his left hand, pulling the base of the tongue up and forward until the leaf-shaped epiglottis appeared.

Behind it, the light at the tip of the laryngoscope showed glimpses of the voice box and the vocal cords. With his right hand, Ray fed the endotracheal tube alongside the laryngoscope, down the back of the throat, past the epiglottis, and past the vocal cords—this part done almost blindly and with a prayer—and into the trachea. Then he connected the squeeze bag to the end of the endotracheal tube and watched the chest rise as he pumped air into the lungs. He nodded, giving the signal for the action to resume.

Now Ray listened with his stethoscope over both sides of the chest as the respiratory therapist bagged the limp young man. He listened for the muffled *whoosh* of air, listened to see if it was equally loud over both lungs.

He heard sounds only over the right lung. The tube had gone down the right main bronchus, a straighter shot than the left.

He pulled the tube back an inch, listened again, and heard air entering both sides. The tube was sitting above the carina, above the point where the trachea bifurcates. He called for another chest x-ray; a radiopaque marker at the end of the tube would confirm its exact position.

With a syringe he inflated the balloon cuff at the end of the endotracheal tube that would keep it snugly in the trachea. Claire would tape around the tube and plastered it down across the young man's cheeks and behind his neck.

The blue in the young man's skin began to wash out and a faint pink appeared in his cheeks. The ECG machine, which had spewed paper into a curly mound on the floor, now showed the original rapid heart rhythm restored.

At this point the young man was alive again, but just barely. The Code Blue had been a success.

In no time, the young man was moved to the intensive care unit (ICU) and hooked up via the endotracheal tube to a machine that looked like a top-loading washer, gauges and dials covering its flat surface. Its bellows took over the work of his tired diaphragm.

He came awake an hour later to the suffocating and gagging sensation of the endotracheal tube lodged in his throat. Even as the respirator tried to pump oxygen into his lungs, he bucked and resisted it, tried to cough out the tube. One can only imagine his terror at this awakening: naked, blazing light shining in his eyes, tubes in his mouth, tubes up his nose, tubes in his penis, transfixed by needles and probes stuck into his arms.

He must have wondered if this was hell.

The Miracle Center ICU nurses who were experienced—at least in theory—with this sort of fright and dislocation, reassured him in loud tones. Because of the tube passing between his vocal cords and because his hands were tied to prevent his snatching at the tube (an automatic gesture in this setting), he could not communicate at all. With every passing second, his terror escalated. His heart rate rose quickly.

He was immediately sedated with a bolus of morphine injected into one of his lines. He was paralyzed with a curare-like agent, a cousin of the paste used on arrow tips by indigenous tribes in the Amazon. As the drug shot through his circulation and reached the billions of junctions where nerve met and directed muscle, it blocked all signals, and he lay utterly still and flaccid.

The respirator sent breaths into him with rhythmic precision at the rate dialed in by Ray, even throwing in a mechanical sigh—a breath larger than usual—to recruit and keep patent the air sacs in the base of the lung.

The young man's parents now arrived at the hospital and were escorted up to their son's bedside. They had been waiting for him at home. Now they stood, I was told, in utter disbelief, trying to see their son through the forest of intravenous poles and the thicket of tubing and wires that covered him, asking again and again *what* had happened. And *why?*

By the next day the pneumonia had progressed. His lungs were even stiffer, making the respirator work overtime to drive oxygen into him. Ray performed a bronchoscopy, sliding a fiber-optic device into the endotracheal tube. Through the bronchoscope he could see the glossy red lining of the trachea and the bronchi. All looked normal. He directed the bronchoscope as far out as it would go, then passed a biopsy forceps through it and took a blind bite of the air sacs of the lung.

Under the microscope, the honeycomb-like air spaces of the lung were congealed with a syrupy outpouring of inflammatory fluid and cells. Embedded in this matrix were thousands upon thousands of tiny, darkly staining, flying-saucer-like discs that the pathologist identified as *Pneumocystis carinii.*

The young man had no predisposing illness like leukemia or cancer that would explain this fulminant pneumonia caused by an innocuous organism.

His immune system *had* to be abnormal.

It was clear, though no one had yet seen a case, that he was Johnson City's first case of the acquired immune deficiency syndrome—AIDS.

Word spread like wildfire through the hospital. All those involved in his care in the ER and ICU agonized over their exposure.

The intern remembered his palms pressed against the clammy breast as he performed closed-chest massage.

Claire remembered starting the intravenous line and having blood trickle out and touch her ungloved skin.

The respiratory therapist recalled the fine spray that landed on his face as he suctioned the tracheal tube.

The emergency room physician recalled the sweat and the wet underwear his fingers encountered as he sought out the femoral artery.

Even those who had not touched the young man—the pharmacist, the orderlies, the transport personnel—were alarmed.

Ray worried too; he had been exposed as much as anyone. In the days to follow, he was stopped again and again in the corridor by people quizzing him about the danger, about their exposure. Ray even felt some anger directed at him. As if he, who had done everything right and diagnosed the case in short order, could have prevented this or warned them.

An ICU nurse told me that the young man's room took on a special aura. In the way a grisly murder or the viewing of an apparition can transform an otherwise ordinary abode, so cubicle 7C was forever transformed. Doctors and others in the ICU peeked through the glass, watching the inert body of the young man. His father was seated beside him. The hometown boy was now regarded as an alien, the father an object of pity.

Ray told me how the parents took the news. The mother froze, staring at Ray's lips as if he was speaking a foreign language. The father turned away, only the sound of his footsteps breaking the silence as he walked out into the corridor and on out into the parking lot, unable to stay in the building where that word had been uttered.

Much later, the father asked, "But *how* did he get it? How could he have gotten this?"

Ray pointed out that he had had no time to get a history: perhaps they could give him some information. Had their son been healthy in the past year and in the days preceding the trip? Lord, yes! (The father did all the answering.) Did he ever use intravenous drugs? Lord, no! And to their knowledge had he ever had a blood transfusion?

No.

Was he married?

No.

Did he live alone? No, he had a friend in New York.

A male friend? Yes . . . they had never met him.

"Oh Lord! Is that what you're saying? Is that how he got it? Is my son a queer?"

Ray just stood there, unable to respond to the father's words.

The father turned to his wife and said, "Mother, do you hear this? Do you hear this?"

She gazed at the floor, nodding slowly, confirming finally what she had always known.

The mother never left the ICU or her son's side. And in a day or so, the father also rallied around his son, spending long hours with him, holding his hand, talking to him. Behind the glass one could watch as the father bent over his son, his lips moving soundlessly.

He balked when his son's buddies flew down from New York. He was angry, on the verge of a violent outburst. This was all too much. This nightmare, these city boys, this new world that had suddenly engulfed his family.

Ray tried to mediate. But only when it seemed his boy's death was inevitable did the father relent and allow the New Yorkers near him. He guarded the space around his son, marshaling his protection.

The two visitors were men with closely cut hair. One had a pierced ear, purple suede boots, tight jeans, and what the ICU ward clerk, Jennie, described to me as a "New York attitude—know what I mean?"

Jennie said the other friend, clearly the patient's lover, was dressed more conservatively and was in his early forties. She thought he was "a computer person." She remembers the tears that trickled continuously down his cheeks and the handkerchief squeezed in his hand. Jennie thought the mother wanted to talk to her son's lover. He, in turn, needed badly to talk to anyone. But in the presence of the father there was no chance for them to speak.

Three weeks after his arrival, the young man died.

The New Yorkers left before the funeral.

The respirator was unhooked and rolled back to the respiratory therapy department. A heated debate ensued as to what to do with it. There were, of course, published and simple recommendations for disinfecting it. But that was not the point. The machine that had sustained the young man had come to symbolize AIDS in Johnson City.

Some favored burying the respirator, deep-sixing it in the swampy land at the back of the hospital. Others were for incinerating it. As a compromise, the machine was opened up, its innards gutted and most replaceable parts changed. It was then gas disinfected several times. Even so, it was a long time before it was put back into circulation.

About two months after the young man died, I returned to Johnson City. I had previously worked there as an intern and resident in internal medicine, and I was now coming back after completing my training in infectious diseases in Boston. People who knew me from my residency days stopped me and told me the sad story of this young man's homecoming.

But it was not always recounted as a sad story. "Did you hear what happened to Ray?" a doctor asked me. He proceeded to tell me how a young man had dropped into the emergency room looking like he had pneumonia but turning out to be "a homo from New York with AIDS." The humor resided in what had happened to the unsuspecting Ray, the pie-in-your-face nature of the patient's diagnosis.

Some of the veteran ICU nurses, perhaps because this case broke through their I've-seen-it-all-and-more-honey attitudes, astonished me with their indignation. In their opinion, this "homo-sex-shual" with AIDS clearly had no right to expect to be taken care of in our state-of-the-art, computerized ICU.

When I heard the story, the shock waves in the hospital had already subsided. Everyone thought it had been a freak accident, a one-time thing in Johnson City. This was a small town in the country, a town of clean living, good country people. AIDS was clearly a big-city problem. It was something that happened in other kinds of lives.

Raymond Carver

WHAT THE DOCTOR SAID

What is the nature of the doctor's skillfulness when there are no real therapeutic options available to a patient? What does it mean for one human being to tell another that he or she is going to die? When does a discussion in "an honest and objective fashion" suddenly turn into a moment of grace?

This poem by Raymond Carver, perhaps his best known, begins with a physician discussing sobering test results with his patient. It presents the limits of one type of skill and the beginnings of another sort altogether, the art of simply being with someone in a difficult moment.

RAYMOND CARVER is one of this country's most famous short-story writers and poets. Carver died of lung cancer in 1988. His short story "A Small, Good Thing" also appears in this anthology.

He said it doesn't look good
he said it looks bad in fact real bad
he said I counted thirty-two of them on one lung before
I quit counting them
I said I'm glad I wouldn't want to know
about any more being there than that
he said are you a religious man do you kneel down
in forest groves and let yourself ask for help
when you come to a waterfall
mist blowing against your face and arms
do you stop and ask for understanding at those moments
I said not yet but I intend to start today
he said I'm real sorry he said
I wish I had some other kind of news to give you
I said Amen and he said something else
I didn't catch and not knowing what else to do
and not wanting him to have to repeat it
and me to have to fully digest it
I just looked at him
for a minute and he looked back it was then
I jumped up and shook hands with this man who'd just given me
something no one else on earth had ever given me
I may even have thanked him habit being so strong

Jeanne Bryner

THIS RED OOZING

This poem reflects the challenge of gathering an "accurate history." Does the single sentence "I was raped" reflect the impact of such an experience or provide enough information to proceed in making clinical judgments? How does the patient convey to the physician the depth of her struggles and the lifelong impact of that simple statement? Jeanne Bryner's poem is powerfully descriptive; it provides imagery that will not be put aside once such a history is taken, recorded, and filed away.

JEANNE BRYNER is an emergency room nurse. She received a Pushcart Prize nomination in 1994. Her poems have appeared in several literary magazines, among them *Hiram Poetry Review, Poetry East, Prairie Schooner,* and an anthology titled *Gathering of Poets.* Her own collection of poetry is titled *Breathless,* from which this poem is taken.

I'm a nurse in emergency.
You're a hostess at Benny's Lounge,
thirty-five, divorced. After three beers,
you can never let the friend of a friend
drop you off at your apartment,
then ask him in for coffee.

Never pee with an accountant in the house,
especially one dragging his briefcase.
See how the balding sheriff shakes
his *I-told-you-so-eyes*
while you tell how the man shoved
your bathroom door open,
pulled out his revolver, grinned.

We know what he said next; we hear it
nearly every week: *I'm gonna fuck you;*
you scream, I'll kill you.
We believe you cried, begged on knees,
told him your kids might be home soon.
You kneeling on the fuzzy pink rug—
he likes that—you genuflecting.

The safety clicks on his forty-five.
You know guns; your father hunted—
black roundness against your right temple,
your hoop earrings clang, train whistles
in your ears and his words squeeze:
suck hard bitch.

We're sorry, but now the doctor
makes you say all of it again,
how a single lamp burns on the nightstand
and your kids smile in their school pictures.

How tight he holds the cold muzzle to your neck,
jerks your dark hair like a mane and rips
you until you bleed, your breath becomes
grunts, your face in a pillow.

Doctors in ER speak like priests,
and they try to explain it, clean it up
when they swab, hunting for sperm, trying
to mount rage on slides—dead or alive.

This red oozing,
this trail from your buttocks to your thighs
will not fill him, and it doesn't matter
how many times you throw up green
or call on God or bruises rise
like small iris on your cheekbones,
the razor moves on.

The friend of your friend
with the pinstriped suit will probably walk.
I think you know that.
What you don't know is how he rapes you
endlessly: how he crawls out of your lipstick
tube in the morning, slithers out of the soapy
washcloth in the shower, snickers every Friday
when you dust those photos on your stand.
How his boots climb the back stairs
of your mind year after year
as he comes and comes and comes.

John Stone

FROM THE LISTENING END OF THE STETHOSCOPE

"What kinds of music, or noise, arrive at the listening end of the stethoscope?" John Stone asks at the outset of this exploration. Stone demonstrates his own thorough skillfulness in presenting the history of listening to the heart, what health care professionals listen for and why, and, above all, what it means to obtain and interpret the language of the heart.

JOHN STONE is a cardiologist and a poet. He is the author of three collections of poetry—*The Smell of Matches, In All the Rain,* and *Renaming the Streets*—and a co-author of *On Doctoring.* This essay is taken from his collection of essays titled *In the Country of Hearts: Journeys in the Art of Medicine.*

He calls my office late Friday afternoon to say that his heart has been running away with him all day. He's thirty-five and has had an artificial aortic valve in place for twelve years. Out of curiosity, I ask him to place the mouthpiece of his phone firmly against his chest wall. I listen closely: the clicks of his artificial valve are easy to hear. His heart rate is very rapid, about 180 beats a minute, and grossly irregular. The diagnosis is clear: He has a rhythm disturbance called "atrial fibrillation." I tell him that I'll phone in a prescription for him. He's to pick it up on his way home, take three of the tablets, and call me back in an hour or so. It's dark outside when the phone rings, but the news is good—a few minutes ago, abruptly, his heart slowed and the sense of "fluttering" in his chest vanished. Over the phone, the clicks of his valve are slow and regular. I've never used the telephone as a kind of long-distance stethoscope before, but the technique worked beautifully. Over the miles between us, he and I are smiling as we say good night.

My stethoscope, by now, is an old friend. It is, after all, the one I bought in medical school, twenty-eight years ago, though it's been replaced several times over, part by worn-out part, like atoms of the body. The earpieces slip into my ears tightly, the sounds of the world diminish. I enter the cave-dark, tone-dense hollow of the chest and tune in to the mother heart. My patient is a mother and she's better this morning, but still very sick. I bend and listen. As I do, I am aware of the film of sweat over the bridge of her nose and a flaring of her nostrils related to the work of her breathing. Her heart tones remind me of a racehorse laboring for the finish line: "lup-*dup*-pah, lup-*dup*-pah," and so forth. This triple cadence, understandably, is called a "gallop rhythm," after the canter of a horse. It connotes heart failure: her heart is unable to pump all the blood that it receives and her lungs are congested. Her heart muscle, the pump itself, is sick and unlikely to get better. As I slip the stethoscope back into my pocket, there is no way for me to know that within two years, she will be dead, suddenly, at the age of forty-one.

But most songs heard by the stethoscope are not as sad. Some are quite happy.

The idea for the stethoscope came to a young man in France as he watched two children at play with a wooden baton; one child scratched his end of the stick while the other, holding the opposite end to his ear, listened expectantly for the scratching to be "telegraphed" to him. The young man's mellifluous name was René Théophile Hyacinthe Laënnec (*lan-eck*). During his short life (1781–1826), he made many contributions to medicine, but he is best known as the father of the stethoscope.

The Ur-stethoscope, in fact, was a rolled-up cylinder of paper improvised by Laënnec in 1816 to better examine an obese young woman with heart disease. Laënnec was impressed with his *cornet de papier*: "I was not a little surprised and pleased to find that I could thereby perceive the action of the heart in a manner much more clear and distinct than I had ever been able to do by the immediate application of the ear." Later, the instrument was crafted out of wood, a hole was bored through the baton to facilitate the passage of sound; and it was divided, for portability, into halves that could be screwed together.

Long before Laënnec, physicians listened to hearts by simply placing the ear directly on the patient's chest. But the technique was not utilized that often because of concerns about modesty and hygiene. Then came the stethoscope, one of the earliest instruments to be physically interposed between doctor and patient. Laënnec's invention, however, despite its rudimentary form, was like the modern version in one important way: There was a human being at either end. As Dr. Dickinson Richards insisted in 1962, to use the stethoscope, "the doctor has to be within thirty inches of the patient," close enough to ensure the intimacy and laying on of hands often said to be lacking in medicine today.

The modern stethoscope—the word derives from the Greek *stethos*, meaning "chest"—evolved with new knowledge about the physics of sound transmission. Thus, the tubing between doctor and patient is of a prescribed bore and length. The earpieces must fit snugly. On the other end, the "heads" of the stethoscope, usually two or occasionally three in number, filter the sound. The flat piece, the diaphragm, picks up high-pitched sounds; the domed piece, the bell, registers low frequencies.

What kinds of music, or noise, arrive at the listening end of the stethoscope? The most common use of the instrument is in the measurement of blood pressure, as the arterial blood column strains to thump under the cuff tightened around the arm. But the stethoscope is useful in decoding all the sounds of the body at work: the tick-tock of the fetal heart tones from the uterus; the rumblings of the gut under the abdominal wall (sounds that carry the aptly onomatopoeic Greek *borborygmos*, meaning "to rumble"); the rush of blood in narrowed vessels, notably the carotid arteries leading to the brain. In Laënnec's time, the stethoscope was most frequently employed to monitor the lungs: fully a third of the patients hospitalized in Paris were there because of tuberculosis. But the most dramatic use of it is in sorting out the cacophony of sound from the heart. Use of the stethoscope in this way is called "auscultation" (L. *auscultare*, "to listen").

The normal heart tones, a poet would note, are *iambic* in rhythm: a weaker followed by a stronger stress—lup-*dup*, lup-*dup*. These sounds, the "lup" and the "dup," are called the first and the second heart sounds, S-1 and S-2. They are due basically to the rhythmic paired closing of the four heart valves (tricuspid and pulmonary valves in the right side of the heart, mitral and aortic valves in the left side). The valves work gracefully and ingeniously to direct blood flow—from the right heart to the lungs, from the left heart to the body. The time between the *lup* and the *dup* defines systole (*sis'toll-ee*), the interval of contraction of the heart. The interval between the second sound and the subsequent first sound defines diastole (*dye-as'toll-ee*), the interval of relaxation. The flow of blood through the heart is often made turbulent (e.g., after exercise or with structural abnormalities of the heart); it is this turbulence that produces cardiac "murmurs." A murmur is often musical in character, and may occur in systole, diastole, or throughout both intervals, depending on the cause.

Many, perhaps most, heart murmurs are not pathological at all. An estimated 50 percent of all children, if their hearts are examined often enough, will have a murmur at some point. The turbulent blood flow in their active, growing bodies is one explanation of such "innocent" murmurs. These are the happiest sounds, joys to find. Similarly, many pregnant women develop murmurs as the torrential blood flow to the gravid uterus places an extra workload on the maternal heart. The revved-up circulation that occurs with anemia or an overactive thyroid may also produce such murmurs.

But what of pathological murmurs? The valves of the heart may dysfunction for many reasons. Basically, dysfunction takes one of two forms: a narrowing of the valve ("stenosis") or a leakage ("insufficiency" or "regurgitation"). Stenosis of the aortic valve, situated between the left ventricle and the aorta, is a good example. With cardiac contraction, the three pliable leaflets of a normal valve are thrown open abruptly, like swinging doors, allowing blood to pass from the left ventricle to the aorta. After contraction, the leaflets recoil and close, halting any retreat of the aortic blood back into the ventricle. If the valve is narrowed by disease and scarring, however, the squeezing of blood through it may produce enough turbulence to cause a systolic murmur.

The loudness of murmurs is graded from 1 to 6 (6 is loud enough to be heard with the stethoscope completely off the chest). Rarely, a murmur is loud enough to be heard several feet away without using a stethoscope. Opening and closing "clicks" of certain artificial heart valves may be audible to others in a quiet waiting room.

A sense of rhythm is helpful in the interpretation of complex cardiac sounds. Generations of medical students, learning auscultation, have used a rhythmic, exaggerated pronunciation of the word *Ken-tuck-y, Ken-tuck-y*, to help time the gallops of the heart. Some conditions produce extra cardiac sounds: a variety of clicks, "rubs," and murmurs. Inflammation of the sac around the heart—pericarditis—results in a distinctive "scratchy" rub (the quality of the rub can be simulated by taking a small punch of hair near the ear and rubbing the fingers together briskly). One of the most dramatic sounds in medicine is called "Hamman's crunch," after the physician who described its typical features. Auscultation of the heart after air has been introduced into the center of the chest (after a stab wound, for example) may reveal a crackling and crunching of the air and fluid around the beating heart, sounds that reminded Hamman (and thousands of clinicians since) of the crunch of snow under heavy boots.

Auscultation is usually done with the patient lying down. But listening with the patient sitting tilts the pendulous heart toward the chest wall, facilitating diagnosis. Listening with the patient standing, squatting, or with his feet elevated off the bed all may be used in special circumstances.

A complete examination of the lungs also includes auscultation: as the patient breathes deeply, air rushing through the bronchial tree may pass over abnormal fluid within the bronchi (in pneumonia, for example), causing soft bubbling sounds.

Another valuable technique for examination of the lungs (less valuable for the heart) is that of *percussion*. In percussion, the long finger of one hand is laid flat against the chest wall while the long finger of the other hand taps or percusses it. Changes in the quality or "timbre" of the thumping sounds thus generated can help detect abnormal collections of fluid at the base of the lungs. Leopold Auenbrugger (1722–1809), a Viennese physician, is the father of percussion; applying the technique to the human chest was suggested to him by wine testers who drummed their fingers over the kegs to check the level of fluid within them.

Years ago, as fledgling medical students in St. Louis, Luis Vasconez and I were assigned to examine the heart and lungs of a patient. While I stood in front of the (patient) patient, attempting to make sense out of his heart sounds, Luis was trying out his newfound technique of percussion over the patient's back: Luis' drumbeats sounded like thunder in my stethoscope. Needless to say, the techniques of auscultation and percussion are not intended to be carried out simultaneously!

Despite the long history of the stethoscope, there is much more to learn about auscultation. Until the 1960s, for example, a click or clicks heard between the *lup* and the *dup* were thought to be noncardiac in origin. Sophisticated studies have now shown that such clicks often arise from the mitral valve in a condition called "mitral valve prolapse." Newer techniques help us understand what we're hearing: these include echocardiography (viewing the heart with ultrasound) and magnetic resonance imaging, a noninvasive technique that gives clear views of cardiac anatomy without the injection of dyes. Thus, as the stethoscope keeps the physician near the bedside of the patient, its messages are continually reinterpreted in light of new information.

Recently, I and my older son, a medical student in Boston, spent a morning at the hospital decoding the heart sounds that emanated from a wondrous electronic teaching mannequin called "Harvey." Harvey can be programmed to simulate a wide variety of murmurs (and pulses). I envy my son the process of discovery that lies before him. It will take some time. Only with time, only after moving the stethoscope like a metal detector over the landscape of countless hearts, does one truly learn how to be still and listen. Such training of the ear comes only with experience. The art of auscultation is remarkably like listening to Mozart's clarinet quintet—after so long a time, one is able to follow the voice of the cello and thus appreciate its individual music within the ensemble.

Physicians and patients, of course, are not the only ones interested in the arcane language of the heart. John Ciardi wrote a fine poem called "Lines From the Beating End of the Stethoscope." And W. H. Auden, in "Lay your sleeping head, my love," speaks knowingly of the "knocking heart." The very first auscultator, surely, was a lover—head pillowed on the drum of the lover's chest—who heard the murmurs and murmurings of the heart and worried what they might mean long before—and long since—Laënnec.

Alyson Porter

LARGE WOMAN, HALF

Leaning down and touching, palpitating, and listening to another human being are necessary parts of developing the skills to perform a complete physical examination. The practitioner works with patients to develop and refine these skills. But how often are these procedures done without regard for the person, the person whose heart we cannot really hear, cannot really appreciate?

ALYSON PORTER had her first writing—a story about space aliens—published by *Cricket* magazine when she was eight years old. Today she is a resident at the University of New Mexico School of Medicine. She lives in Albuquerque with her husband who is also in medical school.

Large woman, half-sitting,
wrecked among the creased sheets, tubes, sharp needles, blue blankets,
incurious.

Her loose white and rain gray hair stripes pillows.
She has the preoccupied jelly gaze of fish.

Under the gown, she has been cracked
down her center
and shut tight again. There is dried blood
traveling the long barbed seam.

Bent to listen, there are gusts
newspaper crackling against the wire fence of suture
new wine bubbling up
a door banging open into an empty room
heavy trucks on an unfamiliar stretch of highway
branches gnashing the tin roof of a shed
or the settling of birds in zoo cages at dusk?

She breathes like a runner
with hard purpose.

I move the stethoscope again
and again.
Again

pressing
it stamps the warm freckled flesh.

Even the fabric murmurs

explaining
Well, I am new to this
I cannot fully appreciate your heart sounds.

Constance Meyd

THE KNEE

The skills required in a complete or limited physical examination are demonstrated and practiced daily in a variety of teaching settings. In almost all instances, the practice and demonstration are done with live patients. Many medical institutions are structured to provide students with multiple opportunities to practice their emerging skills. But do the demonstrations, repeated examinations, and procedures done by the least skilled rather than the most skilled violate patients' rights in the interest of learning or education? This essay takes a hard look at what else is learned in the process of a routine knee examination—by both patient and studying intern.

CONSTANCE MEYD is an assistant professor, Department of Neurology at Johns Hopkins University. She is also a member of Pi Chapter, Sigma Theta Tay International Honor Society of Nursing Past Executives.

We are on attending rounds with the usual group: attending, senior resident, junior residents, and medical students. There are eight of us. Today we will learn how to examine the knee properly. The door is open. The room is ordinary institutional yellow, a stained curtain between the beds. We enter in proper order behind our attending physician. The knee is attached to a woman, perhaps 35 years old, dressed in her own robe and nightgown. The attending physician asks the usual questions as he places his hand on the knee: "This knee bothers you?" All eyes are on the knee; no one meets her eyes as she answers. The maneuvers begin—abduction, adduction, flexion, extension, rotation. She continues to tell her story, furtively pushing her clothing between her legs. Her endeavors are hopeless, for the full range of knee motion must be demonstrated. The door is open. Her embarrassment and helplessness are evident. More maneuvers and a discussion of knee pathology ensue. She asks a question. No one notices. More maneuvers. The door is open. Now the uninvolved knee is examined—abduction, adduction, flexion, extension, rotation. She gives up. The door is open. Now a discussion of surgical technique. Now review the knee examination. We file out through the open door. She pulls the sheet up around her waist. She is irrelevant.

Jean-Dominique Bauby
from THE DIVING BELL AND THE BUTTERFLY

A patient in a French hospital, completely stripped of any ability to move or speak, offers an extraordinary perspective on the skillfulness of the doctors who attend to him, and on the world of the hospital, giving the reader of this excerpt a full measure of an utterly helpless patient's resentment and anger in the face of indifferent, "ungracious" care.

JEAN-DOMINIQUE BAUBY was the forty-three-year-old editor-in-chief of *Elle* when he suffered a stroke that decimated his brain stem. After weeks in a coma, he awoke to find that he suffered from a rare condition known as "locked-in syndrome," which left his mind intact but his body almost completely paralyzed. Bauby "dictated" this story by blinking his one still-functioning eye, one letter at a time. He died two days after *The Diving Bell and the Butterfly* was published in France.

I have known gentler awakenings. When I came to that late-January morning, the hospital ophthalmologist was leaning over me and sewing my right eyelid shut with a needle and thread, just as if he were darning a sock. Irrational terror swept over me. What if this man got carried away and sewed up my left eye as well, my only link to the outside world, the only window to my cell, the one tiny opening of my diving bell? Luckily, as it turned out, I wasn't plunged into darkness. He carefully packed away his sewing kit in padded tin boxes. Then, in the tones of a prosecutor demanding a maximum sentence for a repeat offender, he barked out: "Six months!" I fired off a series of questioning signals with my working eye, but this man—who spent his days peering into people's pupils—was apparently unable to interpret a simple look. With a big round head, a short body, and a fidgety manner, he was the very model of the couldn't-care-less doctor: arrogant, brusque, sarcastic—the kind who summons his patients for 8:00 A.M., arrives at 9:00, and departs at 9:05, after giving each of them forty-five seconds of his precious time. Disinclined to chat with normal patients, he turned thoroughly evasive in dealing with ghosts of my ilk, apparently incapable of finding words to offer the slightest explanation. But I finally discovered why he had put a six-month seal on my eye: the lid was no longer fulfilling its function as a protective cover, and I ran the risk of an ulcerated cornea.

As the weeks went by, I wondered whether the hospital employed such an ungracious character deliberately—to serve as a focal point for the veiled mistrust the medical profession always arouses in long-term patients. A kind of scapegoat, in other words. If he leaves Berck, which seems likely, who will be left for me to sneer at? I shall no longer have the solitary, innocent pleasure of hearing his eternal question:"Do you see double?" and replying—deep inside—"Yes, I see two assholes, not one."

I need to feel strongly, to love and to admire, just as desperately as I need to breathe. A letter from a friend, a Balthus painting on a postcard, a page of Saint-Simon, give meaning to the passing hours. But to keep my mind sharp, to avoid descending into resigned indifference, I maintain a level of resentment and anger, neither too much nor too little, just as a pressure cooker has a safety valve to keep it from exploding.

And while we're on the subject, *The Pressure Cooker* could be a title for the play I may write one day, based on my experiences here. I've also thought of calling it *The Eye* and, of course, *The Diving Bell.* You already know the plot and the setting. A hospital room in which Mr. L., a family man in the prime of life, is learning to live with locked-in syndrome brought on by a serious cerebrovascular accident. The play follows Mr. L.'s adventures in the medical world and his shifting relationships with his wife, his children, his friends, and his associates from the leading advertising agency he helped to found. Ambitious, somewhat cynical, heretofore a stranger to failure, Mr. L. takes his first steps into distress, sees all the certainties that buttressed him collapse, and discovers that his nearest and dearest are strangers. We could carry this slow transformation to the front seats of the balcony: a voice offstage would reproduce Mr. L.'s unspoken inner monologue as he faces each new situation. All that is left is to write the play. I have the final scene already: The stage is in darkness, except for a halo of light around the bed in center stage. Nighttime. Everyone is asleep. Suddenly Mr. L., inert since the curtain first rose, throws aside sheets and blankets, jumps from the bed, and walks around the eerily lit stage. Then it grows dark again, and you hear the voice offstage—Mr. L.'s inner voice—one last time:

"Damn! It was only a dream!"

Lucia Cordell Getsi

LETTER FROM THE REHABILITATION INSTITUTE

On a children's rehabilitation ward, a skillful observer describes the particulars of a set of lives, including those of her own daughter. In so doing, she offers a succinct set of histories, diagnoses, and prognoses, and an understanding of how the patients' conditions affect her own moral condition.

LUCIA CORDELL GETSI has published four collections of poetry, and her poems, fiction, and essays have appeared in several literary magazines. *Intensive Care*, a collection of her poems about her daughter's battle with Guillain-Barré syndrome, won the 1990 Capricorn Poetry Prize.

Mostly bandaged, Joe looks like the Elephant Man
or the Creature from the Black Lagoon, in white.
Without blinking, he says he wished he'd died
in the fire his twelve-year strength failed
to pull his mother from. He still smells her flesh,
like a cinder in his nose, or what is left
of nose. *It's too hard,* he says, *alone, and like this.*

LaToya is quiet in her bed or rolling cart,
seems to be observant. Her small body, amoeba-like,
responds to voice probes: *Sit up, LaToya, raise
your arm.* No one can tell if she understands
her mother was killed by the train that smacked
the speech out of her mouth. One dropped eye
tracks my arms that pivot Manon* to the chair.

Danny tried to beat the express-lane traffic
on foot. He wears seamed legs and crushed hips,
a patchwork body pieced by surgeons who speak of him
as a masterwork. He pops wheelies in his motorized
chair, bothers the girls as though he'll have one.
When he goes home, Frankenstein with cane, his mother
clicks her high heels quickly away, as far ahead
of him as she can get. He jerks along behind.

"G." got shot in the back like the other Black
and Chicago boys here, wears his colon in a pouch.
He walks. The only one who can. These boys call
each other Mutha, slap hands in greeting, manage
a tired strut in their wheelchairs. In art therapy
G. paints a light like a jack-o'-lantern grinning
in a shadow, a richochet of motherlessness
that writhes like an orange ghost trapped in paper.

Arnold "fell" from three storeys, lay on concrete
one whole morning. His mother never visits.
Little cuddler, the nurses vie to tuck him
in. Earphones on his ears, he snaps his fingers and
jives, baby hips rocking to music that sings
him finally to sleep. At 3 A.M. he howls
and whimpers like a puppy lost from the litter.

*Manon is the poet's daughter.

Jimmy dived and struck the bottom he thought was
deeper. He'll never pull water over his head
again, or a blanket when he's cold, or feel
below his broken neck. Bone thin, his body
is flat, enormous eyes grab like hands.
His trache gurgles when he whispers he is scared.

I could tell about Lily, the university student
who woke in a tremor of electric shock up one side
of her body and down the other. After months
of paralysis she can sit well enough to withstand
the long flight home to Japan, strapped
in her seat. Or Aileen, the six-year-old
ballerina who struggles to speak again
after her fourth stroke.

In this place of broken children
I don't know who *you* are—*you* are different
in the way I was different before
I arrived and thought I would be the same,
in the way Manon tries to find an adolescence, falling
in love with a snazzy wheelchair, a funny
story, someone else's need. No,
there is nothing to be done about difference.
It leaves a mark.

Audre Lorde

BREAST CANCER: POWER VS. PROSTHESIS

from The Cancer Journals

Recovery from breast cancer brings with it a transformed life and concerns. In this excerpt from her landmark work *The Cancer Journals*, poet Audre Lorde writes about one of the most powerful issues arising for women in the aftermath of a mastectomy: whether or not to wear a prosthesis.

This essay begins as Lourde goes to the doctor's office for a checkup after her surgery and the nurse asks why she isn't wearing a prosthesis. The nurse's question provides Lourde an opportunity to discuss women with breast cancer as "warriors" and to highlight the importance of seeing therapeutic options in the context of their larger, societal implications.

AUDRE LORDE published more than a dozen collections of poems and six books of prose. She began writing her journal entries six months after having a radical mastectomy. *The Cancer Journals* was first published in 1980. Audre Lorde succumbed to breast cancer in 1992.

On Labor Day, 1978, during my regular monthly self-examination, I discovered a lump in my right breast which later proved to be malignant. During my following hospitalization, my mastectomy and its aftermath, I passed through many stages of pain, despair, fury, sadness, and growth. I moved through these stages, sometimes feeling as if I had no choice, other times recognizing that I could choose oblivion—or a passivity that is very close to oblivion—but did not want to. As I slowly began to feel more equal to processing and examining the different parts of this experience, I also began to feel that in the process of losing a breast I had become a more whole person.

After a mastectomy, for many women including myself, there is a feeling of wanting to go back, of not wanting to persevere through this experience to whatever enlightenment might be at the core of it. And it is this feeling, this nostalgia, which is encouraged by most of the post-surgical counseling for women with breast cancer. This regressive tie to the past is emphasized by the concentration upon breast cancer as a cosmetic problem, one which can be solved by a prosthetic pretense. The American Cancer Society's Reach For Recovery Program, while doing a valuable service in contacting women immediately after surgery and letting them know they are not alone, nonetheless encourages this false and dangerous nostalgia in the mistaken belief that women are too weak to deal directly and courageously with the realities of our lives.

The woman from Reach For Recovery who came to see me in the hospital, while quite admirable and even impressive in her own right, certainly did not speak to my experience nor my concerns. As a 44-year-old Black Lesbian Feminist, I knew there were very few role models around for me in this situation, but my primary concerns two days after mastectomy were hardly about what man I could capture in the future, whether or not my old boyfriend would still find me attractive enough, and even less about whether my two children would be embarrassed by me around their friends.

My concerns were about my chances for survival, the effects of a possibly shortened life upon my work and my priorities. Could this cancer have been prevented, and what could I do in the future to prevent its recurrence? Would I be able to maintain the control over my life that I had always taken for granted? A lifetime of loving women had taught me that when women love each other, physical change does not alter that love. It did not occur to me that anyone who really loved me would love me any less because I had one breast instead of two, although it did occur to me to wonder if they would be able to love and deal with the new me. So my concerns were quite different from those spoken to by the Reach For Recovery volunteer, but one bit less crucial nor less poignant.

Yet every attempt I made to examine or question the possibility of a real integration of this experience into the totality of my life and my loving and my work was ignored by this woman, or uneasily glossed over by her as not looking on "the bright side of things." I felt outraged and insulted, and weak as I was, this left me feeling even more isolated than before.

In the critical and vulnerable period following surgery, self-examination and self-evaluation are positive steps. To imply to a woman that yes, she can be the 'same' as before surgery, with the skillful application of a little puff of lambswool, and/or silicone gel, is to place an emphasis upon prosthesis which encourages her not to deal with herself as physically and emotionally real, even though altered and traumatized. This emphasis upon the cosmetic after surgery reinforces this society's stereotype of women, that we are only what we look or appear, so this is the only aspect of our existence we need to address. Any woman who has had a breast removed because of cancer knows she does not feel the same. But we are allowed no psychic time or space to examine what our true feelings are, to make them our own. With quick cosmetic reassurance, we are told that our feelings are not important, our appearance is all, the sum total of self.

I did not have to look down at the bandages on my chest to know that I did not feel the same as before surgery. But I still felt like myself, like Audre, and that encompassed so much more than simply the way my chest appeared.

The emphasis upon physical pretense at this crucial point in a woman's reclaiming of her self and her body-image has two negative effects:

1. It encourages women to dwell in the past rather than a future. This prevents a woman from assessing herself in the present, and from coming to terms with the changed planes of her own body. Since these then remain alien to her, buried under prosthetic devices, she must mourn the loss of her breast in secret, as if it were the result of some crime of which she were guilty.

2. It encourages a woman to focus her energies upon the mastectomy as a cosmetic occurrence, to the exclusion of other factors in a constellation that could include her own death. It removes her from what that constellation means in terms of her living, and from developing priorities of usage for what-

ever time she has before her. It encourages her to ignore the necessity for nutritional vigilance and psychic armament that can help prevent recurrence.

I am talking here about the need for every woman to live a considered life. The necessity for that consideration grows and deepens as one faces directly one's own mortality and death. Self-scrutiny and an evaluation of our lives, while painful, can be rewarding and strengthening journeys toward a deeper self. For as we open ourselves more and more to the genuine conditions of our lives, women become less and less willing to tolerate those conditions unaltered, or to passively accept external and destructive controls over our lives and our identities. Any short-circuiting of this quest for self-definition and power, however well-meaning and under whatever guise, must be seen as damaging, for it keeps the post-mastectomy women in a position of perpetual and secret insufficiency, infantilized and dependent for her identity upon an external definition by appearance. In this way women are kept from expressing the power of our knowledge and experience, and through that expression, developing strengths that challenge those structures within our lives that support the Cancer Establishment. For instance, why hasn't the American Cancer Society publicized the connections between animal fat and breast cancer for our daughters the way it has publicized the connection between cigarette smoke and lung cancer? These links between animal fat, hormone production and breast cancer are not secret.

Ten days after having my breast removed, I went to my doctor's office to have the stitches taken out. This was my first journey out since coming home from the hospital, and I was truly looking forward to it. A friend had washed my hair for me and it was black and shining, with my new grey hairs glistening in the sun. Color was starting to come back into my face and around my eyes. I wore the most opalescent of my moonstones, and a single floating bird dangling from my right ear in the name of grand assymmetry. With an African kente-cloth tunic and new leather boots, I knew I looked fine, with that brave new-born security of a beautiful woman having come through a very hard time and being very glad to be alive.

I felt really good, within the limits of that grey mush that still persisted in my brain from the effects of the anesthesia.

When I walked into the doctor's office, I was really rather pleased with myself, all things considered, pleased with the way I felt, with my own flair, with my own style. The doctor's nurse, a charmingly bright and steady woman of about my own age who had always given me a feeling of quiet no-nonsense support on my other visits, called me into the examining room. On the way, she asked me how I was feeling.

"Pretty good," I said, half-expecting her to make some comment about how good I looked.

"You're not wearing a prosthesis," she said, a little anxiously, and not at all like a question.

"No," I said, thrown off my guard for a minute. "It really doesn't feel right," referring to the lambswool puff given to me by the Reach For Recovery volunteer in the hospital.

Usually supportive and understanding, the nurse now looked at me urgently and disapprovingly as she told me that even if it didn't look exactly right, it was "better than nothing," and that as soon as my stitches were out I could be fitted for a "real form."

"You will feel so much better with it on," she said. "And besides, we really like you to wear something, at least when you come in. Otherwise it's bad for the morale of the office."

I could hardly believe my ears! I was too outraged to speak then, but this was to be only the first such assault on my right to define and to claim my own body.

Here we were, in the offices of one of the top breast cancer surgeons in New York City. Every woman there either had a breast removed, might have to have a breast removed, or was afraid of having to have a breast removed. And every woman there could have used a reminder that having one breast did not mean her life was over, not that she was less a woman, nor that she was condemned to the use of a placebo in order to feel good about herself and the way she looked.

Yet a woman who has one breast and refuses to hide that fact behind a pathetic puff of lambswool which has no relationship nor likeness to her own breasts, a woman who is attempting to come to terms with her changed landscape and changed timetable of life and with her own body and pain and beauty and strength, that woman is seen as a threat to the "morale" of a breast surgeon's office!

Yet when Moshe Dayan, the prime minister of Israel, stands up in front of parliament or on TV with an eyepatch over his empty eye socket, nobody tells him to go get a glass eye, or that he is bad for the morale of the office.

The world sees him as a warrior with an honorable wound, and a loss of a piece of himself which he has marked, and mourned, and moved beyond. And if you have trouble dealing with Moshe Dayan's empty eye socket, everyone recognizes that it is your problem to solve, not his.

Well, women with breast cancer are warriors, also. I have been to war, and still am. So has every woman who had had one or both breasts amputated because of the cancer that is becoming the primary physical scourge of our time. For me, my scars are an honorable reminder that I may be a casualty in the cosmic war against radiation, animal fat, air pollution, McDonald's hamburgers and Red Dye No. 2, but the fight is still going on, and I am still a part of it. I refuse to have my scars hidden or trivialized behind lambswool or silicone gel. I refuse to be reduced in my own eyes or in the eyes of others from warrior to mere victim, simply because it might render me a fraction more acceptable or less dangerous to the still complacent, those who believe if you cover up a problem it ceases to exist. I refuse to hide my body simply because it might make a woman-phobic world more comfortable.

Raymond Carver

A SMALL, GOOD THING

The agony of parents awaiting word of their child's condition forms the heart of this piece by master storyteller Raymond Carver, one that poignantly illustrates the effect of a doctor's well-intended optimism as it belies the medical crisis at hand.

Shortly after Ann Weiss has ordered a birthday cake for her son Scotty's birthday party, Scotty is hit by a car and taken to the hospital. Life becomes a nightmare of waiting and dwindling hope, as the doctor's initial diagnosis proves itself inaccurate. Carver's story offers a complex examination of parents living the unimaginable, the inability of the hospital to assuage their suffering, and a surprisingly redemptive, unexpected conclusion: the "small, good thing" of the story's title.

Born in Clatskanie, Oregon, in 1938, RAYMOND CARVER'S first collection of short stories was titled *Will You Please Be Quiet, Please?* It was nominated for the National Book Award in 1977, followed by collections titled *What We Talk About When We Talk About Love*—nominated for the Pulitzer Prize in 1984—and *Where I'm Calling From*, published in 1988. Carver was inducted that same year into the American Academy of Arts and Letters. He died of cancer in August 1988, after completing a collection of poems titled *A New Path to the Waterfall*. Carver's poem "What the Doctor Said" also appears in this anthology.

Saturday afternoon she drove to the bakery in the shopping center. After looking through a loose-leaf binder with photographs of cakes taped onto the pages, she ordered chocolate, the child's favorite. The cake she chose was decorated with a spaceship and launching pad under a sprinkling of white stars, and a planet made of red frosting at the other end. His name, SCOTTY, would be in green letters beneath the planet. The baker, who was an older man with a thick neck, listened without saying anything when she told him the child would be eight years old next Monday. The baker wore a white apron that looked like a smock. Straps cut under his arms, went around in back and then to the front again, where they were secured under his heavy waist. He wiped his hands on his apron as he listened to her. He kept his eyes down on the photographs and let her talk. He let her take her time. He'd just come to work and he'd be there all night, baking, and he was in no real hurry.

She gave the baker her name, Ann Weiss, and her telephone number. The cake would be ready on Monday morning, just out of the oven, in plenty of time for the child's party that afternoon. The baker was not jolly. There were no pleasantries between them, just the minimum exchange of words, the necessary information. He made her feel uncomfortable, and she didn't like that. While he was bent over the counter with the pencil in his hand, she studied his coarse features and wondered if he'd ever done anything else with his life besides be a baker. She was a mother and thirty-three years old, and it seemed to her that everyone, especially someone the baker's age—a man old enough to be her father—must have children who'd gone through this special time of cakes and birthday parties. There must be that between them, she thought. But he was abrupt with her—not rude, just abrupt. She gave up trying to make friends with him. She looked into the back of the bakery and could see a long, heavy wooden table with aluminum pie pans stacked at one end; and beside the table a metal container filled with empty racks. There was an enormous oven. A radio was playing country-western music.

The baker finished printing the information on the special order card and closed up the binder. He looked at her and said, "Monday morning." She thanked him and drove home.

On Monday morning, the birthday boy was walking to school with another boy. They were passing a bag of potato chips back and forth and the birthday boy was trying to find out what his friend intended to give him for his birthday that afternoon. Without looking, the birthday boy stepped off the curb at an intersection and was immediately knocked down by a car. He fell on his side with his head in the gutter and his legs out in the road. His eyes were closed, but his legs moved back and forth as if he were trying to climb over something. His friend dropped the potato chips and started to cry. The car had gone a hundred feet or so and stopped in the middle of the road. The man in the driver's seat looked back over his shoulder. He waited until the boy got unsteadily to his feet. The boy wobbled a little. He looked dazed, but okay. The driver put the car into gear and drove away.

The birthday boy didn't cry, but he didn't have anything to say about anything either. He wouldn't answer when his friend asked him what it felt like to be hit by a car. He walked home, and his friend went on to school. But after the birthday boy was inside his house and was telling his mother about it—she sitting beside him on the sofa, holding his hands in her lap, saying, "Scotty, honey, are you sure you feel all right, baby?" thinking she would call the doctor anyway—he suddenly lay back on the sofa, closed his eyes, and went limp. When she couldn't wake him up, she hurried to the telephone and called her husband at work. Howard told her to remain calm, remain calm, and then he called an ambulance for the child and left for the hospital himself.

Of course, the birthday party was canceled. The child was in the hospital with a mild concussion and suffering from shock. There'd been vomiting, and his lungs had taken in fluid which needed pumping out that afternoon. Now he simply seemed to be in a very deep sleep—but no coma, Dr. Francis had emphasized, no coma, when he saw the alarm in the parents' eyes. At eleven o'clock that night, when the boy seemed to be resting comfortably enough after the many X-rays and the lab work, and it was just a matter of his waking up and coming around, Howard left the hospital. He and Ann had been at the hospital with the child since that afternoon, and he was going home for a short while to bathe and change clothes. "I'll be back in an hour," he said. She nodded. "It's fine," she said. "I'll be right here." He kissed her on the forehead, and they touched hands. She sat in the chair beside the bed and looked at the child. She was waiting for him to wake up and be all right. Then she could begin to relax.

Howard drove home from the hospital. He took the wet, dark streets very fast, then caught himself and slowed down. Until now, his life had gone smoothly and to his satisfaction—college, marriage, another year of college for the advanced degree in business, a junior partnership in an investment firm. Fatherhood. He was happy and, so far, lucky—he knew that. His parents were still living, his brothers and his sister were established, his friends from college had gone out to take their places in the world. So far, he had kept away from any real harm, from those forces he knew existed and that could cripple or bring down a man if the luck went bad, if things suddenly turned. He pulled into the driveway and parked. His left leg began to tremble. He sat in the car for a minute and tried to deal with the present situation in a rational manner. Scotty had been hit by a car and was in the hospital, but he was going to be all right. Howard closed his eyes and ran his hand over his face. He got out of the car and went up to the front door. The dog was barking inside the house. The telephone rang and rang while he unlocked the door and fumbled for the light switch. He shouldn't have left the hospital, he shouldn't have. "Goddamn it!" he said. He picked up the receiver and said, "I just walked in the door!"

"There's a cake here that wasn't picked up," the voice on the other end of the line said.

"What are you saying?" Howard asked.

"A cake," the voice said. "A sixteen-dollar cake."

Howard held the receiver against his ear, trying to understand. "I don't know anything about a cake," he said. "Jesus, what are you talking about?"

"Don't hand me that," the voice said.

Howard hung up the telephone. He went into the kitchen and poured himself some whiskey. He called the hospital. But the child's condition remained the same; he was still sleeping and nothing had changed there. While water poured into the tub, Howard lathered his face and shaved. He'd just stretched out in the tub and closed his eyes when the telephone rang again. He hauled himself out, grabbed a towel, and hurried through the house, saying, "Stupid, stupid," for having left the hospital. But when he picked up the receiver and shouted, "Hello!" there was no sound at the other end of the line. Then the caller hung up.

He arrived back at the hospital a little after midnight. Ann still sat in the chair beside the bed. She looked up at Howard, and then she looked back at the child. The child's eyes stayed closed, the head was still wrapped in bandages. His breathing was quiet and regular. From an apparatus over the bed hung a bottle of glucose with a tube running from the bottle to the boy's arm.

"How is he?" Howard said. "What's all this?" waving at the glucose and the tube.

"Dr. Francis's orders," she said. "He needs nourishment. He needs to keep up his strength. Why doesn't he wake up, Howard? I don't understand, if he's all right."

Howard put his hand against the back of her head. He ran his fingers through her hair. "He's going to be all right. He'll wake up in a little while. Dr. Francis knows what's what."

After a time, he said, "Maybe you should go home and get some rest. I'll stay here. Just don't put up with this creep who keeps calling. Hang up right away."

"Who's calling?" she asked.

"I don't know who, just somebody with nothing better to do than call up people. You go on now."

She shook her head. "No," she said, "I'm fine."

"Really," he said. "Go home for a while, and then come back and spell me in the morning. It'll be all right. What did Dr. Francis say? He said Scotty's going to be all right. We don't have to worry. He's just sleeping now, that's all."

A nurse pushed the door open. She nodded at them as she went to the bedside. She took the left arm out from under the covers and put her fingers on the wrist, found the pulse, then consulted her watch. In a little while, she put the arm back under the covers and moved to the foot of the bed, where she wrote something on a clipboard attached to the bed.

"How is he?" Ann said. Howard's hand was a weight on her shoulder. She was aware of the pressure from his fingers.

"He's stable," the nurse said. Then she said, "Doctor will be in again shortly. Doctor's back in the hospital. He's making rounds right now."

"I was saying maybe she'd want to go home and get a little rest," Howard said. "After the doctor comes," he said.

"She could do that," the nurse said. "I think you should both feel free to do that, if you wish." The nurse was a big Scandinavian woman with blond hair. There was the trace of an accent in her speech.

"We'll see what the doctor says," Ann said. "I want to talk to the doctor. I don't think he should keep sleeping like this. I don't think that's a good sign." She brought her hand up to her eyes and let her head come forward a little. Howard's grip tightened on her shoulder, and then his hand moved up to her neck, where his fingers began to knead the muscles there.

"Dr. Francis will be here in a few minutes," the nurse said. Then she left the room.

Howard gazed at his son for a time, the small chest quietly rising and falling under the covers. For the first time since the terrible minutes after Ann's telephone call to him at his office, he felt a genuine fear starting in his limbs. He began shaking his head. Scotty was fine, but instead of sleeping at home in his own bed, he was in a hospital bed with bandages around his head and a tube in his arm. But this help was what he needed right now.

Dr. Francis came in and shook hands with Howard, though they'd just seen each other a few hours before. Ann got up from the chair. "Doctor?"

"Ann," he said and nodded. "Let's just first see how he's doing," the doctor said. He moved to the side of the bed and took the boy's pulse. He peeled back one eyelid and then the other. Howard and Ann stood beside the doctor and watched. Then the doctor turned back the covers and listened to the boy's heart and lungs with his stethoscope. He pressed his fingers here and there on the abdomen. When he was finished, he went to the end of the bed and studied the chart. He noted the time, scribbled something on the chart, and then looked at Howard and Ann.

"Doctor, how is he?" Howard said. "What's the matter with him exactly?"

"Why doesn't he wake up?" Ann said.

The doctor was a handsome, big-shouldered man with a tanned face. He wore a three-piece blue suit, a striped tie, and ivory cuff links. His gray hair was combed along the sides of his head, and he looked as if he had just come from a concert. "He's all right," the doctor said. "Nothing to shout about, he could be better, I think. But he's all right. Still, I wish he'd wake up. He should wake up pretty soon." The doctor looked at the boy again. "We'll know some more in a couple of hours, after the results of a few more tests are in. But he's all right, believe me, except for the hairline fracture of the skull. He does have that."

"Oh, no," Ann said.

"And a bit of a concussion, as I said before. Of course, you know he's in shock," the doctor said. "Sometimes you see this in shock cases. This sleeping."

"But he's out of any real danger?" Howard said. "You said before he's not in a coma. You wouldn't call this a coma, then—would you, doctor?" Howard waited. He looked at the doctor.

"No, I don't want to call it a coma," the doctor said and glanced over at the boy once more. "He's just in a very deep sleep. It's a restorative measure the body is taking on its own. He's out of any real danger, I'd say that for certain, yes. But we'll know more when he wakes up and the other tests are in," the doctor said.

"It's a coma," Ann said. "Of sorts."

"It's not a coma yet, not exactly," the doctor said. "I wouldn't want to call it coma. Not yet, anyway. He's suffered shock. In shock cases, this kind of reaction is common enough; it's a temporary reaction to bodily trauma. Coma. Well, coma is a deep, prolonged unconsciousness, something that could go on for days, or weeks even. Scotty's not in that area, not as far as we can tell. I'm certain his condition will show improvement by morning. I'm betting that it will. We'll know more when he wakes up, which shouldn't be long now. Of course, you may do as you like, stay here or go home for a time. But by all means feel free to leave the hospital for a while if you want. This is not easy, I know." The doctor gazed at the boy again, watching him, and then he turned to Ann and said, "You try not to worry, little mother. Believe me, we're doing all that can be done. It's just a question of a little more time now." He nodded at her, shook hands with Howard again, and then he left the room.

Ann put her hand over the child's forehead. "At least he doesn't have a fever," she said. Then she said, "My God, he feels so cold, though. Howard? Is he supposed to feel like this? Feel his head."

Howard touched the child's temples. His own breathing had slowed. "I think he's supposed to feel this way right now," he said. "He's in shock, remember? That's what the doctor said. The doctor was just in here. He would have said something if Scotty wasn't okay."

Ann stood there a while longer, working her lip with her teeth. Then she moved over to her chair and sat down.

Howard sat in the chair next to her chair. They looked at each other. He wanted to say something else and reassure her, but he was afraid, too. He took her hand and put it in his lap, and this made him feel better, her hand being there. He picked up her hand and squeezed it. Then he just held her hand. They sat like that for a while, watching the boy and not talking. From time to time, he squeezed her hand. Finally, she took her hand away.

"I've been praying," she said.

He nodded.

She said, "I almost thought I'd forgotten how, but it came back to me. All I had to do was close my eyes and say, 'Please God, help us—help Scotty,' and then the rest was easy. The words were right there. Maybe if you prayed, too," she said to him.

"I've already prayed," he said. "I prayed this afternoon—yesterday afternoon, I mean—after you called, while I was driving to the hospital. I've been praying," he said.

"That's good," she said. For the first time, she felt they were together in it, this trouble. She realized with a start that, until now, it had only been happening to her and to Scotty. She hadn't let Howard into it, though he was there and needed all along. She felt glad to be his wife.

The same nurse came in and took the boy's pulse again and checked the flow from the bottle hanging above the bed.

In an hour, another doctor came in. He said his name was Parsons, from Radiology. He had a bushy moustache. He was wearing loafers, a western shirt, and a pair of jeans.

"We're going to take him downstairs for more pictures," he told them. "We need to do some more pictures, and we want to do a scan."

"What's that?" Ann said. "A scan?" She stood between this new doctor and the bed. "I thought you'd already taken all your X-rays."

"I'm afraid we need some more," he said. "Nothing to be alarmed about. We just need some more pictures, and we want to do a brain scan on him."

"My God," Ann said.

"It's perfectly normal procedure in cases like this," this new doctor said. "We just need to find out for sure why he isn't back awake yet. It's normal medical procedure, and nothing to be alarmed about. We'll be taking him down in a few minutes," this doctor said.

In a little while, two orderlies came into the room with a gurney. They were black-haired, dark-complexioned men in white uniforms, and they said a few words to each other in a foreign tongue as they unhooked the boy from the tube and moved him from his bed to the gurney. Then they wheeled him from the room. Howard and Ann got on the same elevator. Ann gazed at the child. She closed her eyes as the elevator began its descent. The orderlies stood at either end of the gurney without saying anything, though once one of the men made a comment to the other in their own language, and the other man nodded slowly in response.

Later that morning, just as the sun was beginning to lighten the windows in the waiting room outside the X-ray department, they brought the boy out and moved him back up to his room. Howard and Ann rode up on the elevator with him once more, and once more they took up their places beside the bed.

They waited all day, but still the boy did not wake up. Occasionally, one of them would leave the room to go downstairs to the cafeteria to drink coffee and then, as if suddenly remembering and feeling guilty, get up from the table and hurry back to the room. Dr. Francis came again that afternoon and examined the boy once more and then left after telling them he was coming along and could wake up at any minute now. Nurses, different nurses from the night before, came in from time to time. Then a young woman from the lab knocked and entered the room. She wore white slacks and a white blouse and carried a little tray of things which she put on the stand beside the bed. Without a word to them, she took blood from the boy's arm. Howard closed his eyes as the woman found the right place on the boy's arm and pushed the needle in.

"I don't understand this," Ann said to the woman.

"Doctor's orders," the young woman said. "I do what I'm told. They say draw that one, I draw. What's wrong with him, anyway?" she said. "He's a sweetie."

"He was hit by a car," Howard said. "A hit-and-run."

The young woman shook her head and looked again at the boy. Then she took her tray and left the room.

"Why won't he wake up?" Ann said. "Howard? I want some answers from these people."

Howard didn't say anything. He sat down again in the chair and crossed one leg over the other. He rubbed his face. He looked at his son and then he settled back in the chair, closed his eyes, and went to sleep.

Ann walked to the window and looked out at the parking lot. It was night, and cars were driving into and out of the parking lot with their lights on. She stood at the window with her hands gripping the sill, and knew in her heart that they were into something now, something hard. She was afraid, and her teeth began to chatter until she tightened her jaws. She saw a big car stop in front of the hospital and someone, a woman in a long coat, get into the car. She wished she were that woman and somebody, anybody, was driving her away from here to somewhere else, a place where she would find Scotty waiting for her when she stepped out of the car, ready to say *Mom* and let her gather him in her arms.

In a little while, Howard woke up. He looked at the boy again. Then he got up from the chair, stretched, and went over to stand beside her at the window. They both stared out at the parking lot. They didn't say anything. But they seemed to feel each other's insides now, as though the worry had made them transparent in a perfectly natural way.

The door opened and Dr. Francis came in. He was wearing a different suit and tie this time. His gray hair was combed along the sides of his head, and he looked as if he had just shaved. He went straight to the bed and examined the boy. "He ought to have come around by now. There's just no good reason for this," he said. "But I can tell you we're all convinced he's out of any danger. We'll just feel better when when he wakes up. There's no reason, absolutely none, why he shouldn't come around. Very soon. Oh, he'll have himself a dilly of a headache when he does, you can count on that. But all of his signs are fine. They're as normal as can be."

"It is a coma, then?" Ann said.

The doctor rubbed his smooth cheek. "We'll call it that for the time being, until he wakes up. But you must be worn out. This is hard. I know this is hard. Feel free to go out for a bite," he said. "It would do you good. I'll put a nurse in here while you're gone if you'll feel better about going. Go and have yourselves something to eat."

"I couldn't eat anything," Ann said.

"Do what you need to do, of course," the doctor said. "Anyway, I wanted to tell you that all the signs are good, the tests are negative, nothing showed up at all, and just as soon as he wakes up he'll be over the hill."

"Thank you, doctor," Howard said. He shook hands with the doctor again. The doctor patted Howard's shoulder and went out.

"I suppose one of us should go home and check on things," Howard said. "Slug needs to be fed, for one thing."

"Call one of the neighbors," Ann said. "Call the Morgans. Anyone will feed a dog if you ask them to."

"All right," Howard said. After a while, he said, "Honey, why don't *you* do it? Why don't you go home and check on things, and then come back? It'll do you good. I'll be right here with him. Seriously," he said. "We need to keep up our strength on this. We'll want to be here for a while even after he wakes up."

"Why don't *you* go?" she said. "Feed Slug. Feed yourself."

"I already went," he said. "I was gone for exactly an hour and fifteen minutes. You go home for an hour and freshen up. Then come back."

She tried to think about it, but she was too tired. She closed her eyes and tried to think about it again. After a time, she said, "Maybe I *will* go home for a few minutes. Maybe if I'm not just sitting right here watching him every second, he'll wake up and be all right. You know? Maybe he'll wake up if I'm not here. I'll go home and take a bath and put on clean clothes. I'll feed Slug. Then I'll come back."

"I'll be right here," he said. "You go on home, honey. I'll keep an eye on things here." His eyes were bloodshot and small, as if he'd been drinking for a long time. His clothes were rumpled. His beard had come out again. She touched his face, and then she took her hand back. She understood he wanted to be by himself for a while, not have to talk or share his worry for a time. She picked her purse up from the nightstand, and he helped her into her coat.

"I won't be gone long," she said.

"Just sit and rest for a little while when you get home," he said. "Eat something. Take a bath. After you get out of the bath, just sit for a while and rest. It'll do you a world of good, you'll see. Then come back," he said. "Let's try not to worry. You heard what Dr. Francis said."

She stood in her coat for a minute trying to recall the doctor's exact words, looking for any nuances, any hint of something behind his words other than what he had said. She tried to remember if his expression had changed any when he bent over to examine the child. She remembered the way his features had composed themselves as he rolled back the child's eyelids and then listened to his breathing.

She went to the door, where she turned and looked back. She looked at the child, and then she looked at the father. Howard nodded. She stepped out of the room and pulled the door closed behind her.

She went past the nurses' station and down to the end of the corridor, looking for the elevator. At the end of the corridor, she turned to her right and entered a little waiting room where a Negro family sat in wicker chairs. There was a middle-aged man in a khaki shirt and pants, a baseball cap pushed back on his head. A large woman wearing a housedress and slippers was slumped in one of the chairs. A teenaged girl in jeans, hair done in dozens of little braids, lay stretched out in one of the chairs smoking a cigarette, her legs crossed at the ankles. The family swung their eyes to Ann as she entered the room. The little table was littered with hamburger wrappers and Styrofoam cups.

"Franklin," the large woman said as she roused herself. "Is it about Franklin?" Her eyes widened. "Tell me now, lady," the woman said. "Is it about Franklin?" She was trying to rise from her chair, but the man had closed his hand over her arm.

"Here, here," he said. "Evelyn."

"I'm sorry," Ann said. "I'm looking for the elevator. My son is in the hospital, and now I can't find the elevator."

"Elevator is down that way, turn left," the man said as he aimed a finger.

The girl drew on her cigarette and stared at Ann. Her eyes were narrowed to slits, and her broad lips parted slowly as she let the smoke escape. The Negro woman let her head fall on her shoulder and looked away from Ann, no longer interested.

"My son was hit by a car," Ann said to the man. She seemed to need to explain herself. "He has a concussion and a little skull fracture, but he's going to be all right. He's in shock now, but it might be some kind of coma, too. That's what really worries us, the coma part. I'm going out for a little while, but my husband is with him. Maybe he'll wake up while I'm gone."

"That's too bad," the man said and shifted in the chair. He shook his head. He looked down at the table, and then he looked back at Ann. She was still standing there. He said, "Our Franklin, he's on the operating table. Somebody cut him. Tried to kill him. There was a fight where he was at. At this party. They say he was just standing and watching. Not bothering nobody. But that don't mean nothing these days. Now he's on the operating table. We're just hoping and praying, that's all we can do now." He gazed at her steadily.

Ann looked at the girl again, who was still watching her, and at the older woman, who kept her head down, but whose eyes were now closed. Ann saw the lips moving silently, making words. She had an urge to ask what those words were. She wanted to talk more with these people who were in the same kind of waiting she was in. She was afraid, and they were afraid. They had that in common. She would have liked to have said something else about the accident, told them more about Scotty, that it had happened on the day of his birthday, Monday, and that he was still unconscious. Yet she didn't know how to begin. She stood looking at them without saying anything more.

She went down the corridor the man had indicated and found the elevator. She waited a minute in front of the closed doors, still wondering if she was doing the right thing. Then she put out her finger and touched the button.

She pulled into the driveway and cut the engine. She closed her eyes and leaned her head against the wheel for a minute. She listened to the ticking sounds the engine made as it began to cool. Then she got out of the car. She could hear the dog barking inside the house. She went to the front door, which was unlocked. She went inside and turned on lights and put on a kettle of water for tea. She opened some dog food and fed Slug on the back porch. The dog ate in hungry little smacks. It kept running into the kitchen to see that she was going to stay. As she sat down on the sofa with her tea, the telephone rang.

"Yes!" she said as she answered. "Hello!"

"Mrs. Weiss," a man's voice said. It was five o'clock in the morning, and she thought she could hear machinery or equipment of some kind in the background.

"Yes, yes! What is it?" she said. "This is Mrs. Weiss. This is she. What is it, please?" She listened to whatever it was in the background. "Is it Scotty, for Christ's sake?"

"Scotty," the man's voice said. "It's about Scotty, yes. It has to do with Scotty, that problem. Have you forgotten about Scotty?" the man said. Then he hung up.

She dialed the hospital's number and asked for the third floor. She demanded information about her son from the nurse who answered the telephone. Then she asked to speak to her husband. It was, she said, an emergency.

She waited, turning the telephone cord in her fingers. She closed her eyes and felt sick at her stomach. She would have to make herself eat. Slug came in from the back porch and lay down near her feet. He wagged his tail. She pulled at his ear while he licked her fingers. Howard was on the line.

"Somebody just called here," she said. She twisted the telephone cord. "He said it was about Scotty," she cried.

"Scotty's fine," Howard told her. "I mean, he's still sleeping. There's been no change. The nurse has been in twice since you've been gone. A nurse or else a doctor. He's all right."

"This man called. He said it was about Scotty," she told him.

"Honey, you rest for a little while, you need the rest. It must be that same caller I had. Just forget it. Come back down here after you've rested. Then we'll have breakfast or something."

"Breakfast," she said. "I don't want any breakfast."

"You know what I mean," he said. "Juice, something. I don't know. I don't know anything, Ann. Jesus, I'm not hungry, either. Ann, it's hard to talk now. I'm standing here at the desk. Dr. Francis is coming again at eight o'clock this morning. He's going to have something to tell us then, something more definite. That's what one of the nurses said. She didn't know any more than that. Ann? Honey, maybe we'll know something more then. At eight o'clock. Come back here before eight. Meanwhile, I'm right here and Scotty's all right. He's still the same," he added.

"I was drinking a cup of tea," she said, "when the telephone rang. They said it was about Scotty. There was a noise in the background. Was there a noise in the background on that call you had, Howard?"

"I don't remember," he said. "Maybe the driver of the car, maybe he's a psychopath and found out about Scotty somehow. But I'm here with him. Just rest like you were going to do. Take a bath and come back by seven or so, and we'll talk to the doctor together when he gets here. It's going to be all right, honey. I'm here, and there are doctors and nurses around. They say his condition is stable."

"I'm scared to death," she said.

She ran water, undressed, and got into the tub. She washed and dried quickly, not taking the time to wash her hair. She put on clean underwear, wool slacks, and a sweater. She went into the living room, where the dog looked up at her and let its tail thump once against the floor. It was just starting to get light outside when she went out to the car.

She drove into the parking lot of the hospital and found a space close to the front door. She felt she was in some obscure way responsible for what had happened to the child. She let her thoughts move to the Negro family. She remembered the name Franklin and the table that was covered with hamburger papers, and the teenaged girl staring at her as she drew on her cigarette. "Don't have children," she told the girl's image as she entered the front door of the hospital. "For God's sake, don't."

She took the elevator up to the third floor with two nurses who were just going on duty. It was Wednesday morning, a few minutes before seven. There was a page for a Dr. Madison as the elevator doors slid open on the third floor. She got off behind the nurses, who turned in the other direction and continued the conversation she had interrupted when she'd gotten into the elevator. She walked down the corridor to the little alcove where the Negro family had been waiting. They were gone now, but the chairs were scattered in such a way that it looked as if people had just jumped up from them the minute before. The tabletop was cluttered with the same cups and papers, the ashtray was filled with cigarette butts.

She stopped at the nurses' station. A nurse was standing behind the counter, brushing her hair and yawning.

"There was a Negro boy in surgery last night," Ann said. "Franklin was his name. His family was in the waiting room. I'd like to inquire about his condition."

A nurse who was sitting at a desk behind the counter looked up from a chart in front of her. The telephone buzzed and she picked up the receiver, but she kept her eyes on Ann.

"He passed away," said the nurse at the counter. The nurse held the hairbrush and kept looking at her. "Are you a friend of the family or what?"

"I met the family last night," Ann said. "My own son is in the hospital. I guess he's in shock. We don't know for sure what's wrong. I just wondered about Franklin, that's all. Thank you." She moved down the corridor. Elevator doors the same color as the walls slid open and a gaunt, bald man in white pants and white canvas shoes pulled a heavy cart off the elevator. She hadn't noticed these doors last night. The man wheeled the cart out into the corridor and stopped in front of the room nearest the elevator and consulted a clipboard. Then he reached down and slid a tray out of the cart. He rapped lightly on the door and entered the room. She could smell the unpleasant odors of warm food as she passed the cart. She hurried on without looking at any of the nurses and pushed open the door to the child's room.

Howard was standing at the window with his hands behind his back. He turned around as she came in.

"How is he?" she said. She went over to the bed. She dropped her purse on the floor beside the nightstand. It seemed to her she had been gone a long time. She touched the child's face. "Howard?"

"Dr. Francis was here a little while ago," Howard said. She looked at him closely and thought his shoulders were bunched a little.

"I thought he wasn't coming until eight o'clock this morning," she said quickly.

"There was another doctor with him. A neurologist."

"A neurologist," she said.

Howard nodded. His shoulders were bunching, she could see that. "What'd they say, Howard? For Christ's sake, what'd they say? What is it?"

"They said they're going to take him down and run more tests on him, Ann. They think they're going to operate, honey. Honey, they *are* going to operate. They can't figure out why he won't wake up. It's more than just shock or concussion, they know that much now. It's in his skull, the fracture, it has something, something to do with that, they think. So they're going to operate. I tried to call you, but I guess you'd already left the house."

"Oh, God," she said. "Oh, please, Howard, please," she said, taking his arms.

"Look!" Howard said. "Scotty! Look, Ann!" He turned her toward the bed.

The boy had opened his eyes, then closed them. He opened them again now. The eyes stared straight ahead for a minute, then moved slowly in his head until they rested on Howard and Ann, then traveled away again.

"Scotty," his mother said, moving to the bed.

"Hey, Scott," his father said. "Hey, son."

They leaned over the bed. Howard took the child's hand in his hands and began to pat and squeeze the hand. Ann bent over the boy and kissed his forehead again and again. She put her hands on either side of his face. "Scotty, honey, it's Mommy and Daddy," she said. "Scotty?"

The boy looked at them, but without any sign of recognition. Then his mouth opened, his eyes scrunched closed, and he howled until he had no more air in his lungs. His face seemed to relax and soften then. His lips parted as his last breath was puffed through his throat and exhaled gently through the clenched teeth.

The doctors called it a hidden occlusion and said it was a one-in-a-million circumstance. Maybe if it could have been detected somehow and surgery undertaken immediately, they could have saved him. But more than likely not. In any case, what would they have been looking for? Nothing had shown up in the tests or in the X-rays.

Dr. Francis was shaken. "I can't tell you how badly I feel. I'm so very sorry, I can't tell you," he said as he led them into the doctors' lounge. There was a doctor sitting in a chair with his legs hooked over the back of another chair, watching an early-morning TV show. He was wearing a green delivery-room outfit, loose green pants and green blouse, and a green cap that covered his hair. He looked at Howard and Ann and then looked at Dr. Francis. He got to his feet and turned off the set and went out of the room. Dr. Francis guided Ann to the sofa, sat down beside her, and began to talk in a low, consoling voice. At one point, he leaned over and embraced her. She could feel his chest rising and falling evenly against her shoulder. She kept her eyes open and let him hold her. Howard went into the bathroom, but he left the door open. After a violent fit of weeping, he ran water and washed his face. Then he came out and sat down at the little table that held a telephone. He looked at the telephone as though deciding what to do first. He made some calls. After a time, Dr. Francis used the telephone.

"Is there anything else I can do for the moment?" he asked them.

Howard shook his head. Ann stared at Dr. Francis as if unable to comprehend his words.

The doctor walked them to the hospital's front door. People were entering and leaving the hospital. It was eleven o'clock in the morning. Ann was aware of how slowly, almost reluctantly, she moved her feet. It seemed to her that Dr. Francis was making them leave when she felt they should stay, when it would be more the right thing to do to stay. She gazed out into the parking lot and then turned around and looked back at the front of the hospital. She began shaking her head. "No, no," she said. "I can't leave him here, no." She heard herself say that and thought how unfair it was that the only words that came out were the sort of words used on TV shows where people were stunned by violent or sudden deaths. She wanted her words to be her own. "No," she said, and for some reason the memory of the Negro woman's head lolling on the woman's shoulder came to her. "No," she said again.

"I'll be talking to you later in the day," the doctor was saying to Howard. "There are still some things that have to be done, things that have to be cleared up to our satisfaction. Some things that need explaining."

"An autopsy," Howard said.

Dr. Francis nodded.

"I understand," Howard said. Then he said, "Oh, Jesus. No, I don't understand, doctor. I can't, I can't. I just can't."

Dr. Francis put his arm around Howard's shoulders. "I'm sorry. God, how I'm sorry." He let go of Howard's shoulders and held out his hand. Howard looked at the hand, and then he took it. Dr. Francis put his arms around Ann once more. He seemed full of some goodness she didn't understand. She let her head rest on his shoulder, but her eyes stayed open. She kept looking at the hospital. As they drove out of the parking lot, she looked back at the hospital.

At home, she sat on the sofa with her hands in her coat pockets. Howard closed the door to the child's room. He got the coffee-maker going and then he found an empty box. He had thought to pick up some of the child's things that were scattered around the living room. But instead he sat down beside her on the sofa, pushed the box to one side, and leaned forward, arms between his knees. He began to weep. She pulled his head over into her lap and patted his shoulder. "He's gone," she said. She kept patting his shoulder. Over his sobs, she could hear the coffee-maker hissing in the kitchen. "There, there," she said tenderly. "Howard, he's gone. He's gone and now we'll have to get used to that. To being alone."

In a little while, Howard got up and began moving aimlessly around the room with the box, not putting anything into it, but collecting some things together on the floor at one end of the sofa. She continued to sit with her hands in her coat pockets. Howard put the box down and brought coffee into the living room. Later, Ann made calls to relatives. After each call had been placed and the party had answered, Ann would blurt out a few words and cry for a minute. Then she would quietly explain, in a measured voice, what had happened and tell them about arrangements. Howard took the box out to the garage, where he saw the child's bicycle. He dropped the box and sat down on the pavement beside the bicycle. He took hold of the bicycle awkwardly so that it leaned against his chest. He held it, the rubber pedal sticking into his chest. He gave the wheel a turn.

Ann hung up the telephone after talking to her sister. She was looking up another number when the telephone rang. She picked it up on the first ring.

"Hello," she said, and she heard something in the background, a humming noise. "Hello!" she said. "For God's sake," she said. "Who is this? What is it you want?"

"Your Scotty, I got him ready for you," the man's voice said. "Did you forget him?"

"You evil bastard!" she shouted into the receiver. "How can you do this, you evil son of a bitch?"

"Scotty," the man said. "Have you forgotten about Scotty?" Then the man hung up on her.

Howard heard the shouting and came in to find her with her head on her arms over the table, weeping. He picked up the receiver and listened to the dial tone.

Much later, just before midnight, after they had dealt with many things, the telephone rang again.

"You answer it," she said. "Howard, it's him, I know." They were sitting at the kitchen table with coffee in front of them. Howard had a small glass of whiskey beside his cup. He answered on the third ring.

"Hello," he said. "Who is this? Hello! Hello!" The line went dead. "He hung up," Howard said. "Whoever it was."

"It was him," she said. "That bastard. I'd like to kill him," she said. "I'd like to shoot him and watch him kick," she said.

"Ann, my God," he said.

"Could you hear anything?" she said. "In the background? A noise, machinery, something humming?"

"Nothing, really. Nothing like that," he said. "There wasn't much time. I think there was some radio music. Yes, there was a radio going, that's all I could tell. I don't know what in God's name is going on," he said.

She shook her head. "If I could, could get my hands on him." It came to her then. She knew who it was. Scotty, the cake, the telephone number. She pushed the chair away from the table and got up. "Drive me down to the shopping center," she said. "Howard."

"What are you saying?"

"The shopping center. I know who it is who's calling. I know who it is. It's the baker, the son-of-a-bitching baker, Howard. I had him bake a cake for Scotty's birthday. That's who's calling. That's who has the number and keeps calling us. To harass us about that cake. The baker, that bastard."

They drove down to the shopping center. The sky was clear and stars were out. It was cold, and they ran the heater in the car. They parked in front of the bakery. All of the shops and stores were closed, but there were cars at the far end of the lot in front of the movie theater. The bakery windows were dark, but when they looked through the glass they could see a light in the back room and, now and then, a big man in an apron moving in and out of the white, even light. Through the glass, she could see the display cases and some little tables with chairs. She tried the door. She rapped on the glass. But if the baker heard them, he gave no sign. He didn't look in their direction.

They drove around behind the bakery and parked. They got out of the car. There was a lighted window too high up for them to see inside. A sign near the back door said THE PANTRY BAKERY, SPECIAL ORDERS. She could hear faintly a radio playing inside and something creak—an oven door as it was pulled down? She knocked on the door and waited. Then she knocked again, louder.

The radio was turned down and there was a scraping sound now, the distinct sound of something, a drawer, being pulled open and then closed.

Someone unlocked the door and opened it. The baker stood in the light and peered out at them. "I'm closed for business," he said. "What do you want at this hour? It's midnight. Are you drunk or something?"

She stepped into the light that fell through the open door. He blinked his heavy eyelids as he recognized her. "It's you," he said.

"It's me," she said. "Scotty's mother. This is Scotty's father. We'd like to come in."

The baker said, "I'm busy now. I have work to do."

She had stepped inside the doorway anyway. Howard came in behind her. The baker moved back. "It smells like a bakery in here. Doesn't it smell like a bakery in here, Howard?"

"What do you want?" the baker said. "Maybe you want your cake? That's it, you decided you want your cake. You ordered a cake, didn't you?"

"You're pretty smart for a baker," she said. "Howard, this is the man who's been calling us." She clenched her fists. She stared at him fiercely. There was a deep burning inside her, an anger that made her feel larger than herself, larger than either of these men.

"Just a minute here," the baker said. "You want to pick up your three-day-old cake? That it? I don't want to argue with you, lady. There it sits over there, getting stale. I'll give it to you for half of what I quoted you. No. You want it? You can have it. It's no good to me, no good to anyone now. It cost me time and money to make that cake. If you want it, okay, if you don't, that's okay, too. I have to get back to work." He looked at them and rolled his tongue behind his teeth.

"More cakes," she said. She knew she was in control of it, of what was increasing in her. She was calm.

"Lady, I work sixteen hours a day in this place to earn a living," the baker said. He wiped his hands on his apron. "I work night and day in here, trying to make ends meet." A look crossed Ann's face that made the baker move back and say, "No trouble, now." He reached to the counter and picked up a rolling pin with his right hand and began to tap it against the palm of his other hand. "You want the cake or not? I have to get back to work. Bakers work at night," he said again. His eyes were small, mean-looking, she thought, nearly lost in the bristly flesh around his cheeks. His neck was thick with fat.

"I know bakers work at night," Ann said. "They make phone calls at night, too. You bastard," she said.

The baker continued to tap the rolling pin against his hand. He glanced at Howard. "Careful, careful," he said to Howard.

"My son's dead," she said with a cold, even finality. "He was hit by a car Monday morning. We've been waiting with him until he died. But, of course, you couldn't be expected to know that, could you? Bakers can't know everything—can they, Mr. Baker? But he's dead. He's dead, you bastard!" Just as suddenly as it had welled in her, the anger dwindled, gave way to something else, a dizzy feeling of nausea. She leaned against the wooden table that was sprinkled with flour, put her hands over her face, and began to cry, her shoulders rocking back and forth. "It isn't fair," she said. "It isn't, isn't fair."

Howard put his hand at the small of her back and looked at the baker. "Shame on you," Howard said to him. "Shame."

The baker put the rolling pin back on the counter. He undid his apron and threw it on the counter. He looked at them, and then he shook his head slowly. He pulled a chair out from under the card table that held papers and receipts, an adding machine, and a telephone directory. "Please sit down," he said. "Let me get you a chair," he said to Howard. "Sit down now, please." The baker went into the front of the shop and returned with two little wrought-iron chairs. "Please sit down, you people."

Ann wiped her eyes and looked at the baker. "I wanted to kill you," she said. "I wanted you dead."

The baker had cleared a space for them at the table. He shoved the adding machine to one side, along with the stacks of notepaper and receipts. He pushed the telephone directory onto the floor, where it landed with a thud. Howard and Ann sat down and pulled their chairs up to the table. The baker sat down, too.

"Let me say how sorry I am," the baker said, putting his elbows on the table. "God alone knows how sorry. Listen to me. I'm just a baker. I don't claim to be anything else. Maybe once, maybe years ago, I was a different kind of human being. I've forgotten, I don't know for sure. But I'm not any longer, if I ever was. Now I'm just a baker. That don't excuse my doing what I did, I know. But I'm deeply sorry. I'm sorry for your son, and sorry for my part in this," the baker said. He spread his hands out on the table and turned them over to reveal his palms. "I don't have any children myself, so I can only imagine what you must be feeling. All I can say to you now is that I'm sorry. Forgive me, if you can," the baker said. "I'm not an evil man, I don't think. Not evil, like you said on the phone. You got to understand what it comes down to is I don't know how to act anymore, it would seem. Please," the man said, "let me ask you if you can find it in your hearts to forgive me?"

It was warm inside the bakery. Howard stood up from the table and took off his coat. He helped Ann from her coat. The baker looked at them for a minute and then nodded and got up from the table. He went to the oven and turned off some switches. He found cups and poured coffee from an electric coffee-maker. He put a carton of cream on the table, and a bowl of sugar.

"You probably need to eat something," the baker said. "I hope you'll eat some of my hot rolls. You have to eat and keep going. Eating is a small, good thing in a time like this," he said.

He served them warm cinnamon rolls just out of the oven, the icing still runny. He put butter on the table and knives to spread the butter. Then the baker sat down at the table with them. He waited. He waited until they each took a roll from the platter and began to eat. "It's good to eat something," he said, watching them. "There's more. Eat up. Eat all you want. There's all the rolls in the world in here."

They ate rolls and drank coffee. Ann was suddenly hungry, and the rolls were warm and sweet. She ate three of them, which pleased the baker. Then he began to talk. They listened carefully. Although they were tired and in anguish, they listened to what the baker had to say. They nodded when the baker began to speak of loneliness, and of the sense of doubt and limitation that had come to him in his middle years. He told them what it was like to be childless all these years. To repeat the days with the ovens endlessly full and endlessly empty. The party food, the celebrations he'd worked over. Icing knuckle-deep. The tiny wedding couples stuck into cakes. Hundreds of them, no, thousands by now. Birthdays. Just imagine all those candles burning. He had a necessary trade. He was a baker. He was glad he wasn't a florist. It was better to be feeding people. This was a better smell anytime than flowers.

"Smell this," the baker said, breaking open a dark loaf. "It's a heavy bread, but rich." They smelled it, then he had them taste it. It had the taste of molasses and coarse grains. They listened to him. They ate what they could. They swallowed the dark bread. It was like daylight under the fluorescent trays of light. They talked on into the early morning, the high, pale cast of light in the windows, and they did not think of leaving.

Timothy J. Fisher

PIES

This piece was written in response to Raymond Carver's story "A Small, Good Thing" in a literature and medicine course offered at Dartmouth Medical School. Students were asked to write about "a small, good thing" they had experienced during their four years of medical school; this story is one result of that assignment.

A fourth-year medical school student recalls his second year of medical school, when he is intent on demonstrating his competence and skill as he takes an "H&P"—a history and physical. The medical student's seriousness is delightfully undermined as a ninety-three-year-old man from Vermont's Northeast Kingdom offers his own diagnostic story about living so long a life.

TIMOTHY J. FISHER is an Ob-Gyn resident at the U.S. Naval Hospital in San Diego.

My white coat still had the wrinkles in it and hadn't yet developed the indelible ring-around-the-collar grunge that it has today. I was a second-year medical student, an impostor of the worst sort, sent out to prey on an unsuspecting inpatient to perform one of my first "H&P's." With clammy sweat on my brow and palms, I introduced myself in my best "I'm-almost-a-doctor-can't-you-tell?" voice and began my interrogation of the ninety-three-year-old man from the Northeast Kingdom. It seemed he had all the time in the world on his hands, while I had a precious, frantic hour in which to gather a history of present illness, to inquire about hemastochezia and tinnitus, to probe and prod, percuss and anscuctate.

"So tell me about your family," I said, doing my best to act as if I, too, had all the time in the world.

He started in, and the beads of sweat started to drip down my temples as I realized he wasn't meeting my agenda. I looked up from my cheat sheet to see him looking straight at me with what could only be described as a glimmer in his eye. It was a startlingly beautiful winter day, frigid and cobalt blue. A little part of me conceded, so I sat back to listen.

"I had four brothers and I was the youngest."

Long pause.

"Oh, the trouble we used to get into."

Pause. Chuckle.

"My mother used to bake pies for the Saturday-night potluck dinner at church. When they came out of the oven, she would put them out on the porch to cool. Each one had a little hole in the top, and my brothers and I would take turns peeing right in that little hole. You should have seen the faces of the people at those church suppers! Oh how they complimented my mother on them pies . . ."

Tears rolled down my face and I almost wet my pants from laughing. We both looked out the window for a long time, and he turned to me and said, "You know, I feel the same inside as I did back then. This body is just failing me."

Sarah Lentz

COMMUNION

This piece is another student response to Raymond Carver's "A Small, Good Thing." Here, a routine examination by an earnest medical student anxious to demonstrate her skill becomes a moment of poignant communion between doctor and patient during, of all things, a rectal examination for cancer.

SARAH LENTZ is a surgery resident at Emory University School of Medicine.

Cardiovascular Surgery Elective. Two weeks of suturing—or so I thought. Within the first two days, Mr. T—returned for rehospitalization following a bivalvular replacement procedure. His first operation had not been entirely successful for he now had regurgitation around one of his new valves. A suture had pulled through, the valve had been defective or his aged tissue could not keep the valve in place—whatever the cause, he could not live in his current state: shortness of breath, fatigue, only being able to play with his grandchildren for minimal periods of time. And so he returned to the surgeons: whatever the risks, he was willing.

I met him the night prior to his surgery. I completed the requisite history and physical. However, the attending inquired whether or not I had performed a rectal examination. "No," I replied, since I had not wanted to put the patient or myself through the embarrassment. Later, I performed the examination, but only after I was sure he and his family had finished dinner and spent some time together.

When he was alone, I timidly entered the room with latex glove and lubricative jelly in hand. He welcomed me in true northern New England style. He had been through this many times and so had no qualms. I talked, questioned, and listened to pass the time and make this easier—for both of us.

Whether or not I did, I will never know.

We chatted about his family and past operations. We got around to what was scheduled for tomorrow. Firm and assured, he told me, just like he had "the attendings," he could not live like he was now. He was ready.

And that was that.

Well, he went to surgery the next day for a double valve replacement at 82. It was not successful.

He held on for a couple of days, but inevitably, I guess, he passed on.

What was I to think?

I was perhaps best acquainted with this gentleman. For gentleman he certainly was. I can't help but think that almost the last knowledge of him was my finger over his prostate. Nevertheless, he told me—and I do firmly believe—this is what he wanted. He could not live the way he was.

Yet questions remain. And always will.

Several days after Mr. T passed on and I navigated through my days with guarded feelings, Doctor R stepped on an elevator with me. He was a cardiologist I had seen around but was not working with directly. Without pretense, he said to me, "Sorry to hear about Mr. T. I know you were working with him."

"Yeah," I said, not knowing what else to say.

But when the elevator stopped and Doctor R got off, everything felt a little more balanced.

Eric J. Cassel

THE NATURE OF SUFFERING AND THE GOALS OF MEDICINE

Eric J. Cassel's landmark essay, first published in the *New England Journal of Medicine*, explores a paradox—that suffering is often caused during treatment of the sick by those entrusted with healing. Cassel probes the delicate relationship between pain and suffering, and the role of the physician in understanding both. He makes a plea for understanding "all the known dimensions of personhood and their relations to illness and suffering."

ERIC J. CASSEL serves on the National Bioethics Advisory Commission's Subcommittee on Human Subjects. He is the author of *Changing Values in Medicine; The Nature of Suffering and the Goals of Medicine*, a book based on this essay;. *Talking with Patients; The Healer's Art*; and *Doctoring: The Nature of Primary Care Medicine.*

The obligation of physicians to relieve human suffering stretches back into antiquity. Despite this fact, little attention is explicitly given to the problem of suffering in medical education, research, or practice. I will begin by focusing on a modern paradox: Even in the best settings and with the best physicians, it is not uncommon for suffering to occur not only during the course of a disease but also as a result of its treatment. To understand this paradox and its resolution requires an understanding of what suffering is and how it relates to medical care.

Consider this case: A 35-year-old sculptor with metastatic disease of the breast was treated by competent physicians employing advanced knowledge and technology and acting out of kindness and true concern. At every stage, the treatment as well as the disease was a source of suffering to her. She was uncertain and frightened about her future, but she could get little information from her physicians, and what she was told was not always the truth. She had been unaware, for example, that the irradiated breast would be so disfigured. After an oophorectomy and a regimen of medications, she became hirsute, obese, and devoid of libido. With tumor in the supraclavicular fossa, she lost strength in the hand that she had used in sculpturing, and she became profoundly depressed. She had a pathologic fracture of the femur, and treatment was delayed while her physicians openly disagreed about pinning her hip.

Each time her disease responded to therapy and her hope was rekindled, a new manifestation would appear. Thus, when a new course of chemotherapy was started, she was torn between a desire to live and the fear that allowing hope to emerge again would merely expose her to misery if the treatment failed. The nausea and vomiting from the chemotherapy were distressing, but no more so than the anticipation of hair loss. She feared the future. Each tomorrow was seen as heralding increased sickness, pain, or disability, never as the beginning of better times. She felt isolated because she was no longer like other people and could not do what other people did. She feared that her friends would stop visiting her. She was sure that she would die.

This young woman had severe pain and other physical symptoms that caused her suffering. But she also suffered from some threats that were social and from others that were personal and private. She suffered from the effects of the disease and its treatment on her appearance and abilities. She also suffered unremittingly from her perception of the future.

What can this case tell us about the ends of medicine and the relief of suffering? Three facts stand out: The first is that this woman's suffering was not confined to her physical symptoms. The second is that she suffered not only from her disease but also from its treatment. The third is that one could not anticipate what she would describe as a source of suffering; like other patients, she had to be asked. Some features of her condition she would call painful, upsetting, uncomfortable, and distressing, but not a source of suffering. In these characteristics her case was ordinary.

In discussing the matter of suffering with lay persons, I learned that they were shocked to discover that the problem of suffering was not directly addressed in medical education. My colleagues of a contemplative nature were surprised at how little they knew of the problem and how little thought they had given it, whereas medical students tended to be unsure of the relevance of the issue to their work.

The relief of suffering, it would appear, is considered one of the primary ends of medicine by patients and lay persons, but not by the medical profession. As in the care of the dying, patients and their friends and families do not make a distinction between physical and nonphysical sources of suffering in the same way that doctors do.

A search of the medical and social-science literature did not help me in understanding what suffering is; the word "suffering" was most often coupled with the word "pain," as in "pain and suffering." (The databases used were *Psychological Abstracts*, the *Citation Index*, and the *Index Medicus*.)

This phenomenon reflects a historically constrained and currently inadequate view of the ends of medicine. Medicine's traditional concern primarily for the body and for physical disease is well known, as are the widespread effects of the mind-body dichotomy on medical theory and practice. I believe that this dichotomy itself is a source of the paradoxical situation in which doctors cause suffering in their care of the sick. Today, as ideas about the separation of mind and body are called into question, physicians are concerning themselves with new aspects of the human condition. The profession of medicine is being pushed and pulled into new areas, both by its technology and by the demands of its patients. Attempting to understand what suffering is and how physicians might truly be devoted to its relief will require that medicine and its critics overcome the dichotomy between mind and body and the associated dichotomies between subjective and objective and between person and object.

In the remainder of this paper I am going to make three points. The first is that suffering is experienced by persons. In the separation between mind and body, the concept of the person, or personhood, has been associated with that of mind, spirit, and the subjective. However, as I will show, a person is not merely mind, merely spiritual, or only subjectively knowable. Personhood has many facets, and it is ignorance of them that actively contributes to patients' suffering. The understanding of the place of the person in human illness requires a rejection of the historical dualism of mind and body.

The second point derives from my interpretation of clinical observations: Suffering occurs when an impending destruction of the person is perceived; it continues until the threat of disintegration has passed or until the integrity of the person can be restored in some other manner. It follows, then, that although suffering often occurs in the presence of acute pain, shortness of breath, or other bodily symptoms, suffering extends beyond the physical. Most generally, suffering can be defined as the state of severe distress associated with events that threaten the intactness of the person.

The third point is that suffering can occur in relation to any aspect of the person, whether it is in the realm of social roles, group identification, the relation with self, body, or family, or the relation with a transpersonal, transcendent source of meaning. Below is a simplified description or "topology" of the constituents of personhood.

"Person" Is Not "Mind"

The split between mind and body that has so deeply influenced our approach to medical care was proposed by Descartes to resolve certain philosophical issues. Moreover, Cartesian dualism made it possible for science to escape the control of the church by assigning the noncorporeal, spiritual realm to the church, leaving the physical world as the domain of science. In that religious age, "person," synonymous with "mind," was necessarily off limits to science.

Changes in the meaning of concepts like that of personhood occur with changes in society, while the word for the concept remains the same. This fact tends to obscure the depth of the transformations that have occurred between the seventeenth century and today. People simply *are* "persons" in this time, as in past times, and they have difficulty imagining that the term described something quite different in an earlier period when the concept was more constrained.

If the mind-body dichotomy results in assigning the body to medicine, and the person is not in that category, then the only remaining place for the person is in the category of mind. Where the mind is problematic (not identifiable in objective terms), its very reality diminishes for science, and so, too, does that of the person. Therefore, so long as the mind-body dichotomy is accepted, suffering is either subjective and thus not truly "real"—not within medicine's domain—or identified exclusively with bodily pain. Not only is such an identification misleading and distorting, for it depersonalizes the sick patient, but it is itself a source of suffering. It is not possible to treat sickness as something that happens solely to the body without thereby risking damage to the person. An anachronistic division of the human condition into what is medical (having to do with the body) and what is nonmedical (the remainder) has given medicine too narrow a notion of its calling. Because of this division, physicians may, in concentrating on the cure of bodily disease, do things that cause the patient as a person to suffer.

An Impending Destruction of Person

Suffering is ultimately a personal matter. Patients sometimes report suffering when one does not expect it, or do not report suffering when one does expect it. Furthermore, a person can suffer enormously at the distress of another, especially a loved one.

In some theologies, suffering has been seen as bringing one closer to God. This "function" of suffering is at once its glorification and its relief. If, through great pain or deprivation, someone is brought closer to a cherished goal, that person may have no sense of having suffered but may instead feel enormous triumph. To an observer, however, only the deprivation may be apparent. This cautionary note is important because people are often said to have suffered greatly, in a religious context, when they are known only to have been injured, tortured, or in pain, not to have suffered.

Although pain and suffering are closely identified in the medical literature, they are phenomenologically distinct. The difficulty of understanding pain and the problems of physicians in providing adequate relief of physical pain are well known.

The greater the pain, the more it is believed to cause suffering. However, some pain, like that of childbirth, can be extremely severe and yet considered rewarding. The perceived meaning of pain influences the amount of medication that will be required to control it. For example, a patient reported that when she believed the pain in her leg was sciatica, she could control it with small doses of codeine, but when she discovered that it was due to the spread of malignant disease, much greater amounts of medication were required for relief. Patients can writhe in pain from kidney stones and by their own admission not be suffering, because they "know what it is"; they may also report considerable suffering from apparently minor discomfort when they do not know its source. Suffering in close relation to the intensity of pain is reported when the pain is virtually overwhelming, such as that associated with a dissecting aortic aneurysm. Suffering is also reported when the patient does not believe that the pain can be controlled. The suffering of patients with terminal cancer can often be relieved by demonstrating that their pain truly can be controlled; they will then often tolerate the same pain without any medication, preferring the pain to the side effects of their analgesics. Another type of pain that can be a source of suffering is pain that is not overwhelming but continues for a very long time.

In summary, people in pain frequently report suffering from the pain when they feel out of control, when the pain is overwhelming, when the source of the pain is unknown, when the meaning of the pain is dire, or when the pain is chronic.

In all these situations, persons perceive pain as a threat to their continued existence—not merely to their lives, but to their integrity as persons. That this is the relation of pain to suffering is strongly suggested by the fact that suffering can be relieved, in the presence of continued pain, by making the source of the pain known, changing its meaning, and demonstrating that it can be controlled and that an end is in sight.

It follows, then, that suffering has a temporal element. In order for a situation to be a source of suffering, it must influence the person's perception of future events. ("If the pain continues like this, I *will be* overwhelmed"; "If the pain comes from cancer, I *will* die"; "If the pain cannot be controlled, I *will not* be able to take it.") At the moment when the patient is saying, "If the pain continues like this, I will be overwhelmed," he or she is not overwhelmed. Fear itself always involves the future. In the case with which I opened this paper, the patient could not give up her fears of her sense of future, despite the agony they caused her. As suffering is discussed in the other dimensions of personhood, note how it would not exist if the future were not a major concern.

Two other aspects of the relation between pain and suffering should be mentioned. Suffering can occur when physicians do not validate the patient's pain. In the absence of disease, physicians may suggest that the pain is "psychological" (in the sense of not being real) or that the patient is "faking." Similarly, patients with chronic pain may believe after a time that they can no longer talk to others about their distress. In the former case the person is caused to distrust his or her perceptions of reality, and in both instances social isolation adds to the person's suffering.

Another aspect essential to an understanding of the suffering of sick persons is the relation of meaning to the way in which illness is experienced. The word "meaning" is used here in two senses. In the first, to mean is to signify, to imply. Pain in the chest may imply heart disease. We also say that we know what something means when we know how important it is. The importance of things is always personal and individual, even though meaning in this sense may be shared by others or by society as a whole. What something signifies and how important it is relative to the whole array of a person's concerns contribute to its personal meaning. "Belief" is another word for that aspect of meaning concerned with implications, and "value" concerns the degree of importance to a particular person.

The personal meaning of things does not consist exclusively of values and beliefs that are held intellectually; it includes other dimensions. For the same word, a person may simultaneously have a cognitive meaning, an affective or emotional meaning, a bodily meaning, and a transcendent or spiritual meaning. And there may be contradictions in the different levels of meaning. The nuances of personal meaning are complex, and when I speak of personal meanings I am implying this complexity in all its depth—known and unknown. Personal meaning is a fundamental dimension of personhood, and there can be no understanding of human illness or suffering without taking it into account.

A Simplified Description of the Person

A simple topology of a person may be useful in understanding the relation between suffering and the goals of medicine. The features discussed below point the way to further study and to the possibility of specific action by individual physicians.

Persons have personality and character. Personality traits appear within the first few weeks of life and are remarkably durable over time. Some personalities handle some illnesses better than others. Individual persons vary in character as well. During the heyday of psychoanalysis in the 1950s, all behavior was attributed to unconscious determinants: No one was bad or good; they were merely sick or well. Fortunately, that simplistic view of human character is now out of favor. Some people do in fact have stronger characters and bear adversity better. Some are good and kind under the stress of terminal illness, whereas others become mean and offensive when even mildly ill.

A person has a past. The experiences gathered during one's life are a part of today as well as yesterday. Memory exists in the nostrils and the hands, not only in the mind. A fragrance drifts by, and a memory is evoked. My feet have not forgotten how to roller-skate, and my hands remember skills that I was hardly aware I had learned. When these past experiences involve sickness and medical care, they can influence present illness and medical care. They stimulate fear, confidence, physical symptoms, and anguish. It damages people to rob them of their past and deny their memories, or to mock their fears and worries. A person without a past is incomplete.

Life experiences—previous illness, experiences with doctors, hospitals, and medications, deformities and disabilities, pleasures and successes, miseries and failures—all form the nexus for illness. The personal meaning of the disease and its treatment arises from the past as well as the present. If cancer occurs in a patient with self-confidence from past achievements, it may give rise to optimism and a resurgence of strength. Even if it is fatal, the disease may not produce the destruction of the person but, rather, reaffirm his or her indomitability. The outcome would be different in a person for whom life had been a series of failures.

The intensity of ties to the family cannot be overemphasized; people frequently behave as though they were physical extensions of their parents. Events that might cause suffering in others may be borne without complaint by someone who believes that the disease is part of his or her family identity and hence inevitable. Even diseases for which no heritable basis is known may be borne easily by a person because others in the family have been similarly afflicted. Just as the person's past experiences give meaning to present events, so do the past experiences of his or her family. Those meanings are part of the person.

A person has a cultural background. Just as a person is part of a culture and a society, these elements are part of the person. Culture defines what is meant by masculinity or femininity, what attire is acceptable, attitudes toward the dying and sick, mating behavior, the height of chairs and steps, degrees of tolerance for odors and excreta, and how the aged and the disabled are treated. Cultural definitions have an enormous impact on the sick and can be a source of untold suffering. They influence the behavior of others toward the sick person and that of the sick toward themselves. Cultural norms and social rules regulate whether someone can be among others or will be isolated, whether the sick will be considered foul or acceptable, and whether they are to be pitied or censured.

Returning to the sculptor described earlier, we know why that young woman suffered. She was housebound and bedbound, her face was changed by steroids, she was masculinized by her treatment, one breast was scarred, and she had almost no hair. The degree of importance attached to these losses—that aspect of their personal meaning—is determined to a great degree by cultural priorities.

With this in mind, we can also realize how much someone devoid of physical pain, even devoid of "symptoms," may suffer. People suffer from what they have lost of themselves in relation to the world of objects, events, and relationships. We realize, too, that although medical care can reduce the impact of sickness, inattentive care can increase the disruption caused by illness.

A person has roles. I am a husband, a father, a physician, a teacher, a brother, an orphaned son, and an uncle. People are their roles, and each role has rules. Together, the rules that guide the performance of roles make up a complex set of entitlements and limitations of responsibility and privilege. By middle age, the roles may be so firmly set that disease can lead to the virtual destruction of a person by making the performance of his or her roles impossible. Whether the patient is a doctor who cannot doctor or a mother who cannot mother, he or she is diminished by the loss of function.

No person exists without others; there is no consciousness without a consciousness of others, no speaker without a hearer, and no act, object, or thought that does not somehow encompass others. All behavior is or will be involved with others, even if only in memory or reverie. Take away others, remove sight or hearing, and the person is diminished. Everyone dreads becoming blind or deaf, but these are only the most obvious injuries to human interaction. There are many ways in which human beings can be cut off from others and then suffer the loss.

It is in relationships with others that the full range of human emotions finds expression. It is this dimension of the person that may be injured when illness disrupts the ability to express emotion. Furthermore, the extent and nature of a sick person's relationships influence the degree of suffering from a disease. There is a vast difference between going home to an empty apartment and going home to a network of friends and family after hospitalization. Illness may occur in one partner of a long and strongly bound marriage or in a union that is falling apart. Suffering from the loss of sexual function associated with some diseases will depend not only on the importance of sexual performance itself but also on its importance in the sick person's relationships.

A person is a political being. A person is in this sense equal to other persons, with rights and obligations and the ability to redress injury by others and the state. Sickness can interfere, producing the feeling of political powerlessness and lack of representation. Persons who are permanently handicapped may suffer from a feeling of exclusion from participation in the political realm.

Persons do things. They act, create, make, take apart, put together, wind, unwind, cause to be, and cause to vanish. They know themselves, and are known, by these acts. When illness restricts the range of activity of persons, they are not themselves.

Persons are often unaware of much that happens within them and why. Thus, there are things in the mind that cannot be brought to awareness by ordinary reflection. The structure of the unconscious is pictured quite differently by different scholars, but most students of human behavior accept the assertion that such an interior world exists. People can behave in ways that seem inexplicable and strange even to themselves, and the sense of powerlessness that the person may feel in the presence of such behavior can be a source of great distress.

Persons have regular behaviors. In health, we take for granted the details of our day-to-day behavior. Persons know themselves to be well as much by whether they behave as usual as by any other set of facts. Patients decide that they are ill because they cannot perform as usual, and they may suffer the loss of their routine. If they cannot do the things that they identify with the fact of their being, they are not whole.

Every person has a body. The relation with one's body may vary from identification with it to admiration, loathing, or constant fear. The body may even be perceived as a representation of a parent, so that when something happens to the person's body it is as though a parent were injured. Disease can so alter the relation that the body is no longer seen as a friend but, rather, as an untrustworthy enemy. This is intensified if the illness comes on without warning, and as illness persists, the person may feel increasingly vulnerable. Just as many people have an expanded sense of self as a result of changes in their bodies from exercise, the potential exists for a contraction of this sense through injury to the body.

Everyone has a secret life. Sometimes it takes the form of fantasies and dreams of glory; sometimes it has a real existence known to only a few. Within the secret life are fears, desires, love affairs of the past and present, hopes, and fantasies. Disease may destroy not only the public or the private person but the secret person as well. A secret beloved friend may be lost to a sick person because he or she has no legitimate place by the sickbed. When that happens, the patient may have lost the part of life that made tolerable an otherwise embittered existence. Or the loss may be only of a dream, but one that might have come true. Such loss can be a source of great distress and intensely private pain.

Everyone has a perceived future. Events that one expects to come to pass vary from expectations for one's children to a belief in one's creative ability. Intense unhappiness results from a loss of the future—the future of the individual person, of children, and of other loved ones. Hope dwells in this dimension of existence, and great suffering attends the loss of hope.

Everyone has a transcendent dimension, a life of the spirit. This is most directly expressed in religion and the mystic traditions, but the frequency with which people have intense feelings of bonding with groups, ideals, or anything larger and more enduring than the person is evidence of the universality of the transcendent dimension. The quality of being greater and more lasting than an individual life gives this aspect of the person its timeless dimension. The profession of medicine appears to ignore the human spirit. When I see patients in nursing homes who have become only bodies, I wonder whether it is not their transcendent dimension that they have lost.

The Nature of Suffering

Injuries to the integrity of the person may be expressed by sadness, anger, loneliness, depression, grief, unhappiness, melancholy, rage, withdrawal, or yearning. We acknowledge the person's right to have and express such feelings.

But we often forget that the affect is merely the outward expression of the injury, not the injury itself. We know little about the nature of the injuries themselves, and what we know has been learned largely from literature, not medicine.

If the injury is sufficient, the person suffers. The only way to learn what damage is sufficient to cause suffering, or whether suffering is present, is to ask the sufferer. We all recognize certain injuries that almost invariably cause suffering: the death or distress of loved ones, powerlessness, helplessness, hopelessness, torture, the loss of a life's work, betrayal, physical agony, isolation, homelessness, memory failure, and fear. Each is both universal and individual. Each touches features common to all of us, yet each contains features that must be defined in terms of a specific person at a specific time. With the relief of suffering in mind, however, we should reflect on how remarkably little is known of these injuries.

The Amelioration of Suffering

One might inquire why everyone is not suffering all the time. In a busy life, almost no day passes in which one's intactness goes unchallenged. Obviously, not every challenge is a threat. Yet I suspect that there is more suffering than is known. Just as people with chronic pain learn to keep it to themselves because others lose interest, so may those with chronic suffering.

There is another reason why every injury may not cause suffering. Persons are able to enlarge themselves in response to damage, so that instead of being reduced, they may indeed grow. This response to suffering has encouraged the belief that suffering is good for people. To some degree, and in some persons, this may be so. If a leg is injured so that an athlete cannot run again, the athlete may compensate for the loss by learning another sport or mode of expression. So it is with the loss of relationships, loves, roles, physical strength, dreams, and power. The human body may lack the capacity to gain a new part when one is lost, but the person has it.

The ability to recover from loss without succumbing to suffering is sometimes called resilience, as though nothing but elastic rebound were involved, but it is more as though an inner force were withdrawn from one manifestation of a person and redirected to another. If a child dies and the parent makes a successful recovery, the person is said to have "rebuilt" his or her life. The term suggests that the parts of the person are structured in a new manner, allowing expression in different dimensions. If a previously active person is confined to a wheelchair, intellectual pursuits may occupy more time.

Recovery from suffering often involves help, as though people who have lost parts of themselves can be sustained by the personhood of others until their own recovers. This is one of the latent functions of physicians: to lend strength. A group, too, may lend strength: Consider the success of groups of the similarly afflicted in easing the burden of illness (e.g., women with mastectomies, people with ostomies, and even the parents or family members of the diseased).

Meaning and transcendence offer two additional ways by which the suffering associated with destruction of a part of personhood is ameliorated. Assigning a meaning to the injurious condition often reduces or even resolves the suffering associated with it. Most often, a cause for the condition is sought within past behaviors or beliefs. Thus, the pain or threat that causes suffering is seen as not destroying a part of the person, because it is part of the person by virtue of its origin within the self. In our culture, taking the blame for harm that comes to oneself because of the unconscious mind serves the same purpose as the concept of karma in Eastern theologies; suffering is reduced when it can be located within a coherent set of meanings. Physicians are familiar with the question from the sick, "Did I do something that made this happen?" It is more tolerable for a terrible thing to happen because of something that one has done than it is to be at the mercy of chance.

Transcendence is probably the most powerful way in which one is restored to wholeness after an injury to personhood. When experienced, transcendence locates the person in a far larger landscape. The sufferer is not isolated by pain but is brought closer to a transpersonal source of meaning and to the human community that shares those meanings. Such an experience need not involve religion in any formal sense; however, in its transpersonal dimension, it is deeply spiritual. For example, patriotism can be a secular expression of transcendence.

When Suffering Continues

But what happens when suffering is not relieved? If suffering occurs when there is a threat to one's integrity or a loss of a part of a person, then suffering will continue if the person cannot be made whole again. Little is known about this aspect of suffering. Is much of what we call depression merely unrelieved suffering? Considering that depression commonly follows the loss of loved ones, business reversals, prolonged illness, profound injuries to self-esteem, and other damages to personhood, the possibility is real. In many chronic or serious diseases, persons who "recover" or who seem to be successfully treated do not return to normal function. They may never again be employed, recover sexual function, pursue career goals, reestablish family relationships, or reenter the social world, despite a physical cure. Such patients may not have recovered from the nonphysical changes occurring with serious illness. Consider the dimensions of personhood described above, and note that each is threatened or damaged in profound illness. It should come as no surprise, then, that chronic suffering frequently follows in the wake of disease.

The paradox with which this paper began—that suffering is often caused by the treatment of the sick—no longer seems so puzzling. How could it be otherwise, when medicine has concerned itself so little with the nature and causes of suffering? This lack is not a failure of good intentions. None are more concerned about pain or loss of function than physicians. Instead, it is a failure of knowledge and understanding. We lack knowledge, because in working from a dichotomy contrived within a historical context far from our own, we have artificially circumscribed our task in caring for the sick.

Attempts to understand all the known dimensions of personhood and their relations to illness and suffering present problems of staggering complexity. The problems are no greater, however, than those initially posed by the question of how the body works—a question that we have managed to answer in extraordinary detail. If the ends of medicine are to be directed to the relief of human suffering, the need is clear.

I am indebted to Rabbi Jack Bemporad, Dr. Joan Cassell, Peter Dineen, Nancy McKenzie, and Robert Zaner, to Mrs. Dawn McGuire, to the members of the research group on Death, Suffering, and Well-Being of the Hastings Center for their advice and assistance, and to the Arthur Vining Davis Foundations for support of the research group.

REFERENCES

Bakan, D. *Disease, Pain and Sacrifice: Toward a Psychology of Suffering.* Chicago: Beacon Press, 1971.

Casell, E. "Being and Becoming Dead." *Physicians for Social Responsibility.* 1972; 39: 528–42.

Goodwin, J. S., Goodwin, J. M., Vogel, A. V. "Knowledge and Use of Placebos by House Officers and Nurses." *Annals of Internal Medicine.* 1979; 91: 106–10.

Kanner, R. M., Foley, K. M. "Patterns of Narcotic Use in a Cancer Pain Clinic." *Annals of the New York Academy of Science.* 1981; 362: 161–72.

Marks, R. M., Sachar, E. J. "Undertreatment of Medical Inpatients with Narcotic Analgesics." *Annals of Internal Medicine.* 1973; 78: 173–81.

Zaner, R. *The concept of Self: A Phenomenologic Inquiry Using Medicine as a Clue.* Athens, Ohio: Ohio University Press, 1981.

Matt Dugan

REPOSE

A medical student struggles to reconcile the needs of his young patient with his ability to bear the pain associated with his feelings for that patient. He has embraced the patient, learned from his family, tasted the food of the patient's homeland, and enjoyed the warmth of the patient's family; he struggles with the unfairness of the patient's condition and senses what his young friend needs. In the end, the student answers his own question about his ability to be all the things his young patient asks him to be.

MATT DUGAN is a graduate of the University of New England's College of Osteopathic Medicine and an oncology fellow at the University of Vermont.

It is 3 A.M. and it has begun to snow again. I am lying on a cot, hospital sheets softened by years of use. These winter nights are long. Daylight is at a premium, not that I've seen it in a while. This is my third call night in the past six days, and I know that sleep will once again evade me. But now as I close my eyes, memories come rushing up to greet me. I think of Sarah, long asleep now, under the layers of our down comforter, warm, dreaming, so far away. All I want is to join her, if only in simultaneous sleep, but I know that tonight I cannot.

I make the long walk from my tiny call room to the tenth floor. Immaculate tile and ethereal white walls encompass me. A hospital ward at night is like a ghost town. It echoes with memories of its patients. Whispering stories of souls come and gone. I can almost see them if I look close enough, but tonight I see no one. The nurses' station is dimly lit, like the helm of a ship running at night, I think. The captain is fast asleep.

I approach his room and gently open the door. It is humid in here, the small antechamber where all visitors must wash their hands and don the mask that prevents us from spreading potential pathogens to Faisal. I catch myself in the mirror above the sink—top half of a face. Eyes for a moment look foreign to me. It is me, but I am just older.

There, cradled in his bed, he looks so small. Suspended by the countless tubes and wires that sustain his ravished immune system, Faisal is sleeping. I am thankful for this. I can see the discoloration extending from his hands up his twig-like arms where they disappear under his white gown. His skin is dark, like wet sand. His head is crowned with a shock of black hair, wavy and wild. I joke with him sometimes that he looks like Elvis. He is my friend.

Faisal came here from India only two months ago to stay with his aunt while studying at a prestigious boarding school. He is eleven years old. It was shortly after he arrived that he noticed the bruises. Then came the nosebleeds. Then came fatigue for a long visit. By the time he was admitted, he had very few platelets and barely detectable white cells. Pancytopenia. He has been diagnosed with aplastic anemia and he is at the beginning of his disease. He still feels well on rare days. But he does understand that he is sick. He understands that his immune system cannot work without the cells it needs to perform. What he does not understand is that this illness will eventually kill him. It will snatch his life from him.

I sit down in a large red chair at the foot of the bed. I think of events that day. His family in the States come to see him in droves. The women wear traditional dress—saris of beautiful color and fabric. They welcome me with smiles and hugs and looks of adoration and trust. How can I tell them that he has only a one in five chance of survival?

I was late today to see him. Hours late. When I finally came in and sat down, Faisal just stared at me. "Where were you today?" he demanded. I had a hundred valid excuses, but I just smiled and apologized. We watched cartoons on television and laughed together. We drew caricatures of each other and laughed so hard that the nurses came in to hush us. I ate the curried lamb his grandmother left for him, since he cannot. He has only juice, Jell-O and occasional bland soup.

On some days, when the fever is high, he cries to me. He misses his mother, he misses his father. He feels his body fight, betray him and grow weaker. But still, he never complains.

This is taking too much from me. I can feel it. I cannot leave this room anymore. I am still there, even in my sleep, watching over him. Trying to make sense of things. Working the puzzle. Why has this child with so much promise, so much potential, been divined to suffer like this? I strive for understanding. Or at least acceptance.

I rise, and at once I realize that I have dozed off, but time is of no consequence to me as this night blurs along. Faisal rustles. I stand over him. He is framed like an angel in this pale pink light. I know that he will wake soon with the needle stick from the early-morning blood draw. And I know that then he will need me. A friendly face and reassurance. I want to be strong for him, but I am terrified.

I walk out of his room and back down the hall.

William Carlos Williams

THE GIRL WITH THE PIMPLY FACE

No collection of stories about health care professionals and patients would be complete without a selection by American writer William Carlos Williams. Reprinted here is his classic story—one regularly anthologized—about a chance meeting between a busy physician making house calls among the poor and a fifteen-year-old girl with acne who is "as fresh as paint and seeming about as indifferent." As much a story about Williams's keen diagnostic powers as it is a portrait of life among the working poor, "The Girl with the Pimply Face" is a timeless examination of human nature through the practice of medicine.

WILLIAM CARLOS WILLIAMS was born in 1883 in Rutherford, New Jersey, where he practiced medicine his entire professional life. While obtaining his M.D. from the University of Pennsylvania, Williams met Ezra Pound, who was an important influence on Williams's poetry. Williams's poetic works include *Kora in Hell, Spring and All,* and the five-volume epic poem *Paterson.* Robert Coles compiled Williams's short stories into a volume called *The Doctor Stories,* from which this selection is taken.

One of the local druggists sent in the call: 50 Summer St., second floor, the door to the left. It's a baby they've just brought from the hospital. Pretty bad condition I should imagine. Do you want to make it? I think they've had somebody else but don't like him, he added as an afterthought.

It was half past twelve. I was just sitting down to lunch. Can't they wait till after office hours?

Oh I guess so. But they're foreigners and you know how they are. Make it as soon as you can. I guess the baby's pretty bad.

It was two-thirty when I got to the place, over a shop in the business part of town. One of those street doors between plate-glass show windows. A narrow entry with smashed mail boxes on one side and a dark stair leading straight up. I'd been to the address a number of times during the past years to see various people who had lived there.

Going up I found no bell so I rapped vigorously on the wavy-glass door-panel to the left. I knew it to be the door to the kitchen, which occupied the rear of that apartment.

Come in, said a loud childish voice.

I opened the door and saw a lank haired girl of about fifteen standing chewing gum and eyeing me curiously from beside the kitchen table. The hair was coal black and one of her eyelids drooped a little as she spoke. Well, what do you want? she said. Boy, she was tough and no kidding but I fell for her immediately. There was that hard, straight thing about her that in itself gives an impression of excellence.

I'm the doctor, I said.

Oh, you're the doctor. The baby's inside. She looked at me. Want to see her?

Sure, that's what I came for. Where's your mother?

She's out. I don't know when she's coming back. But you can take a look at the baby if you want to.

All right. Let's see her.

She led the way into the bedroom, toward the front of the flat, one of the unlit rooms, the only windows being those in the kitchen and along the facade of the building.

There she is.

I looked on the bed and saw a small face, emaciated but quiet, unnaturally quiet, sticking out of the upper end of a tightly rolled bundle made by the rest of the baby encircled in a blue cotton blanket. The whole wasn't much larger than a good sized loaf of rye bread. Hands and everything were rolled up. Just the yellowish face showed, tightly hatted and framed around by a corner of the blanket.

What's the matter with her, I asked.

I dunno, said the girl as fresh as paint and seeming about as indifferent as though it had been no relative of hers instead of her sister. I looked at my informer very much amused and she looked back at me, chewing her gum vigorously, standing there her feet well apart. She cocked her head to one side and gave it to me straight in the eye, as much as to say, Well? I looked back at her. She had one of those small, squeezed up faces, snub nose, overhanging eyebrows, low brow and a terrible complexion, pimply and coarse.

When's your mother coming back do you *think*, I asked again.

Maybe in an hour. But maybe you'd better come some time when my father's here. He talks English. He ought to come in around five I guess.

But can't you tell me something about the baby? I hear it's been sick. Does it have a fever?

I dunno.

But has it diarrhea, are its movements green?

Sure, she said, I guess so. It's been in the hospital but it got worse so my father brought it home today.

What are they feeding it?

A bottle. You can see that yourself. There it is.

There was a cold bottle of half-finished milk lying on the coverlet the nipple end of it fallen behind the baby's head.

How old is she? It's a girl, did you say?

Yeah, it's a girl.

Your sister?

Sure. Want to examine it?

No thanks, I said. For the moment at least I had lost all interest in the baby. This young kid in charge of the house did something to me that I liked. She was just a child but nobody was putting anything over on her if she knew it, yet the real thing about her was the complete lack of the rotten smell of a liar. She wasn't in the least presumptive. Just straight.

But after all she wasn't such a child. She had breasts you knew would be like small stones to the hand, good muscular arms and fine hard legs. Her bare feet were stuck into broken down leather sandals such as you see worn by children at the beach in summer. She was heavily tanned too, wherever her skin showed. Just one of the kids you'll find loafing around the pools they have outside towns and cities everywhere these days. A tough little nut finding her own way in the world.

What's the matter with your legs? I asked. They were bare and covered with scabby sores.

Poison ivy, she answered, pulling up her skirts to show me.

Gee, but you ought to seen it two days ago. This ain't nothing. You're a doctor. What can I do for it?

Let's see, I said.

She put her leg up on a chair. It had been badly bitten by mosquitoes, as I saw the thing, but she insisted on poison ivy. She had torn at the affected places with her fingernails and that's what made it look worse.

Oh that's not so bad, I said, if you'll only leave it alone and stop scratching it.

Yeah, I know that but I can't. Scratching's the only thing makes it feel better.

What's that on your foot?

Where? looking.

That big brown spot there on the back of your foot.

Dirt I guess. Her gum chewing never stopped and her fixed defensive non-expression never changed.

Why don't you wash it?

I do. Say, what could I do for my face?

I looked at it closely. You have what they call acne, I told her. All those blackheads and pimples you see there, well, let's see, the first thing you ought to do, I suppose, is to get some good soap.

What kind of soap? Lifebuoy?

No. I'd suggest one of those cakes of Lux. Not the flakes but the cake.

Yeah, I know, she said. Three for seventeen.

Use it. Use it every morning. Bathe your face in very hot water. You know, until the skin is red from it. That's to bring the blood up to the skin. Then take a piece of ice. You have ice, haven't you?

Sure, we have ice.

Hold it in a face cloth—or whatever you have—and rub that all over your face. Do that right after you've washed it in the very hot water—before it has cooled. Rub the ice all over. And do it every day—for a month. Your skin will improve. If you like, you can take some cold cream once in a while, not much, just a little and rub that in last of all, if your face feels too dry.

Will that help me?

If you stick to it, it'll help you.

All right.

There's a lotion I could give you to use along with that. Remind me of it when I come back later. Why aren't you in school?

Agh, I'm not going any more. They can't make me. Can they?

They can try.

How can they? I know a girl thirteen that don't go and they can't make her either.

Don't you want to learn things?

I know enough already.

Going to get a job?

I got a job. Here. I been helping the Jews across the hall. They give me three fifty a week—all summer.

Good for you, I said. Think your father'll be here around five?

Guess so. He ought to be.

I'll come back then. Make it all the same call.

All right, she said, looking straight at me and chewing her gum as vigorously as ever.

Just then a little blond-haired thing of about seven came in through the kitchen and walked to me looking curiously at my satchel and then at the baby.

What are you, a doctor?

See you later, I said to the older girl and went out.

At five-thirty I once more climbed the wooden stairs after passing two women at the street entrance who looked me up and down from where they were leaning on the brick wall of the building talking.

This time a woman's voice said, Come in, when I knocked on the kitchen door.

It was the mother. She was impressive, a bulky woman, growing toward fifty, in a black dress, with lank graying hair and a long seamed face. She stood by the enameled kitchen table. A younger, plumpish woman with blond hair, well cared for and in a neat house dress—as if she had dolled herself up for the occasion—was standing beside her. The small blank child was there too and the older girl, behind the others, overshadowed by her mother, the two older women at least a head taller than she. No one spoke.

Hello, I said to the girl I had been talking to earlier. She didn't answer me.

Doctor, began the mother, save my baby. She very sick. The woman spoke with a thick, heavy voice and seemed overcome with grief and apprehension. Doctor! Doctor! she all but wept.

All right, I said to cut the woman short, let's take a look at her first.

So everybody headed toward the front of the house, the mother in the lead. As they went I lagged behind to speak to the second woman, the interpreter. What happened?

The baby was not doing so well. So they took it to the hospital to see if the doctors there could help it. But it got worse. So her husband took it out this morning. It looks bad to me.

Yes, said the mother who had overheard us. Me got seven children. One daughter married. This my baby, pointing to the child on the bed. And she wiped her face with the back of her hand. This baby no do good. Me almost crazy. Don't know who can help. What doctor, I don't know. Somebody tell me take to hospital. I think maybe do some good. Five days she there. Cost me two dollar every day. Ten dollar. I no got money. And when I see my baby, she worse. She look dead. I can't leave she there. No. No. I say to everybody, no. I take she home. Doctor, you save my baby. I pay you. I pay you everything—

Wait a minute, wait a minute, I said. Then I turned to the other woman. What happened?

The baby got like a diarrhea in the hospital. And she was all dirty when they went to see her. They got all excited—

All sore behind, broke in the mother—

The younger woman said a few words to her in some language that sounded like Russian but it didn't stop her—

No. No. I send she to hospital. And when I see my baby like that I can't leave she there. My babies no that way. Never, she emphasized. Never! I take she home.

Take your time, I said. Take off her clothes. Everything off. This is a regular party. It's warm enough in here. Does she vomit?

She no eat. How she can vomit? said the mother.

But the other woman contradicted her. Yes, she was vomiting in the hospital, the nurse said.

It happens that this September we had been having a lot of such cases in my hospital also, an infectious diarrhea which practically all the children got when they came in from any cause. I supposed that this was what happened to this child. No doubt it had been in a bad way before that, improper feeding, etc., etc. And then when they took it in there, for whatever had been the matter with it, the diarrhea had developed. These things sometimes don't turn out so well. Lucky, no doubt, that they had brought it home when they did. I told them so, explaining at the same time: One nurse for ten or twenty babies, they do all they can but you can't run and change the whole ward every five minutes. But the infant looked too lifeless for that only to be the matter with it.

You want all clothes off, asked the mother again, hesitating and trying to keep the baby covered with the cotton blanket while undressing it.

Everything off, I said.

There it lay, just skin and bones with a round fleshless head at the top and the usual pot belly you find in such cases.

Look, said the mother, tilting the infant over on its right side with her big hands so that I might see the reddened buttocks. What kind of nurse that. My babies never that way.

Take your time, take your time, I told her. That's not bad. And it wasn't either. Any child with loose movements might have had the same half an hour after being cared for. Come on. Move away, I said and give me a chance. She kept hovering over the baby as if afraid I might expose it.

It had no temperature. There was no rash. The mouth was in reasonably good shape. Eyes, ears negative. The moment I put my stethoscope to the little boney chest, however, the whole thing became clear. The infant had a severe congenital heart defect, a roar when you listened over the heart that meant, to put it crudely, that she was no good, never would be.

The mother was watching me. I straightened up and looking at her told her plainly: She's got a bad heart.

That was the sign for tears. The big woman cried while she spoke. Doctor, she pleaded in blubbering anguish, save my baby.

I'll help her, I said, but she's got a bad heart. That will never be any better.

But I knew perfectly well she wouldn't pay the least attention to what I was saying.

I give you anything, she went on. I pay you. I pay you twenty dollar. Doctor, you fix my baby. You good doctor. You fix.

All right, all right, I said. What are you feeding it?

They told me and it was a ridiculous formula, unboiled besides. I regulated it properly for them and told them how to proceed to make it up. Have you got enough bottles, I asked the young girl.

Sure, we got bottles, she told me.

O.K., then go ahead.

You think you cure she? The mother with her long, tearful face was at me again, so different from her tough female fifteen-year-old.

You do what I tell you for three days, I said, and I'll come back and see how you're getting on.

Tank you, doctor, so much. I pay you. I got today no money. I pay ten dollar to hospital. They cheat me. I got no more money. I pay you Friday when my husband get pay. You save my baby.

Boy! what a woman. I couldn't get away.

She my baby, doctor. I no want to lose. Me got seven children—

Yes, you told me.

But this my baby. You understand. She very sick. You good doctor—

Oh my God! To get away from her I turned again to the kid. You better get going after more bottles before the stores close. I'll come back Friday morning.

How about that stuff for my face you were gonna give me.

That's right. Wait a minute. And I sat down on the edge of the bed to write out a prescription for some lotio alba comp. such as we use in acne. The two older women looked at me in astonishment—wondering, I suppose, how I knew the girl. I finished writing the thing and handed it to her. Sop it on your face at bedtime, I said, and let it dry on. Don't get it into your eyes.

No, I won't.

I'll see you in a couple of days, I said to them all.

Doctor! the old woman was still after me. You come back. I pay you. But all a time short. Always tomorrow come milk man. Must pay rent, must pay coal. And no got money. Too much work. Too much wash. Too much cook.

Nobody help. I don't know what's a matter. This door, doctor, this door. This house make sick. Make sick.

Do the best I can, I said as I was leaving.

The girl followed on the stairs. How much is this going to cost, she asked shrewdly holding the prescription.

Not much, I said, and then started to think. Tell them you only got half a dollar. Tell them I said that's all it's worth.

Is that right, she said.

Absolutely. Don't pay a cent more for it.

Say, you're all right, she looked at me appreciatively.

Have you got half a dollar?

Sure. Why not.

What's it all about, my wife asked me in the evening. She had heard about the case. Gee! I sure met a wonderful girl, I told her.

What! another?

Some tough baby. I'm crazy about her. Talk about straight stuff . . . And I recounted to her the sort of case it was and what I had done. The mother's an odd one too. I don't quite make her out.

Did they pay you?

No. I don't suppose they have any cash.

Going back?

Sure. Have to.

Well, I don't see why you have to do all this charity work. Now that's a case you should report to the Emergency Relief. You'll get at least two dollars a call from them.

But the father has a job, I understand. That counts me out.

What sort of a job?

I dunno. Forgot to ask.

What's the baby's name so I can put it in the book?

Damn it. I never thought to ask them that either. I think they must have told me but I can't remember it. Some kind of a Russian name—

You're the limit. Dumbbell, she laughed. Honestly—Who are they anyhow?

You know, I think it must be that family Kate was telling us about. Don't you remember. The time the little kid was playing there one afternoon after school, fell down the front steps and knocked herself senseless.

I don't recall.

Sure you do. That's the family. I get it now. Kate took the brat down there in a taxi and went up with her to see that everything was all right. Yop, that's it. The old woman took the older kid by the hair, because she hadn't watched her sister. And what a beating she gave her. Don't you remember Kate telling us afterward. She thought the old woman was going to murder the child she screamed and threw her around so. Some old gal. You can see they're all afraid of her. What a world. I suppose the damned brat drives her cuckoo. But boy, how she clings to that baby.

The last hope, I suppose, said my wife.

Yeah, and the worst bet in the lot. There's a break for you.

She'll love it just the same.

More, usually.

Three days later I called at the flat again. Come in. This time a resonant male voice. I entered, keenly interested.

By the same kitchen table stood a short, thickset man in baggy working pants and a heavy cotton undershirt. He seemed to have the stability of a cube placed on one of its facets, a smooth, highly colored Slavic face, long black moustaches and widely separated, perfectly candid blue eyes. His black hair, glossy and profuse, stood out carelessly all over his large round head. By his look he reminded me at once of his blond-haired daughter, absolutely unruffled. The shoulders of an ox. You the doctor, he said. Come in.

The girl and the small child were beside him, the mother was in the bedroom.

The baby no better. Won't eat, said the man in answer to my first question.

How are its bowels?

Not so bad.

Does it vomit?

No.

Then it is better, I objected. But by this time the mother had heard us talking and came in. She seemed worse than the last time. Absolutely inconsolable. Doctor! Doctor! She came up to me.

Somewhat irritated I put her aside and went in to the baby. Of course it was better, much better. So I told them. But the heart, naturally, was the same.

How she heart? the mother pressed me eagerly. Today little better?

I started to explain things to the man who was standing back giving his wife precedence but as soon as she got the drift of what I was saying she was all over me again and the tears began to pour. There was no use my talking. Doctor, you good doctor. You do something fix my baby. And before I could move she took my left hand in both hers and kissed it through her tears. As she did so I realized finally that she had been drinking.

I turned toward the man, looking a good bit like the sun at noonday and as indifferent, then back to the woman and I felt deeply sorry for her.

Then, not knowing why I said it nor of whom, precisely, I was speaking, I felt myself choking inwardly with the words: Hell! God damn it. The sons of bitches. Why do these things have to be?

The next morning as I came into the coat room at the hospital there were several of the visiting staff standing there with their cigarettes, talking. It was about a hunting dog belonging to one of the doctors. It had come down with distemper and seemed likely to die.

I called up half a dozen vets around here, one of them was saying. I even called up the one in your town, he added turning to me as I came in. And do you know how much they wanted to charge me for giving the serum to that animal?

Nobody answered.

They had the nerve to want to charge me five dollars a shot for it. Can you beat that? Five dollars a shot.

Did you give them the job, someone spoke up facetiously.

Did I? I should say I did not, the first answered. But can you beat that. Why we're nothing but a lot of slop-heels compared to those guys. We deserve to starve.

Get it out of them, someone rasped, kidding. That's the stuff.

Then the original speaker went on, buttonholing me as some of the others faded from the room. Did you ever see practice so rotten. By the way, I was called over to your town about a week ago to see a kid I delivered up here during the summer. Do you know anything about the case?

I probably got them on my list, I said. Russians?

Yeah, I thought as much. Has a job as a road worker or something. Said they couldn't pay me. Well, I took the trouble of going up to your court house and finding out what he was getting. Eighteen dollars a week. Just the type. And they had the nerve to tell me they couldn't pay me.

She told me ten.

She's a liar.

Natural maternal instinct, I guess.

Whisky appetite, if you should ask me.

Same thing.

O.K., buddy. Only I'm telling you. And did I tell *them*. They'll never call me down there again, believe me. I had that much satisfaction out of them anyway. You make 'em pay you. Don't you do anything for them unless they do. He's paid by the county. I tell you if I had taxes to pay down there I'd go and take it out of his salary.

You and how many others?

Say, they're bad actors, that crew. Do you know what they really do with their money? Whisky. Now I'm telling you. That old woman is the slickest customer you ever saw. She's drunk all the time. Didn't you notice it?

Not while I was there.

Don't you let them put any of that sympathy game over on you. Why they tell me she leaves that baby lying on the bed all day long screaming its lungs out until the neighbors complain to the police about it. I'm not lying to you.

Yeah, the old skate's got nerves, you can see that. I can imagine she's a bugger when she gets going.

But what about the young girl, I asked weakly. She seems like a pretty straight kid.

My confrere let out a wild howl. That thing! You mean that pimply-faced little bitch. Say, if I had my way I'd run her out of the town tomorrow. There's about a dozen wise guys on her trail every night in the week. Ask the cops. Just ask them. They know. Only nobody wants to bring in a complaint. They say you'll stumble over her on the roof, behind the stairs, anytime at all. Boy, they sure took you in.

Yes, I suppose they did, I said.

But the old woman's the ringleader. She's got the brains. Take my advice and make them pay.

The last time I went I heard the Come in! from the front of the house. The fifteen-year-old was in there at the window in a rocking chair with the tightly wrapped baby in her arms. She got up. Her legs were bare to the hips. A powerful little animal.

What are you doing? Going swimming? I asked.

Naw, that's my gym suit. What the kids wear for Physical Training in school.

How's the baby?

She's all right.

Do you mean it?

Sure, she eats fine now.

Tell your mother to bring it to the office some day so I can weigh it. The food'll need increasing in another week or two anyway.

I'll tell her.

How's your face?

Gettin' better.

My God, it *is*, I said. And it was much better. Going back to school now?

Yeah, I had tuh.

Michael Weingarten

HEALERS: THE PHYSICIAN AND THE MORI

Just when a doctor or nurse thinks he or she might have the answer to a patient's medical problem, the patient blows a hole in the solution, taking the caregiver's ego right along with it. Michael Weingarten understands the cultural context of the patient's life, respecting and honoring the processes of diagnoses and treatment and their place in the patient's life and treatment.

But the issue is more complex and goes beyond mere acknowledgment. It requires that we also consider what happens to the patient's culture when it is relocated to another world. For both patients and practitioners, understanding these issues for the vast foreign-born populations of this country is highlighted by this simple story.

MICHAEL WEINGARTEN is the director of the Department of Family Medicine at the Rabin Medical Center near Tel Aviv and editor of the *Israel Journal of Family Practice*.

I was thirty-three; she was sixty-six. I had been in my new practice for six months and Naomi had been to see me at least a dozen times already. Hers was one of the few faces I could put a name to. She had come to Israel from

Yemen in 1950, flying through the darkness of a clandestine airlift. Overnight she crossed the centuries between the medieval culture of her childhood and the modernity of her new and progressive young state.

Her file was fat with tests which failed to solve the enigma of her recurrent abdominal cramps. I told her I thought it pointless to order any more. She was silent but looked relieved. "What now?" I ventured. "I don't know," she replied. I asked if she had been to the mori (a traditional Yemenite Jewish rabbi-healer). She had, of course, but had been shy to talk to me about it. Actually, she said, the mori wanted me, the doctor, to write him a note to say that he could go ahead with his treatment. He wanted to give her makweh over all the upper part of her body. I knew all about makweh by now; 70 percent of my Yemenite patients had scars from this healing method—branding by red-hot iron nails. They had it for sciatica—on the side of the ankle; for renal colic—in the loin; for impotence—on the forehead. I thought it was an admirable caution of the mori to check with me first, so I wrote the note for Naomi, who was looking quite apprehensive. "Do you think it'll help?" I asked.

"I don't really know, Doctor," she answered. "In Yemen it certainly would have worked, but here, in Israel, God has taken the right to heal away from the mori, and He has given it to you, the doctors. But you're not so good at it."

PART FOUR

Physicians Must Be Dutiful

PHYSICIANS must feel obliged to collaborate with other health professionals and to use systematic approaches for promoting, maintaining, and improving the health of individuals and populations. They must be knowledgeable about the risk factors for disease and injury; must understand how to utilize disease- and injury-prevention practices in the care of individual patients and their families, and in public education and action; must actively support traditional public health practices in their communities; and must be advocates for improving access to care for everyone, especially those who are members of traditionally underserved populations. They must understand the economic, psychological, occupational, social, and cultural factors that contribute to the development and/or perpetration of conditions that impair health. In caring for individual patients, they must apply the principles of evidence-based medicine and cost-effectiveness in making decisions about the utilization of limited resources. They must be committed to working collaboratively with other physicians, other health care professionals (including administrators of hospitals, health care organizations, and systems of care), and individuals representing a wide variety of community agencies. As members of a team addressing individual or population-based health care issues, they must be willing both to provide leadership when appropriate and to defer to the leadership of others when indicated. They must acknowledge and respect the roles of other health professions in providing needed services to individual patients, populations, or communities.

David Hilfiker

from NOT ALL OF US ARE SAINTS

Is a physician dedicated to working on behalf of the poor wasting his professional education? "Why," the author of this piece is asked by a distinguished professor of pediatric surgery, "should a person go through four years of medical school and at least three years of postgraduate hospital training to take care of problems that are so obviously social and societal in nature?"

Writing about serving the medical needs of the poor in Washington, D.C., physician David Hilfiker observes that "one of the first things a doctor of poverty medicine gives up is the power the physician wields within the American medical system." Hilfiker's ruminations and stories demonstrate powerful advocacy "for improving access to care for everyone, especially those who are members of traditionally underserved communities."

DAVID HILFIKER wrote *Healing Wounds* about his practice in rural Minnesota. In *Not All of Us Are Saints*, Hilfiker describes his practice among the poor in Washington, D.C., where he moved in 1983.

The absence of clear guidelines is virtually the hallmark of medical practice among the poor. "Poverty medicine" sometimes seems related to the rest of American medicine but more often it plunges me headlong into a world for which my medical school training never prepared me. There are, of course, varieties of poverty medicine: Doctoring in Appalachia will look different from doctoring in Washington, will require one set of skills in a Harlem walk-in clinic and another in a Florida migrant worker camp; nevertheless, these varieties have more in common with each other than any of them do with mainstream American medicine.

It is not the diseases that are different. Though heart disease and cancer kill a disproportionate number of poor people, the illnesses are the same in the suburbs as in the inner city. Because they frequently lie concealed behind well-constructed façades, addictions to cocaine or alcohol are less noticeable in upper- and middle-class neighborhoods, but substance abuse with all its consequences is a part of any physician's practice. Though the stresses of suburban and inner-city life may be very different, the stress-related illnesses—headaches, stomachaches, back pain—are the same on Belmont Street and in rural Minnesota. The strictly medical, scientific training a doctor needs to practice among the very poor is essentially the same as preparation for any other primary-care practice.

It's not the science that is different.

Kathy Bartlow is a severely alcoholic, forty-year-old white woman in our neighborhood. Sober, she is one of my favorite patients, actively attending AA, trying to help her neighbors, earnestly working toward her own recovery. Drunk—as she is this particular afternoon—she is a nightmare.

Kathy has a seizure disorder, but I have never been able to determine whether all of her "spells" are genuine seizures. The regularity with which she starts twitching and shaking whenever I begin to refuse some drunken demand of hers seems more than coincidental. Today she wants to go to Sibley Hospital to "dry out." A year ago, when she came to the clinic with pancreatitis and impending delirium tremens, we finagled her admission into Sibley, a wealthy, private hospital in far-northwest Washington that had recently agreed to accept a small number of nonpaying patients from our clinic. Kathy loved it. Now, a year later, she has decided for the umpteenth time to quit drinking and—although she has no acute physical illness at this point—wants to be readmitted to Sibley for detoxification. Since Sibley is not a detox center but a hospital that, as an act of charity, allows me to admit the occasional indigent patient, I feel I can't risk alienating the hospital staff by admitting Kathy (who is loud and demanding when drunk) just for detox.

"I don't think that'll work out, Kathy. The hospital is just for when people are sick. What you need right now is detox. Let me call down to detox and see if they have a bed. Maybe Lois could take you down there."

She sits disheveled in the corner, her short, tight skirt muddy and pushed up high on her thighs. Spittle hangs from the corner of her mouth. She straightens up and teeters on the edge of her chair, trying to look me in the eye but seeming to lose focus. "I ain't going to that hole. I wanna go o'er ta Shibley!" She slurs her words in what seems like a parody of drunkenness.

I notice that the side of her face is beginning to twist and distort. "Well, I don't think that'll be possible, Kathy. But we have to get you help somewhere."

She suddenly screams, "You gotta help me, David!" Still sitting in the chair, she lunges forward, grabs my hand, and hangs on hard. "You gotta help me." She stares into my eyes and then loses focus. Suddenly she lets out a grunt, halfway between a moan and a curse. Her face stiffens in a hideous grimace. She flops back in her chair and begins sliding down to the floor. (Is it only my cynical imagination, or she is gently lowering herself with her arms?) Reaching the floor, she seems to position herself carefully with her head between the chair and the wall and then begins shaking irregularly, spit frothing on her lips in what is either a seizure or a remarkable imitation of one.

I've been through this before.

I call Lois to stand guard while Angie phones for an ambulance. Fifteen minutes later the rescue squad appears. By this time Kathy is up once again and hanging on to Lois. As I come into the room, she lurches toward me, clumsily hooking an arm around my neck. "You gotta send me to Sibley, David. I can't go on like this." On seeing the rescue squad, she squeezes my neck in a violent bear hug. "I love you, David. I love you. Don't let them take me. Don't let them take me." Suddenly she flops back in the chair, and her seizure, or whatever it is, begins again.

Members of the rescue squad, dressed in the rubber suits of the fire department (in Washington, firefighters are the first to answer *all* emergency calls), have been watching through the door. "She did that last time," says a tall white man with a mustache. "She can really put on a good one. She started scratchin' my eyes out when she got to the ambulance. You call the police. I'm calling the ambulance off. We ain't takin' her again."

Kathy is still shaking on the floor. "She needs to go to detox," I say.

"Well, then, you call the police. That's their department."

Within a minute they're gone, and I ask Angie to call the police.

Angie buzzes me right back. "They said if she's having a seizure call the ambulance. They won't take her if she's having a seizure."

Kathy soon passes out in the exam room, while I do my best to see other patients. Harlaney Pearson, the medical assistant working with me this afternoon, watches over Kathy. Fifteen minutes later Kathy decides she'll come back "a little later" and stumbles out of the office.

One of the first things a doctor of poverty medicine gives up is the power the physician wields within the American medical system. Kathy Bartlow, my patient, has come into the office asking—at some level—for healing. But I have the power to accomplish next to nothing. I can spend hours with Kathy and yet be unable to provide what I would have considered in Minnesota the most basic medical care. The way the police and ambulance systems work in the inner city is not responsive to the needs of the poor—or their doctors—so I sometimes don't even have the power to get my patient transported to the hospital. In Kathy's particular case, I *do* have the authority to admit her to Sibley, but must use that authority sparingly for fear of alienating the institution or even having that privilege taken away. What can I offer Kathy Bartlow?

What *did* I offer Kathy Bartlow? What did she receive in this encounter that accomplished nothing? My undivided attention. My respect for her and for her heartrending struggle. My willingness to be there, to listen, and to offer what little I had: to call the ambulance, to protect her from immediate harm (at least for the few minutes she was with us), to care whether or not she got better. I find frequently that those are about the only things I can give my patients.

I spend an hour with Maggie Walker, a thirty-three-year-old heroin addict who desperately wants out. Her family has fallen apart, she is facing jail, and she is being threatened with having her children taken away from her. She is willing to "do anything to get clean," but there is no inpatient drug treatment available in Washington for addicts who have no insurance or other means of payment. All that's available is a public methadone clinic where Maggie would be seen for a few minutes daily as an outpatient to receive a narcotic substitute for the heroin she is already taking. As far as the rest of her life is concerned, she will remain in her drug-infested neighborhood; she will receive only minimal psychological help or group support to help her break her habit; she will get no practical assistance with the insurmountable problems that confront all poor people—lack of housing, security, work, cash. Even the methadone clinic, the sole program accessible to her, has a waiting list five weeks long. Although I'm her doctor, I can't open the door she so desperately wants to walk through. She and I know full well—though neither of us articulates it—that in five weeks, when her appointment at the methadone clinic comes up, the moment will have passed, and she will be in no shape to take advantage of it. The time is now; but there is nothing I can do. I can only maintain hope (against our shared hopelessness), offer my presence, and try to introduce some modicum of concern into an environment in which it's so often absent.

For all my supposed authority as a physician, I have only a little more power than my patients to improve the conditions under which they live. I may be able to diagnose Vaneida Thomas's hypertension, but I can't offer her an apartment, get her kids out of trouble with the police, get her a job, protect her from an enraged boyfriend, or provide her the tools for fashioning a new and healthier life. I can tell Donald Marshall why and how he should change his diet and take his insulin, but I can do nothing about the inadequate education that prevents him from understanding the diet, or about the economic obstacles that, in any case, make it impossible for him to buy the appropriate foods. I am powerless to affect his despair, his certainty that nothing a doctor could suggest would fundamentally alter his life or his options.

Lois and Teresa and I work for months with the Roberts family as they search for housing with the "assistance" of the city's various programs for the homeless. Mr. Roberts is severely, often psychotically, depressed, in real need of hospitalization; Mrs. Roberts has a borderline-low IQ and life-threatening diabetes that—though she is only in her thirties—has wreaked havoc throughout her body. The family, homeless for months, has passed through the shelter system several times. Medical care has been virtually impossible. They come to the clinic infrequently, take their medicine sporadically, under stresses that make control of diabetes, to say nothing of depression, a fantasy.

Mr. Roberts finally finds housing for the family, but six weeks later he reports that the landlord refuses to fix a multitude of defeats that render the apartment almost uninhabitable. It is winter; windows are out, the plumbing doesn't work, and the back door can't be locked. The apartment has been broken into once already in their brief tenancy. When the Roberts family was at the city shelter, their fifteen-year-old daughter was sexually assaulted, so now Mr. Roberts stays awake all night to guard the unlockable back door. Mr. Roberts tells us that the landlord wants the family out, and it seems likely he is (illegally) refusing to maintain the apartment as a means of pressuring them to leave. No one within the city system responds to Mr. Roberts's complaints or pleas for help, and within two months the family finds itself in the shelter system again, having "voluntarily" (according to the social worker's report) left their apartment. During this time Mr. Roberts has given his wife insulin only from time to time, if at all, and she has been hospitalized at least three times for dangerously high blood sugar. I am as helpless as they are to find them housing or redress even a few of the injustices and humiliations they suffer.

On Belmont Street, health is not so much a question of disease. The strictly medical factors are rarely the most crucial to healing. While a patient's lifestyle and environment are important elements to be considered in *any* medical evaluation, traditional medicine nevertheless finds its power by breaking problems down into their constituent parts, isolating individual issues and dealing with them as discrete clinical entities. But the complex, interrelated web of troubles that confront the poor make it impossible for me to treat the medical portion of their lives in isolation. I cannot address James Martin's hypertension without worrying about his economic status (how is he going to fill his prescription?), his educational level (does he understand the need to take medicines—especially given their side effects—that will not, in the short run, seem to do anything for him?), or his family situation (how does the incarceration of his oldest son or the pregnancy of his daughter affect the hypertension?).

Within traditional medicine, the physician is the central player because he holds the keys to wellness. The doctor who chooses poverty medicine, however, not only finds his own power circumscribed by the same forces that dominate the lives of his patients but also quickly discovers that he is not the most important player on the team. At any given time, it may be the nurse, the social worker, the nurses' aide, the counselor, or the receptionist who offers what is most needed.

Defined by usual medical expectations, the "success rate" in our practice is abysmal, and inevitably so. As a physician, I know how to treat high blood pressure. It's not difficult, but it requires regular office visits, a certain familiarity with basic medical language, patients' compliance with treatment recommendations, money for medication, and the ability of patient and physician to work problems out collegially. When patient after patient returns to the clinic with blood pressure wildly out of control, it's sometimes hard to remember that my patients' medical failures are not always and necessarily my own professional failures.

I am speaking to a group of university medical students and faculty about the living and health conditions of my patients. I can sense that the stories are touching the hearts of many of the students and young doctors. During the question-and-answer period at the end of the session, a distinguished professor of pediatric surgery, garbed in a long white coat, rises and says earnestly, "I can only applaud your commitment to the poor, Dr. Hilfiker, but don't you think it's a waste of your professional education? Why should a person go through four years of medical school and at least three years of postgraduate hospital training to take care of problems that are so obviously social and societal in nature? It seems to me that your job might better be done by a social worker or nurse practitioner, while you used your talents more effectively elsewhere."

The surgeon, I suspect, is trying to persuade his students and residents not to "waste" their own educations by choosing work as "useless" as what I do, but he articulates the doubts any doctor whose patients are poor people will experience: Am I throwing away my education and training, possibly letting my competence erode? What if—after years of this kind of practice—I get to the point where I am unqualified to be a "real doctor"?

In clearer moments we who practice poverty medicine are aware that the surgeon's questions and our self-doubts are only part of the story. It takes all the medical judgment we possess to discern when to let go and when to press a homeless patient. It takes every bit of our medical authority to get such patients into the health care system. It takes as much medical knowledge as we can muster to diagnose across cultural barriers. But—since our work is so different from a doctor's standard routine—it is easy, from the medical point of view, to mistake it for no work at all.

At a practical level, the usual professional support systems—continuing education, journals, conferences, societies, and academies—have not yet been developed to meet the needs of a physician who has decided to work with the poor. There are professional associations for gastroendoscopists and medical journals for ophthalmologists specializing solely in diseases of the retina, but there is no Academy of Poverty Doctors, no *Journal of Poverty Medicine.* There is no curriculum for poverty medicine: no one teaches "The Art of Medical Decision Making with Limited Funds" or "Medical Compromise within Cultural Strictures." Medical practice in a community of poor people often seems a solitary specialty without research, common cause, or shared experience. I and my few partners are isolated professionally, with no way even to assess our own record.

In a culture that measures success and competence in dollars, it's easy—when the stresses of practice become overwhelming—to feel that a relatively low salary is further proof of professional lack of worth. The same goes for prestige: As a physician for the poor, I know there will be no "professional advancement." The bottom rung of the ladder is the same as the top rung: working as a clinic doctor, seeing patients day-to-day.

Looked at from one angle, the limitations this environment imposes require an almost indecent compromise of professional standards. From another perspective, however, we who practice in poor communities are in the process of creating new "medical" approaches to dilemmas the profession has too long ignored or mishandled. Most of my patients have already, after all, fared badly in the traditional medical system and are often disinclined to submit to standard procedures like interviews and examinations, not to speak of expensive tests for vague or minor complaints . . . or even for serious ones. A new art of caring is needed for the poor.

Mr. Tanner, an elderly gentleman with anemia and intermittent traces of blood in his stool over the past six months, arrives at the clinic today for a visit . . . but only because Teresa called him and insisted that he come in for follow-up. "No," he says of the colonoscopy I've been recommending every visit for the last six months. "I think I'll wait a little on that bowel test." I explain for at least the third time the danger of bowel cancer, doing whatever I know how to impress on him that blood in the stool is a dangerous sign and that such a cancer would threaten his life. But he looks down at the floor, hems and haws, mumbles something under his breath. If he would even let me off the hook by refusing my request outright, it might be professionally easier; that is, he could help me create a more recognizably middle-class medical exchange, in which individual decision and individual responsibility—his and mine—are clearly delineated.

"I'll need to think about it," he says and smiles, almost mischievously. "Maybe I could check the tests again in a month or two. Maybe it'll be gone."

"Even if the stool samples are okay the next time," I argue, "it's important to have the colonoscopy because just a single stool sample with blood in it can be a sign of danger."

He looks up triumphantly, "Well, I sure don't want to get that bowel test if we don't find no blood there. I'll let you know."

Six months from now we will have the same conversation. . . .

The practice of poverty medicine often takes place in the absence of shared assumptions, which only increases the disorder and uncertainty. To my patients my questions must often seem unrelated to their primary concerns, while the history of their symptoms—easily the most important part of any evaluation—remains a mystery to me. When I am trying, for instance, to determine the likelihood of pregnancy or the significance of vaginal bleeding, I frequently ask a woman the date of her last menstrual period. The invariable answer is either "This month" or "Last month." When I ask her to be more precise, she often seems confused by my question. It's not really a matter of memory; my inquiry seems senseless to her. For many of the women in my practice, menstrual cycles are bound to the calendar months rather than to a cycle of so many weeks and days. A woman will sometimes come to the office worried because "my period came twice this month," by which she means that the first menstrual period began on January 2 and the next on January 30. She will then be concerned because she "misses a period" during February. This simple difference in the way we understand things can usually be compensated for, but there are other, more complex gaps in communication that leave my patients feeling ignored or misunderstood.

Trust—that crucial ingredient between physician and patient—is often lacking in the sort of medicine I now practice. I want to make sure, for instance, that Tajuana Billins, a fifteen-year-old girl with symptoms of a serious pelvic infection, does not have a pregnancy in her fallopian tubes (a so-called ectopic pregnancy, which doctors sometimes mistake for a pelvic infection). I explain that we must determine whether she is pregnant and I ask her about her last menstrual period and her most recent episode of sexual intercourse. She tells me that her period came "last month," but assures me that she has not had sex in over two months. Several minutes later, examining a specimen of her vaginal fluid under the microscope to check for venereal disease, I see sperm vigorously moving about. I return to ask again about her history of intercourse, and she resolutely asserts that she has not had intercourse in over two months, a story she sticks to even after I reemphasize the importance of the question.

Why is she lying to me? Perhaps, for reasons that I don't begun to understand, her story isn't a lie to her. Perhaps talking about sex to a male, especially a white male, is worse than lying. Perhaps in her mind the consequences of opening the door to her personal life, even a crack, are too dire. Perhaps an overly strict or abusive home environment has made hiding her personal life a necessity. Perhaps it is just adolescence. A lot of possible explanations flood my mind, but are any of them correct? In the end, I go with my gut instinct (not always right, either): I decide against confronting her with what is so obviously untrue. I do not blame Tajuana; but our inability to communicate effectively, whatever the cause, leaves me with little reliable information on which to base either a diagnosis or a relationship.

In my Minnesota practice as well, of course, I was sometimes told incomplete or false stories. But my patient and I generally shared a common language, so that someone who did not want to reveal everything to me could nonetheless communicate her reluctance, and I could at least recognize the gaps in my own understanding. Or—when caught in an outright lie—a patient could find a way to backtrack, to give me enough of the truth to get me off her case.

Tajuana and I, however, speak such different languages that I'm far from certain about the real nature of her disease. I know there is something else wrong, something going on behind the present complaint, but here—unlike in my middle-class clinic—my intuition is of minimal value. Because my patients and I face each other across barriers of culture and language, I usually cannot "get inside" their heads to find out what is wrong.

It is not possible to discuss poverty medicine without talking about yet another formidable barrier—that of racial difference. While in absolute numbers most poor people in our country are white, African Americans and Hispanics are three times more likely than whites to be poor, and the inner-city patient is likely to be a person of color. Yet poverty medicine—at least in urban areas—is largely practiced by white professionals. In medicine, as in so many other areas of American life, the person with power is still white; the person needing help, black or Hispanic.

In the 1960s, in the days of Black Power, a white physician practicing in a black neighborhood might have been asked by black people what he was doing there, why he wasn't fighting racism in his own environment. But thirty years later certain dreams have died. No black person has ever said to me directly or, as far as I can remember, even implied that I don't belong on Belmont Street. The reason, I think, is obvious, the reality as clear as it is lamentable: If the white doctors and nurses and lawyers leave Belmont Street, no one will replace us. White theorists and organizers will, from time to time, accuse us of disempowering the people with whom we work, but until those critics show me how I can practice without disempowering my patients or where my patients will receive good medical care when I leave, I find it hard to justify departure.

But despite my pragmatic response to these issues, a problem persists. American history is often read as a long legacy of white people telling black people what to do; and the work of the inner-city doctor can seem like just another instance of this unequal dynamic. White people have historically exploited black communities—have come in, taken the money, and left. The poor inner-city black person has reason to see the white inner-city doctor as someone who comes into the community and earns handsome fees (even my "austerity salary" at Community of Hope is three times what many of my patients earn working full time), while his patients haven't enough to pay the rent. I live at Christ House, but "upstairs," where the patients never go; I live "in" the community, but not directly on Belmont Street. The history of American social reform is filled with white people "helping" black people by "doing for" them. The medical model itself, in which the doctor does *for* and does *to* the patient, is an inherently disempowering one.

So the white doctor of poverty medicine practices within a deeply troubled historical context. How do I deal with the sneaking suspicions (which I, on bad days, share) that I am—despite my best intentions—exploiting my patients? Racial prejudice is so thoroughly ingrained that no one of us—black or white—can be free of the charge of "racism." The best we can do is acknowledge racism, try to understand it, and move on.

These reflections inevitably return me to the same questions: What am I doing here? What can I offer my patients? If I do so little good by traditional medical standards, if my very presence may be disempowering, what *can* I do? Ultimately, the answer is the same one every good doctor anywhere must come to: I can offer myself and my presence as a healer. The recent tide of technological medicine has tended to erode our understanding of the fundamental imperative for any physician—to be a healing presence. Because our antibiotics and our CAT scans and our heart transplants promise such power, we risk confusing the use of those tools with the most basic task of doctoring: to understand, to comfort, to encourage, to *be with* the patient in his or her distress. With its potentially distracting techniques and technology, traditional medicine may *need* poverty medicine as a reminder that the primary role of the good physician is to offer unconditional acceptance of the patient's being; to clarify (without judging) the cause of the illness; to honor the pain, to recognize the fear, and to hold on to hope.

James Wright
IN TERROR OF HOSPITAL BILLS

James Wright's poem describes life on the street for a Native American man. What is striking in this poem is the declaration by the homeless man that life is worth living and was never as precious to him as now. Understanding this has broad implications for practitioners who encounter the poor. The word "terror" in the title is particularly interesting, given that there is no mention of illness or hospitals in the poem.

JAMES WRIGHT (1927–1980) was a postwar poet and prose writer. This poem is taken from his collection titled *Shall We Gather at the River?*

I still have some money
To eat with, alone
And frightened, knowing how soon
I will waken a poor man.

It snows freely and freely hardens
On the lawns of my hope, my secret
Hounded and flayed. I wonder
What words to beg money with.

Pardon me, sir, could you?
Which way is St. Paul?
I thirst.
I am a full-blooded Sioux Indian.

Soon I am sure to become so hungry
I will have to leap barefoot through gas-fire veils of shame,
I will have to stalk timid strangers
On the whorsehouse corners.

Oh moon, sow leaves on my hands,
On my seared face, oh I love you.
My throat is open, insane,
Tempting pneumonia.

But my life was never so precious
To me as now.
I will have to beg coins
After dark.

I will learn to scent the police,
And sit or go blind, stay mute, be taken for dead
For your sake, oh my secret,
My life.

Veneta Masson

ANOTHER CASE OF CHRONIC PELVIC PAIN

A busy clinic is visited; the frequent complaint and its standard answer are heard. How to deconstruct the complaint and find the source of pain for the woman in the poem, when the source of her pain is woven inextricably into her life? If health care professionals are to identify factors that put individuals at risk for disease or injury—whether psychological or physical—aren't they then obliged to begin that commitment with the *first* complaint?

VENETA MASSON is a family nurse practitioner. She has been a nurse for thirty-five years. Most of her poems and essays are based on the seventeen years she spent at a small, inner-city clinic she helped to found in Washington, D.C. This poem is taken from her collection of poetry titled *Rehab at the Florida Avenue Grill.*

Like the others, she is not from here
and when she came she left
all of what matters behind—
four children, a village
a father (not well), the lingering
scent of her man (who had fled)
Sunday walks in the plaza after mass
on days when the soldiers were gone
on days when no bodies were found.

The journey from home was perilous—
sometimes on foot, or crowded
into the back of a truck, over hills
through dense forests, arroyos
dark rivers, toward menacing lights,
the eyes of hostile cities.

The trip cost her more than
she wanted to pay—
all the crumpled bills
from the earthenware jar
in the wall of the house,
the silver bracelets and earrings
passed down from her mother.
Her body they took along the way
again and again as if for a debt
that can never be paid.
What drove her on was a woman's
fixed and singular faith that
she is the giver of life
the mother of God.

By bus from the border
by phone from the station
by foot to the room of the friend

of a cousin who knew of a place
and jobs cleaning offices at night
where no questions were asked
and dollars were paid
unless you missed work
or were caught by the migra—
all this distance she came
numb to the pain in her feet and back
and the ache in her lower heart.

She spent her days trying to sleep.
Nights she roamed large empty halls
as wide as the streets
that gave onto the plaza
pushing a cart full of cleaning supplies
bagging the trash, sweeping the floors
washing away the stains of another
day in the upper world.
Paydays she sent her money home
by the man at Urgente Express.
Sunday she sometimes walked
down the street at the edge
of the park, watching
with shaded eyes among the men
for one she might know.

Months passed this way
and with each one she wept
the tears of blood that women weep
and felt the ache in her belly
grow stronger until at last
there was no relief,
come new moon or full,
and no poultice, tea or prayer
that helped her bear
what she must bear.

She sits in the clinic—
"a 32-year-old Hispanic female
complaining of chronic pelvic pain."

The results of all the tests
are negative, they say.
That means there's nothing we can find
to blame for all the pain.
There is a cause, of course—
perhaps a scar deep inside.
Surgery might tell us more—or not,
but then there's the matter of money.

I see, she says simply.
Well, if you can't find
anything wrong—and you know
there is no money . . .

There are some pills
you could take, they say,
for the pain, when it
bothers you most.

You are kind, she says
and stands up to go,
like the others,
from here to her job,
her room, and perhaps twice a year
to a telephone that spans the miles
of dense forest, dark river
to the house of a friend
of an aunt of her father
to ask if the children
are well and in school
on days when the soldiers are gone
on days when no bodies are found.

I will send for them
one day soon, she says.
For now there is only the ache in her belly,
come new moon or full,
and no poultice, pill or prayer
to help her bear
what she must bear.

What drives her on is a woman's
fixed and singular faith that
she is the giver of life
the mother of God.

Lori Arviso Alvord

from THE SCALPEL AND THE SILVER BEAR

This selection by Navajo surgeon Lori Arviso Alvord is her attempt to understand "the economic, psychological, occupational, social, and cultural factors that contribute to the development and/or perpetration of conditions that impair health." Alvord writes about the patients she sees at the Indian Medical Center in Gallup, New Mexico, many of whose difficulties "had a common denominator: alcohol." She describes in detail how alcohol, "through its pervasiveness and its availability, . . . has touched the lives of Navajos on many levels." The issue is personally as well as professionally relevant for Alvord, whose father died in an alcohol-related car crash.

LORI ARVISO ALVORD is the first Navajo female surgeon. She is associate dean of minority and student affairs at Dartmouth Medical School.

ELIZABETH COHEN VAN PELT co-authored *The Scalpel and the Silver Bear* with Lori Arviso Alvord. She is a staff writer for the *New York Post.*

I was on morning rounds in the intensive care unit. The smell of coffee, cooling in the bottom of Styrofoam cups, mixed with the smell of freshly cleaned linens. A computer screen, divided into bright purple and green lines, traced the activities of the patients' hearts, a stack of their charts lay on the counter.

With my fellow surgeon Susan Stuart and a specialist in internal medicine, Terry Sloan, I waited for everyone else to arrive. As people filed in, several nurses chatted by the doorway. An old audiotape was playing, and music poured through the serious air like honey. Then someone turned down the music, and we began to make our rounds, going over the histories of each patient.

Bed 66: Slim, Ray, a 38-year-old male with early cirrhosis and active hepatitis, fevers, a high white count, and pancreatitis. He was described as a "binge-type drinker who spends his weekends intoxicated."

Bed 65: Thompson, Robert, a 51-year-old male with severe cirrhosis, ulcers, and internal bleeding. Needs an esophagogastroduodenoscopy, or "scope," to locate the source of bleeding in his intestinal tract.

Bed 67: Redhouse, Betty, a 29-year-old woman with a bleeding ulcer, heart condition, and severe liver damage. In the hospital because of a beating that was believed to have been the result of a domestic violence incident. She has lacerations and cuts to the head and neck, as well as a long knife wound to the abdomen.

Bed 64: Antonio, Henry, a 38-year-old man with massive trauma to the neck, mild wheezing, mild hypoxia, severely lacerated tongue, a lumbar fracture, and multiple fractures in the left ankle.

As the physicians talked, this last patient's story began to unfold. Henry Antonio had been jailed the previous night for drunk and disorderly behavior and had tried to hang himself in his jail cell. He suffered back and ankle injuries when he fell. It was believed he had a seizure after the hanging attempt. That was when he bit off part of his tongue.

Listening to the doctors describe these patients in detail on that late winter morning, the fractured and unharmonious parts of our community came into focus, as did one of its chief causes. These patient cases and many of those that followed on that round had a common denominator: alcohol. Much of what I was dealing with medically in the intensive care unit was either directly related to or a side effect of alcohol. Daily, again and again, I found myself forced to consider this toxic substance and the serious damage it was doing to people.

I was not naive about alcohol. In some ways drugs are not unknown to Native cultures, which traditionally used some form of hallucinogenic or mind-altering substance as a part of their religious practices. Yet alcohol is different. It has a devastating, dramatic, and negative effect. Very early on in our history, alcohol was outlawed on reservations, possibly for paternalistic reasons, but bars and liquor stores always spring up nearby.

The lives of the patients at GIMC* were scarred by the disease of alcoholism. Making rounds in the intensive care unit made it obvious: this was an epidemic.

Gallup has about fifty bars to serve fifty thousand people, and arrests for driving intoxicated exceed ten thousand a year. The opening of several new government alcohol treatment programs and the city of Gallup's ban on drive-up liquor sales improved the situation somewhat, but the problem did not go away. The incidence of fetal alcohol syndrome, a condition caused by mothers drinking during pregnancy, is the highest in the country among Native people. Through its pervasiveness and its availability, alcohol has touched the lives of Navajos on many levels.

Alcohol has been called one of the "lubricants of domination," given to non-Europeans by Europeans. Every day I saw cirrhosis, hepatitis, ulcers, internal bleeding, pancreatitis, domestic violence–related injuries—all pathologies that could be associated with the excessive or habitual ingestion of alcohol. We bandaged them up, dried them out, and sent them on their way, but many times they'd be back.

Even after I had been in Gallup only a short while I had already encountered a vast number of patients whose lives were trapped and tangled in alcohol-related problems.

One day as I was operating at GIMC with Greg Stephens and one of our anesthesiologists, Daryl Smith, both of whom were black, I overheard their conversation about people they'd grown up with. They cited the well-known tragedy about young black men in this country: that many of their male child-

*Gallup Indian Medical Center.

hood friends have been killed or were in jail. They named names, ticking them off on their fingers, and remembered the casualties. Suddenly it dawned on me: many of the children I grew up with on the reservation were no longer alive either—but nobody ever really talked about the high number of teenage Indian casualties: Rena Craig, Ernie Henry, Adrian Tenequer, Alfred Chavez, Peter and David Howard, Rickey Estevan, Perryson Perry, Elmer Morgan, Leroy Etcitty, Roger Etcitty. Dead not from guns and drugs but from alcohol, suicide, and automobiles—our own lethal combination.

The leading cause of death among Navajos isn't liver disease or pancreatitis—it is motor vehicle accidents. The rate is three times higher for men than for women; the highest percentage of all is for men in the 25-to-34 age range. Indian Health Service statistics estimate that 60 percent of those accidents are alcohol related, and the numbers are rising.

Besides accidents, other alcohol-related incidents were also common. Everett Nelson, a teenager, was brought in with long tears and crisscross rips in his body from knife wounds. He said his brother and he had gotten in a fight, but his tattoos and clothing told a different story. Gangs on the reservation had been increasing for a decade or so and I was seeing the result.

Young Navajo men like Everett, not yet seventeen, would come in with gunshot or stab wounds. There was even a gang-related fatality in Shiprock: a fourteen-year-old Navajo boy named Shoshonnie Francisco. The gang culture was yet one more outside influence—this time of imported violence and territoriality—that threatened Navajo culture. No one knows for sure how it first infiltrated the far-flung sheep camps and washes of the rez, but it did. Before long Navajo schoolchildren were wearing the symbols and colors of the Bloods and Crips of the West Coast gangs. Soon afterward they began to show up in GIMC, like Everett, and were some of my most seriously injured patients. Navajo communities have become increasingly alarmed by this trend. The elders say that it is a result of the fact that parents have not taught their children the traditional ways. Without the teachings of Walking in Beauty, these children attempted to create their own tribe, but with devastating effects. The blueprint for tribal lifeways had not been handed down to them. Alcohol only made the violence and gang-related crime worse. Usually it took place when they were drunk.

Standing in the intensive care unit that morning and many other mornings in the years that followed, surrounded by patients whose illnesses could all be traced to the abuse of alcohol, I realized that in my profession as a surgeon, I would see the saddest side of this disease—the casualties. I would treat their sick livers and stomachs, and I would treat their bleeding bodies. But there would be little I could do about their souls, the captives of a cruel substance that would probably never let them go. Almost every Navajo family had a member with an alcohol problem.

In my own family that person was my father. Soon after I arrived in Gallup and began practicing surgery at GIMC, my medical work and my personal life came together in a tragic intersection.

My father's story showed me in a personal way how alcohol is destroying our community. When I got back to Dinetah, I saw his alcoholism differently than I had before I left. Before, I had seen it as a problem in our family, but now I also saw it as a disease, in a clinical fashion. Because of him I was able to look at my patients as individuals, each with their own particular story and paths to this illness. Our historic grief had led to a collectively experienced plague; my father was the window through which I could see it.

Robert Cupp, my father, was by any culture's standards an extraordinary man. He had a gift for speaking to animals. Almost everywhere we went, on the reservation or off, he knew the dogs, and they recognized him and came running. Rez dogs. Chocolate and black-splotched or the color of coyote and mesa and riverbed mud. One blue eye, one brown, or two piercing green. They are everywhere on the reservation, used to watch the sheep or guard the hogan, and when you arrive they appear magically, just like those annoying friends who materialize at mealtime. My father knew them. Crows also seemed to gather in groups or come and stand on a fencepost whenever my father was around. Sometimes I'd turn a corner and find my father standing deep in a philosophical discussion with a crow.

In the Navajo world, where everything is connected, talking to animals or acknowledging their presence is not as unusual as it is in other places. In addition to fluent crow and rez dog, my dad sometimes seemed to know the dialects of deer, elk, and even trout—he could easily decipher their language of leaps and cautious lingering in the pools made by rocky eddies. He taught his daughters how to hunt, how to look at a certain set of tracks and determine instantly what type of animal it was from its size, and how long ago it had passed. My two sisters became accomplished hunters. I would usually go along but sit on a rock and read. He also taught us camping and boating and showed us how to hand tie fishing flies.

But perhaps the most important thing about my father was that he taught us the simplest things—Navajo things—like how to just sit and be quiet, to blend in and watch, or to move so silently we'd become a part of the forest. My father taught us how to live the concepts of our culture, especially the importance of communicating with the natural world.

For most Native people the animals and environment have a spirit and life of their own that is respected and protected. Part of the Beauty Way ceremony teaches us that humans should live in harmony with the animal world and the natural world—the earth, plants, water, air, everything that surrounds us. Navajo chantways are beautiful in their descriptions of the world we live in. For example, the Mountain Chantway has passages that capture the power and glory of nature:

The voice that beautifies the land!
The voice above
The voice of the thunder
Within the dark cloud,
Again and again it sounds,
The voice that beautifies the land!
The voice of the grasshopper
Among the plants,
Again and again it sounds,
The voice that beautifies the land![7]

My father taught us that before a hunt traditionally raised Navajos sang sacred songs. He also taught us that part of the meat must be given away, and that nothing should be wasted.

Our family honored that tradition by providing meat for my father's grandparents and other elder relatives, and by wasting nothing. We could not even leave any meat on the ribs we ate.

In their childhoods both my father and my grandmother had been punished for speaking Navajo in school. Navajos were told by white educators that, in order to be successful, they would have to forget their language and culture and adopt American ways. They were warned that if they taught their children to speak Navajo, the children would have a harder time learning in school, and would therefore be at a disadvantage.

A racist attitude existed. Navajo children were told that their culture and lifeways were inferior, and they were made to feel they could never be as good as white people. This pressure to assimilate, along with the physical, social, psychological, and economic destruction of the tribes following the Indian wars of the 1800s, the poverty due to poor grazing lands and forced stock reduction, and the lack of available jobs all combined to bring the Navajo people to their knees. The physical genocide of the 1800s, followed by the cultural genocide of the 1900s, left behind a tribe whose roots and foundation were shattered.

My father suffered terribly from these events and conditions. He had been a straight-A student and was sent away to one of the best prep schools in the state. He wanted to be like the rich white children who surrounded him there, but the differences were too apparent. My father resented the limitations that being Navajo presented in the 1940s and 1950s. He went to the University of New Mexico, majoring in premed and Latin. It was there that he met my mother.

"She looked so angelic," he often said about their first encounter. To the Navajo boy who was taught to feel shame about the color of his skin, she must have. My mother has blond hair and blue eyes, and she probably represented everything that he felt he was not. When they married, my dad left college and went to White Horse Lake to run the trading post, leaving behind his academic dreams. Not long afterward he began to hate himself for being unable to fit into the white world and for not fulfilling his dreams. He escaped his grief with alcohol and would disappear for days, sometimes weeks. I remember the empty seat at the dinner table when he was gone. At those times his absence was a presence. We'd walk around the house, acutely aware of all the places he wasn't—his workshop, the yard, his favorite chair in the living room.

Once, in the middle of the night I was lying with my sisters in the backseat of the car in my pajamas. It was like so many other nights, that night, but somehow it has stayed intact in my memory, almost like a film.

Karen, Robyn, and I waited amid a heap of blankets and pillows while my mother searched for my dad in the bars on Gallup's main strip. We'd already been by the police stations in both Gallup and Crownpoint. Our last stop was the Gallup morgue, where an unidentified Indian man lay dead. Mom had heard about it from a man in one of the bars and didn't want to explain it to us. But we knew where we were, and we knew why we were there. Karen, Robyn, and I huddled together in our blankets while she went in to see if the face beneath the white sheet was his. It wasn't, but when she came out, she looked stark white and shaken.

After I went away to college, my father cut way back on his binges. But always, whenever he was gone, there was uncertainty and fear. I would wonder if he was okay, if he'd been arrested, or if he lay hurt somewhere, the victim of an accident, or if someone else had been injured as well. In our house, whenever the phone rang and Dad was away, we would exchange heavy glances. Such calls often brought bad news.

My father really was two people. One was the man who took pride in everything we did. He never missed a single one of Karen's basketball games. He played for hours with Robyn's baby son, B. J., and read *Parents* magazine.

The other man had black fire streaming through his veins, his life dreams scattered like frightened crows. Alcohol had erased these dreams. It had also enslaved him, as it had so many patients I saw. When I came into work and saw so many cases involving the deterioration of the body through alcohol, I would remind myself that each one had a story, each one a reason why.

Two or three generations of our tribe had been taught to feel shame about our culture, and parents had often not taught their children traditional Navajo beliefs—the very thing that would have shown them how to live, the very thing that could keep them strong.

Today the tire marks have faded, where they left the highway on Interstate 40 near mile marker 47. I saw them all winter in 1993, two years after I came home to practice medicine. A pair of bright black parallel lines veered off the pavement to the right. The site was located between my house in Gallup and my parents' house near Grants, so I had no choice but to drive by it again and again as I came to visit my family. One day I noticed that I could no longer see the tracks, but it didn't matter, I'd memorized them. It was the place where my father's car had rolled four times before smashing into an iron rail.

Each time I saw that place I whispered, *"Ayóó ninshné." I love you, Dad.*

My father is buried in a beautiful, manicured cemetery in Albuquerque.

But that is not where he is. I have been in that cemetery many times; I do not feel his presence. In fact, I often forget that he is there at all. Not so at mile marker 47. To the east is Mount Taylor, our beautiful, sacred Tsoodzil. It seems ironic that nearby, also, was the Top of the World, his favorite bar, at the town of Continental Divide.

It is as though this place were chosen for him.

Mile marker 47. My father's spirit pulled me each time I passed it. It was as though he cast out with his fly-fishing rod there, and it hooked my soul.

Kirsten Emmott

UNWED

Entering another human being's world in a brief medical encounter is particularly difficult in the birthing suite. As this poem bluntly portrays, birth can trigger expletives and rage that go far beyond a response to the pain of giving birth. This raging reflects another life, one unknown to practitioners in the birthing suite. Admission to that other life is denied the practitioner in this poem, despite her gentle ministrations.

KIRSTEN EMMOTT is a general practitioner and poet living in British Columbia. This poem and another, titled "1852: J. Marion Sims Perfects a Repair for Vesicovaginal Fistula," which also appears in this anthology, are taken from Emmott's collection *How Do You Feel?*

Donna
comes from a different world
and will stay there.
She will not return
for her six-week checkup.
She will not breastfeed
nor recycle.

Donna
put on a lot of weight,
got up to two twenty-five,
her face swollen, sullen, still.
Her tattoos announce
she is not like the slim lawyers
who have been to birthing class.
She is not polite in labor;
she yells and curses and wants out.

Though I mothered her
with respectful hands
as she gave birth,
she would not smile for me.
Her small smiles were for the baby
she showed her real mother.
They turned away from me,
traced the absent boyfriend's looks
together.

Though I mothered her
and delivered her very well,
her body knowing what to do,
noisy and efficient as a cow,
when I looked up
she was back in her world,
clutching her boy.

The silence back in place,
Donna said she was sorry
for yelling "Fuck!" so much.

That's all right, I said.

Penny Armstrong and Sheryl Feldman

from A WISE BIRTH

Writing of her work as a nurse-midwife among the Amish and Mennonite communities in rural Lancaster County, Pennsylvania, Penny Armstrong recalls that, during her early days there, for all her professional training, she was "undone by the infrequency of the need . . . to display [her] masterly [medical] strokes. Birth appeared to be another animal out in the country." Labors were generally shorter, pain less severe, cuts and tears fewer. Yet when Amish women went into the hospital to deliver their babies, they had more difficulties than those giving birth at home. Why? The question—and the answers to it Armstrong finds—underscore the need for health professionals to "actively support traditional public health practices in their communities," bringing together the best of natural childbirth with modern medicine.

PENNY ARMSTRONG is a nurse-midwife in private practice. She is co-author, with Sheryl Feldman, of *A Midwife's Story* and former director of the University of New England College of Osteopathic Medicine's Behavioral Science and Community Health Project.

SHERYL FELDMAN co-authored *A Wise Birth* and *A Midwife's Story* with Penny Armstrong. She lives in Seattle.

I had just gotten my accreditation as a certified nurse-midwife when I responded to a call from a general practitioner out in agricultural Lancaster County, Pennsylvania. He was interested in expanding his practice among the Amish people and wanted a midwife as part of his service team. I had been raised in the country and it appealed to me to return.

When I went out for the interview, I was disturbed to find that I would be expected to do home births. All my experience with birth had been in the hospital and I was keen on having emergency equipment nearby and doctors available. I wondered if the doctor wasn't being a bit cavalier about his Amish clients. They had only eighth-grade educations, they did not sue, and so could easily be taken advantage of.

But he took me around to chat with some of the women in their homes and they told me in their own words that they preferred to have their babies at home because it was economical and it suited their farm- and family-centered, low-tech lives. Until recently, Dr. Grace Kaiser had assisted them at home, but she had retired, and they were forced to choose between the hospital or one other home birth practitioner—a person whose methods, when I heard about them, I couldn't condone. What the couples said convinced me that one didn't force mainstream standards—that is, everyone goes to the hospital—on the Amish. I accepted the job and its requirement of attending home births.

I was a well-prepared midwife, exacting of myself and, in one way, ambitious. I was determined that the women I cared for would have the safest, best births possible. I immediately assessed the realities of home birth—being alone in the middle of the night at an Amish farm with my work area lit by gaslight and the closest phone a five- or ten-minute walk away—and compensated. I bought a two-way radio. I equipped my suitcase with all the drugs that midwives are licensed to carry. I put in Pitocin for the resistant placenta, Methergine for postpartum bleeding, Valium to counteract a suddenly elevating blood pressure, Epinephrine to compensate for the sometimes ill effects of numbing drugs used for episiotomy, pills for severe afterpains, antibiotics for the person at risk of infection. I put in Amni-hooks (plastic instruments for breaking the bag of waters), syringes, intravenous (IV) fluids, a ring forceps for examining the cervix, a variety of clamps and scissors, a suture kit, needles, a DeLee's suction catheter for clearing the baby's air passageway, a heavy oxygen tank, a laryngoscope for viewing the baby's throat, an endotracheal (ET) tube to slip down its airway to get oxygen to the lungs, and a bag for forcing oxygen into the baby's lungs.

The doctor and I eliminated (we call it risking out) those women whom we thought unsuitable for home birth. No mothers whose babies were in an odd position, no mothers having their tenth child (or more), no twins, no women with high blood pressure, no women with severe medical problems, no small-bodied women who seemed to be carrying big babies. Any known chance of a complication sent a woman to the hospital.

Meanwhile, I began attending births at home. I hadn't made many forays before I realized that I was seeing births for which I had not been prepared. Accustomed as I was to the taut, often breathless birth atmosphere of hospital births, I was struck by the casual, comfortable movements of the women laboring in their kitchen and giving birth among quilts. Having based much of my assessment of myself as a practitioner on my ability to respond swiftly and accurately to emergency situations, I was undone by the infrequency of the need for me to display my masterly strokes. Birth appeared to be another animal out in the country. Labors were shorter than I was accustomed to. Pain appeared to be less severe. Cuts and tears fewer. Hemorrhage controllable. Babies did not need my suctioning devices or my tubes pressed down their throats; they gurgled when they were born and began to breathe. Their mothers took them to their breasts and nursed without much complication. If problems did arise anytime during a birth, most of them appeared to resolve themselves in short order.

I had an eerie sense of unreality. The births had not only power, but grace and simplicity. Coming home at four or five in the morning after births, each one seeming to unwind to a fruitful, healthy end, I groped for explanation. I wondered if I was witnessing a statistically aberrant population of women, ones who were, by genetic predisposition, good birthers. At other times, bewitched by the grace of the starry landscape and disarmed by the humility of the Amish, I indulged in the magical idea that God rewarded people who followed a religious way of life by giving them easier births. By daylight, the clinician in me credited the food the women ate, the number of hours they spent squatting in the garden, the herbs they took, and their experience with animals giving birth. Sometimes, when sleep-deprived, I considered the self-serving possibility that it was me making all the difference. Finally I countenanced the possibility that I had stumbled upon—as I vaguely put it—something extraordinary.

I yearned to have a more experienced professional explain to me what was going on but I was reluctant to discuss my statistics, which were becoming astounding, with my mentors back at Booth Maternity Center in Philadelphia. Once I mumbled something about them and it was suggested that I wait for the other shoe to drop. That sounded like good advice, so I kept my mouth shut and maintained my style of attending women. I kept the hospital ways I had been able to bring with me into homes. I stayed with the women through the early parts of their labor, I scrubbed carefully, I watched the clock, I shone a strong flashlight on the perineum while I worked, I recorded elaborate detail on charts.

One August night, I was led yet another time by a typical Amish husband into a typical Amish bedroom. Silla, the mother, was propped up in her bed in a moonlit room calmly awaiting my arrival. She smiled, and then, conspiratorially, placed her index finger to her lips. She beckoned me to her side, pulled my head down so my ear was next to her mouth, and whispered. Would it suit me, she wanted to know, to leave the lamp unlit and to talk quietly? Her two-year-old, Joseph, was asleep in the corner of the bedroom and she didn't want to wake him.

My first reaction was to disabuse her of her easygoing confidence by lecturing her on the disasters that can accompany birth: how babies' lives had been saved because practitioners had picked up a tint in the amniotic fluid (waters), because they had been able to use their scissors precisely, because they were able to see when the color of a baby's face shifted. But while I was preparing this speech, my eyes followed Silla's over to damp, tousled Joseph, sleeping in his crib as contented as a puddle after a summer rain; I glanced at Silla's husband, who had competently assisted me at Joseph's birth, and I realized what was bothering me. If I assisted Silla as she requested I would be admitting that birth probably could be trusted.

My decision to do so was based on a number of considerations. I knew, for example, that Silla had had four births, each of them manifestly uncomplicated. This pregnancy had proceeded in perfect order. I knew that she was a responsible person, one who would not cling to her request for quiet and darkness if circumstances changed. I knew Joseph could flare up a lantern in an instant. I acknowledged that Joseph and Silla had a mature and subtle religious faith, one that embraced, as God's will, the unpredictable turnings of nature. I decided, in other words, to trust the accumulation of my experience among the Amish and the judgments that followed from it.

I held the flaps on the locks of my medical case so they wouldn't click; I stepped out into the kitchen to tear open the packages of rubber gloves; I laid my flashlight on the doily on the bureau so it wouldn't startle; I used my stethoscope instead of a doptone (which throws the sound of the baby's heartbeat around the room); I heard the bedsprings creak when Silla's husband climbed onto the bed beside her. Within the half-hour, I felt the slippery dome of a baby's head filling my palm and their little girl eased out. I slid her onto the mounded landscape of her mother's abdomen.

I reached over toward her and saw that she was breathing, that her eyes were open, that they were avidly exploring the bedroom around her. She was as alert and as clear-sighted as a person who has just risen out of deep meditation. When a smile slipped across her face, her perfection skimmed through me. She had come up as effortlessly and as reassuringly as the sun.

I had never seen a smile on the face of a child at birth; indeed, I'd never heard of such a thing. And even supposing, as I did later, that it was just a look of contentment I'd seen, the impact remained the same. If birth could be as easy for a mother as it was for Silla and as comfortable as it apparently was for her baby, then I needed to be able to explain why and how. Urged along by that confounding child, I began to think systematically about the causes of power and grace.

I knew that my clients' births were favorably influenced by the women's general good health. They scrub floors on their hands and knees, sling baskets of wet wash about, climb stairs, work out in the fields, and squat in their gardens. The air they breathe is relatively unpolluted. They don't drink or smoke and, while their diets are not ideal, they are quite adequate. Also, their bodies are not assaulted every day by the psychological stresses of urban life. These are such important physical advantages that, in theory, they should have served the women equally well no matter where they gave birth.

The theory, however, held up no further than the local hospital where, I knew from experience, the general population of Amish women had more difficulties than those who gave birth at home. There seemed to be several possible explanations for this phenomenon: It was something that doctors, who practiced in hospitals, did at delivery; it was something that midwives, when they practiced in hospitals, did at delivery; it was the hospital environment itself; or it was some combination thereof.

As I considered the first possibility, the doctor-assisted hospital delivery, I recalled the description one Amish woman had given me of her first birth. Mary seemed to be a good case for analysis because she's a serene person, one unlikely to exaggerate problems. Furthermore, unusual in an Amish person, she's quite well read. Instead of marrying at twenty or twenty-one as so many do, she taught in an Amish school for eight to ten years before she met Jonas, also a schoolteacher, and they married.

Pregnant with their first child, they asked around and found a physician who was reputed to be both kind and informative. They went to the library and got out books on painless childbirth, which they read at night, sitting at the kitchen table. Attending classes on how to have a baby naturally, they learned that shaves and enemas were outmoded and that lying on one's back during labor was "the worst."

"Apparently," she said, telling me about her first labor, "the hospital staff and my doctor . . . hadn't been informed [about the innovations in childbirth]. No one had told me I needed to lie on my back so the nurse in attendance could watch my contractions on the screen." With typical Amish humility, she added, "But who was I to inconvenience the nurse"—who was constantly checking her and adjusting the "cold" monitor on her stomach "which made the contractions seem worse."

She, a woman accustomed to backbreaking farmwork, found the pain "well-nigh unbearable. . . . With each contraction I felt as though a nerve was being pinched in the vagina. I wanted to scream but dared not, fearing I would lose all control." Entreating God to keep her from screaming, finding her praying capacity weak, she turned to Jonas and asked him to pray for her. He did, but told her later he thought she was contemplating death. "It was unthinkable," she said, describing the retreat of her dream of having a houseful of children, "that there'd be another time."

When she was ready to push, the nurse said that the doctor had not yet arrived and that she should pant through her contractions. In the meantime, while she panted, they moved her from bed to stretcher and from stretcher to delivery table. "The doctor breezed in cool as a cucumber" just as a contraction rose and she moaned.

" 'Don't you start screaming!' [he said].

"His abrupt tone of voice was not lost on me.

" 'Slide over,' came the next command.

"Apparently I wasn't dead center on the table.

"Flat on my back, feet in stirrups, sheet hiding the lower part of my body, the doctor, and some of his gazing companions, I gave birth to a son. I heard his cry. I thought he was mine. I wanted him on my stomach and at my breast."

She wanted to hold him, the first-born child of a long-awaited family-to-be and she wanted him for the sake of her body, she said, remembering her reading and that his suckling at her breast would contract her uterus naturally and force the placenta out. Instead, empty-armed, she felt a shot of Pitocin, the contraction-stimulating drug, stinging her thigh. Only after they extracted the placenta did they give her the baby. He was "blanketed, blond, wide-eyed" and "I laughed for the joy of him."

She wasn't allowed to keep him, however, because the episiotomy gaped. They took the baby away; she began to shiver and begged for a blanket, which they brought: a "nice skinny" one, "suitable for a July night." The doctor began a long sew. It went "on and on. I hadn't known this doctor to be a seamstress or a tailor. . . . I was no longer numb . . . I'd feel him sewing." The pain from the stitches kept her from sitting for a week.

"So much," she said cynically, "for the most lauded event of a woman's life. I cried until I couldn't cry anymore."

The nurses, by contrast, called it a "lovely" birth. And for them, encountering this quiet, loving, and well-educated couple, it probably was. One becomes accustomed to routines—including cutting of the flesh—and can get in the habit of not questioning their necessity.

But if you are not accustomed to it, it is shocking to see vibrant muscle cut. I think of muscles as being strung out on our bones like strings on a cello—vibrating with potential, as if for an extended concert. I dream about a batter with his shirt off and the graceful cresting of power that curves up from the small of his back, across his shoulders, and down his arms. To interrupt that progression of movement is an esthetic crime, and I feel sure we wouldn't do it if it were avoidable.

If a ballplayer was on a table in the operating room and if there was no other remedy but surgery, the prospect of cutting his muscles would still be sobering. Seeing him prepped and draped, we would know that everything possible had been done. Physical therapists with their baths, exercises, and massages would have exhausted their repertoire, specialists with slings and elastic bandages would have signed off. Only then would they resort to the knife.

Maybe we don't think of these women's muscles with the same regard because of where they are located. We don't see them crossing and gliding as they make our hips swing; we don't watch them spreading into broad ribbony bands when we squat down. We don't imagine them roiling with sex. Because we can't see them, maybe we think of them as static, a crude vessel fit only for containing entrails, bowels, and other oozy organs. Maybe that's what makes them easier to cut.

But I have seen the muscles in women. In the delivery room, when the cut was made across three or four major muscle groups, I've seen them retreat and lie there, shrunk back into themselves, and I felt the same way I would if a ballplayer's muscles had been cut. The same way I feel when a cellist's string snaps during a concert. The music of the body, the resonance and the potential for rapture are interrupted.

Replaying Mary's unwieldy birth advanced me only a little in my effort to analyze the benefits of home birth. As many practitioners today would admit, there was too much wrong. The back-lying labor, the cold monitor, the painful vaginal "checks," the waiting to push, the moves from bed to stretcher to delivery table, the strapping down, the stirrups, the harshness of the doctor's orders, the withholding of the baby, the neglected postbirth chill, the shot, and the long sew—all of these seemingly insignificant, routine factors are known to increase anxiety and exacerbate pain. Even a nonlaboring person would find them awkward, uncomfortable, and inhibiting. It would be almost impossible for a birth to flow—as Silla's did—in such circumstances.

I considered the second possible variation in the hospital delivery. What about the perfectly healthy Amish woman who had her baby in the hospital with a midwife's care? Would her birth be compromised simply by being in the hospital? Was a healthy birth dependent upon the environment in which it took place?

The majority of women I attended in the hospital were having their first babies—"primips," we call them. Primip births are challenging for several reasons. In the first place, the women don't have any personal experience of birth. They are likely to be frightened or anxious, which works against relaxation, which works against easy birth. Second, their muscles are tight, and the baby has to travel against their resistance. Their hormonal systems, too, are inexperienced at birth and may be slow to blend. These psychological and physiological factors combine and create the major challenge of a primip birth: the long labor. As a midwife attending a first-time birther, I had a major interest in preserving a woman's energy so that she would have enough strength left at the end to push the baby out.

I managed hospital births differently than most of the doctors did. I told the women they could labor in any position they found comfortable, I did very few vaginal checks, I encouraged them to walk the halls and inhabit the showers at will, I spoke to them kindly, chatted with them about their families and farms, I said they could give birth on their sides, half-sitting, or squatting. Even with these advantages, however, the result results were disappointing. While a good proportion of the primips delivered without intervention, there were several who should have, but couldn't. They would dilate fully, but ultimately needed forceps or a section to give birth.

I knew energy loss was a major problem. The hospital, assessing a set of complicated risk factors, had decided it was prudent to tell women not to eat once they were in labor. While I disagreed with their analysis of the risks, I respected it. Thus the women, doing hard physical work, ran out of energy before it was time for them to push.

There were other factors too, things that felt wrong but defied clinical analysis. In comparison to the home births I attended, hospital births were awkward. They were out of sync with Amish life. I'd tried to ease the transition: I often picked primips up at home and drove them to the hospital. I always guarded their rooms, trying to protect them from the invasion of strangers who spoke a language, bureaucratic and medical, that they couldn't understand; against fluorescent light, which they, being accustomed to lantern lighting, found painful; and against the uncommon, for them, sounds of machinery and phones. Obviously, I could only be partially successful.

What felt more damaging was the distrustful atmosphere of the hospital staff. Laboring women could not be helped by nurses who, not approving of my tolerance for a prolonged first stage (the pre-pushing part), would say disdainfully, "Is she still in labor?" or "Hasn't that girl delivered yet?" A woman in labor hears the doubt and loses confidence. Also, by similar but less direct means, the clinical review committee (it sets hospital policy) influenced the labors. They measured the time women were in labor against a table called the "Friedman labor curve." Designed to *de*scribe the average length of labor, many practitioners and the review committee used it the other way around—to *pre*scribe how long a labor might be. One either began pushing after twelve hours of active labor or one was a candidate for intervention. When the committee reviewed my labor records—which showed my tolerance for individual variation—they expressed unease. Although my outcomes were excellent by any hospital standards, the women I attended were not following the prescribed pattern.

That wasn't all. The administration expected women to give birth on a delivery table and my birthing room with its mattress and box springs did not conform; neither did my informal style. In time, their discomfort sprung up in me as anxiety and I'm sure I passed that feeling on to the laboring women. Perhaps I encouraged them too much, perhaps I implied urgency, perhaps they began to push before they were quite ready and so, in spite of their wholesome advantage, they failed. . . .

As a practitioner, I am guided by the strengths in my material. Like a cabinetmaker eyeing the pattern in wood, like a seamstress feeling the weight of a fabric, I search for the design of birth implicit in a woman. I can anticipate a birth best when I concentrate on information that comes to me through my hands. I glide them up over the bathed and talced mound of a woman's belly. In first-time mothers, when I pull my hands down, tracing the path the baby will take, I feel smooth, strong muscles and a baby who rides in a taut pouch. With experienced birthers, I can close my eyes and feel the revelation of work done, of skin that has stretched and reknit, of muscles that have spread and drawn back together. I can feel tenacious parts and those that are more lax. I can anticipate muscular dynamics. I can feel whether there is a good pool of waters, whether the baby has sufficient mass, and how vital it is.

Birth is infinitely dynamic. We cannot adequately understand it by naming anatomical parts and describing physiological processes, nor are we done when we describe its choreography. Birth functions in the context of mind and spirit. They act directly on birth and give it the complexity we associate with life. When we acknowledge this, we invite the power of birth.

Becca, John's wife, weighed ninety-five pounds and was as shy as a blade of new grass. Her skin was translucent; her bones were slender and fine as light. Fragility dominated her being, easily overwhelming the mere, plain fact that her pregnancy was normal. I could not imagine her having the capacity to throw her baby out. I could not think how to embolden her. The only way I could comfort myself was to dwell on her hot-ember hair and all the passion that superstition credits to redheaded women, but even that didn't really do, because she wore it as all Amish women do, carved in a center part and pulled back into a humble, restricted, "It's only me" knot.

Her husband, John, whom I wanted as an ally, was of the rough-and-tumble, dog tail–pulling type. I wished he would evoke some pacing lioness in her, but all he could do was poke her in the ribs. At childbirth classes, she blushed and he feigned indifference.

When the call came, I went out and found her coiled on her couch. When she pulled her skirt up and I saw a cupped-out space underneath her navel, I knew we had our share of work ahead. The baby was in what we call a "persistent posterior position," which means that labor may be long and back pain relentless. If our little Becca continued to conceal herself, as she seemed bound to do, the baby would stay in retreat and her energy would pour out, wasted. If she continued to curl up like a snail in its shell, we would be undone. Her eyes, I noticed, wandered over to John, beseeching his attention.

"You know," I said to her experimentally, "when you're canning pears, you sometimes shake the jar to get halves to find their space?"

She nodded.

"Well, that's what we need to do for your baby. Jiggle him up a little, so his head can find the easy way out."

"How should I do that, Penny?" she asked, without a trace of confidence.

And John sat, careless as the devil, in a lounge chair by the window.

As I looked over at him, thinking about giving one of his casually flung out legs a good kick, I noticed the window behind him. It framed sunlight and a pasture that spilled down to a spot in a stream where the water coiled and made a pool. Ducks glided about on it. Feeling drawn to it myself, I said I thought it might be well for Becca to take a walk, on the condition that John go along. "You'll have to hold her hand so she doesn't fall, of course, and let her lean up against you when she has a contraction."

"We often walk down by the creek," he said, agreeably and comfortably—as if this was something he knew how to do. And so I left them alone for a while.

When I returned some time later, Becca was serving sandwiches. She raised hers to her mouth, apparently determined—per my instructions—to keep up her strength. Try as she might, she could not comply, and when I said she needn't eat if she didn't want to, she dropped her sandwich on her plate and her head on her arms. I looked hopefully at John, thinking that he might, by now, be following her reactions, but instead he was picking up her sandwich. As soon as he finished it, however, he rose with purpose, went into the bathroom, and returned with a hairbrush. Standing behind Becca, he loosened the knot of her bandana, undid her hair, and let it unfurl in red licks around her shoulders. Then he ran his fingertips gently up the side of her head, gathered a mass of her hair in one hand and sank the brush deep into its thick waves with the other. As he brushed, her head swayed gently. Her neck became loose and languid, and the sighs that flushed out of her were heavy.

Seeing that they were finding their way, I slipped as quickly as I could out into the yard and down to the stream, where I sat and waited for an outcome utterly beyond my control. When the sun dropped out of sight and I saw the flash and glow of a lantern lighting in the kitchen window, I rose, thinking that I had better go back in to work. Even as I gathered myself up, however, I stopped: Music was coming from the house. Music, so alien in an Amish household, coming out of this one, streaming out of windows, lapping down over the pasture, trailing into the stream. I stood a long time—unthinkable to break the thread of melody—then found that it was strong and continuous and so I followed it to its source. On my toes, peering in the farmhouse window, I saw Becca, head high and proud, red hair streaming and gallant down her back. She was pacing round the kitchen table, John following her, now playing "Swing Low, Sweet Chariot" on his harmonica.

I turned away once more and leaned against the clapboards while more songs followed and until the music drained away; until I heard Becca's groan. As I went in, John was helping her to bed; then he held her hand, smoothed her forehead, and ultimately he cradled her shoulders in his arms. In that position she threw out a boy baby, for whom John reached, held, and gave over to her.

Anne Fadiman

from THE SPIRIT CATCHES YOU AND YOU FALL DOWN

Lia is a young Hmong patient with a catastrophic seizure disorder. The struggle of her parents, Foua and Nao Kao, to provide care for their daughter results in clashes with both the medical system and the child welfare agencies. In the end, Lia is declared legally "brain dead," and the debate rages as to who was to blame: the parents, who failed, in the early part of Lia's illness, to provide the prescribed medicine, or the American doctors and nurses, who failed to understand the Hmong culture and work out a resolution when their values and beliefs collided.

The Spirit Catches You and You Fall Down is an in-depth examination of the struggle between value systems and cultures, one having applicability to every encounter mainstream medicine has with patients from other cultures. The "ability to communicate effectively" with patients and their families is a complex and challenging charge in a multicultural world.

ANNE FADIMAN is a journalist and editor of *The American Scholar. The Spirit Catches You and You Fall Down* was awarded a National Book Critics Circle Award for Nonfiction.

Since Lia's brain death, whatever scant trust Foua and Nao Kao had once had in American medicine had shrunk almost to zero. (I say "almost" because Foua exempted Neil and Peggy, Lia's primary care physicians.) When their daughter May broke her arm, and the doctors in the MCMC (Merced Community Medical Center) emergency room told them it needed a cast, Nao Kao marched her straight home, bathed her arm in herbs, and wrapped it in a poultice for a week. May's arm regained its full strength. When a pot of boiling oil fell from the electric stove onto Foua's skirt, setting it on fire and burning her right hip and leg, she sacrificed two chickens and a pig. When Foua got pregnant with her sixteenth child, and had an early miscarriage, she did nothing. When she got pregnant with her seventeenth child and had a complicated miscarriage in her fourth month, Nao Kao waited for three days, until she started to hemorrhage and fell unconscious to the living room floor, before he called an ambulance. He consented to her dilation and curettage only after strenuous—in fact, desperate—persuasion by the MCMC resident on obstetric rotation. Nao Kao also sacrificed a pig while Foua was in the hospital and a second pig after she returned home.

Before she was readmitted to Schelby, Lia was routinely vaccinated against diphtheria, pertussis, and tetanus. At about the same time, she started to develop occasional seizurelike twitches. Because they were brief, infrequent, and benign—and also, perhaps, because he had learned from bitter experience—Neil decided not to prescribe anticonvulsants. Foua and Nao Kao were certain that the shots had caused the twitches, and they told Neil that they did not want Lia to be immunized ever again, for anything.

Dan Murphy, who became the director of MCMC's Family Practice Residency Program, once told me that when you fail one Hmong patient, you fail the whole community. I could see that this was true. Who knew how many Hmong families were giving the hospital a wide berth because they didn't want their children to end up like the second-youngest Lee daughter? Everyone in Merced's Lee and Yang clans knew what had happened to Lia (those bad doctors!), just as everyone on the pediatric floor at MCMC knew what had happened to Lia (those bad parents!). Lia's case had confirmed the Hmong community's worst prejudices about the medical profession and the medical community's worst prejudices about the Hmong.

At the family practice clinic, the staff continued to marvel at the quality of care the Lees provided to their clean, sweet-smelling, well-groomed child. But at the hospital next door, where the nurses had had no contact with Lia since 1986, the case metastasized into a mass of complaints that grew angrier with each passing year. Why had the Lees been so ungrateful for their daughter's free medical care? (Neil—who did not share the nurses' resentment—once calculated that, over the years, Lia had cost the United States government about $250,000, not counting the salaries of her doctors, nurses, and social workers.) Why had the Lees always insisted on doing everything *their* way? Why—this was still the worst sin—had the Lees been noncompliant? As Sharon Yates, a nurse's aide, told me, "If only the parents had given Lia the medicine, she wouldn't be like this. I bet when she came back from that foster home, they just didn't give her any medicine."

But I knew that when she returned from foster care, Foua and Nao Kao *had* given Lia her medicine—4 ccs of Depakene, three times a day—exactly as prescribed. Hoping to clear up some questions about Lia's anticonvulsants, I went to Fresno to talk with Terry Hutchison, the pediatric neurologist who had overseen her care at Valley Children's Hospital. I had noticed that in one of his discharge notes, written nine months before her neurological crisis, he had described Lia as "a very pretty Hmong child" and her parents as "very interested and very good with Lia." I had never seen phrases like that in her MCMC chart.

Bill Selvidge had told me that Dr. Hutchison was "a known eccentric," beloved by his residents for his empathy but dreaded for his insistence on doing rounds at 4:00 A.M. He had an exiguous crewcut and on the day I met him was wearing a necktie decorated with a large bright-yellow giraffe. A sign in the hall outside his office, hung at toddler eye level, read:

KIDS ZONE
ENTER WITH CARE AND LOVE

When I asked him about the relationship between Lia's medications and her final seizure, he said, "Medications probably had nothing to do with it."

"Huh?" I said.

"Lia's brain was destroyed by septic shock, which was caused by the *Pseudomonas aeruginosa* bacillus in her blood. I don't know how Lia got it and I will never know. What I do know is that the septic shock caused the seizures, not the other way around. The fact that she had a preexisting seizure disorder probably made the status epilepticus worse or easier to start or whatever, but the seizures were incidental and not important. If Lia had not had seizures, she would have presented in a coma and shock, and the outcome would probably have been the same, except that her problem might have been more easily recognized. It was too late by the time she got to Valley Children's. It was probably too late by the time she got to MCMC."

"Did her parents' past noncompliance have anything to do with it?"

"Absolutely nothing. The only influence that medications could have had is that the Depakene we prescribed might have compromised her immune system and made her more susceptible to the *Pseudomonas*." (Depakene occasionally causes a drop in white blood cells that can hamper the body's ability to fight infection.) "I still believe Depakene was the drug of choice, and I would prescribe it again. But, in fact, if the family was giving her the Depakene as instructed, it is conceivable that by following our instructions, they set her up for septic shock."

"Lia's parents think that the problem was caused by too much medicine."

"Well," said Dr. Hutchison, "that may not be too far from the truth."

I stared at him.

"Go back to Merced," he said, "and tell all those people at MCMC that the family didn't do this to the kid. We did."

Driving back to Merced, I was in a state of shock myself. I had known about Lia's sepsis, but I had always assumed that her seizure disorder had been the root of the problem. *The Lees were right after all,* I thought. *Lia's medicine did make her sick!*

That night I told Neil and Peggy what Dr. Hutchison had said. As usual, their desire to ferret out the truth outweighed their desire—if indeed they had one—to defend their reputation for infallibility. They immediately asked for my photocopy of Lia's medical chart, and they sat together on Bill Selvidge's sofa, combing Volume 5 for evidence, overlooked during the crisis, that Lia might already have been septic at MCMC. Murmuring to each other in their shared secret language ("calcium 3.2," "platelets 29,000," "hemoglobin 8.4"), they might have been—in fact, were—a pair of lovers exchanging a set of emotionally charged intimacies.

"I always thought Lia got septic down at Children's when they put all those invasive lines in," said Peggy. "But maybe not. There are some signs here."

"I did too," said Neil. "If I'd thought she was septic here at MCMC, I would have done a lumbar puncture. I didn't start her on antibiotics because every single time Lia had come in before that, she was not septic. Every other time, the problem was her seizure disorder, and this was obviously the worst seizure of her life. I stabilized her, I arranged for her transport, and then I went home before all the lab results were back." He didn't sound defensive. He sounded curious.

After Neil and Peggy went home, I asked Bill Selvidge whether he thought Neil had made a mistake in not recognizing and treating Lia's sepsis, even though Dr. Hutchison believed that her fate was probably sealed before she arrived in the MCMC emergency room—and even though the increasing severity of her epilepsy might eventually have led to serious brain damage if sepsis had never entered the picture.

"Neil leaves no stone unturned," said Bill. "If Neil made a mistake, it's because every physician makes mistakes. If it had been a brand-new kid walking off the street, I guarantee you Neil would have done a septic workup and he would have caught it. But this was Lia. *No one* at MCMC would have noticed anything but her seizures. Lia *was* her seizures."

To MCMC's residents, Lia continued to be her seizures—the memory of those terrifying nights in the emergency room that had taught them how to intubate or start IVs or perform venous cutdowns. They always spoke of Lia in the past tense. In fact, Neil and Peggy themselves frequently referred to "Lia's demise," or "what may have killed Lia" or "the reason Lia died." Dr. Hutchison did the same thing. He had asked me, "Was Lia with the foster parents when she died?" And although I reminded him that Lia was alive, five minutes later he said, "Noncompliance had nothing to do with her death." It wasn't just absentmindedness. It was an admission of defeat. Lia was dead to her physicians (in a way, for example, that she was never dead to her social workers) because medicine had once made extravagant claims on her behalf and had had to renounce them.

Once I asked Neil if he wished he had done anything differently. He answered as I expected, focusing not on his relationship with the Lees but on his choice of medication. "I wish we'd used Depakene sooner," he said. "I wish I'd accepted that it would be easier for the family to comply with one medicine instead of three, even if three seemed medically optimal."

Then I asked, "Do you wish you had never met Lia?"

"Oh, no, no, no!" His vehemence surprised me. "Once I might have said yes, but not in retrospect. Lia taught me that when there is a very dense cultural barrier, you do the best you can, and if something happens despite that, you have to be satisfied with little successes instead of total successes. You have to give up total control. That is very hard for me, but I do try. I think Lia made me into a less rigid person."

The next time I saw Foua, I asked her whether she had learned anything from what had happened. "No," she said. "I haven't learned. I just feel confused." She was feeding Lia at the time, making baby noises as she spooned puréed *zaub* the spinachlike green she grew in the parking lot, into the slack mouth. "I don't understand how the doctors can say she is going to be like this for the rest of her life, and yet they can't fix her. How can they know the future but not know how to change it? I don't understand that."

"Well, what do *you* think Lia's future will hold?" I asked.

"I don't know these things," said Foua. "I am not a doctor. I am not a *txiv neeb*. But maybe Lia will stay hurt like this, and that makes me cry about what will happen. I gave birth to Lia, so I will always take care of her with all my heart. But when her father and I pass away, who will take care of Lia? Lia's sisters do love her, but even though they love her, maybe they will not be able to take care of her. Maybe they will need to study too hard and work too hard. I am crying to think that they are just going to give Lia away to the Americans." Foua wept soundlessly. May Ying embraced her and stroked her hair.

"I know where the Americans put children like Lia," she continued. "I saw a place like that in Fresno where they took Lia once, a long time ago." (Foua was recalling a chronic care facility for retarded and disabled children where Lia had been temporarily placed, before her year in foster care, while her medications were monitored and stabilized.) "It was like a house for the dead. The children were so poor and so sad that they just cried. They cried all over. One child had a big head and a really small body. Other children had legs that were all dried up and they just fell on the floor. I have seen this. If the Americans take Lia there she will want to die, but instead she will suffer."

Foua brushed her tears from her cheeks with the back of her hand, in a quick, brusque gesture. Then she wiped Lia's mouth, far more gently, and slowly started to rock her. "I am very sad," she said, "and I think a lot that if we were still in Laos and not in the United States, maybe Lia would never be like this. The doctors are very very knowledgeable, your high doctors, your best doctors, but maybe they made a mistake by giving her the wrong medicine and they made her hurt like this. If it was a *dab* that made Lia sick like this in Laos, we would know how to go to the forest and get herbs to fix her and maybe she could be able to speak. But this happened here in the United States, and Americans have done this to her, and our medicine cannot fix that."

It was also true that if the Lees were still in Laos, Lia would probably have died before she was out of her infancy, from a prolonged bout of untreated status epilepticus. American medicine had both preserved her life and compromised it. I was unsure which had hurt her family more.

Since that night with Foua, I have replayed the story over and over again, wondering if anything could have made it turn out differently. Despite Dr. Hutchison's revisionist emendation of the final chapter, no one could deny that if the Lees had given Lia her anticonvulsants from the beginning, she might have had—might still be having—something approaching a normal life. What was not clear was who, if anyone, should be held accountable. What if Neil *had* prescribed Depakene earlier? What if, instead of placing Lia in foster care, he had arranged for a visiting nurse to administer her medications? What if he had sought out Blia Yao Moua or Jonas Vangay or another Hmong leader who straddled both cultures, and had asked him to intervene with the Lees, thus transferring the issue of compliance to a less suspect source? What if MCMC had had better interpreters?

When I presented my "what if" list to Dan Murphy one day in the MCMC cafeteria, he was less interested in the Depakene than in the interpreters. However, he believed that the gulf between the Lees and their doctors was unbridgeable, and that nothing could have been done to change the outcome. "Until I met Lia," he said, "I thought if you had a problem you could always settle it if you just sat and talked long enough. But we could have talked to the Lees until we were blue in the face—we could have sent the Lees to *medical school* with the world's greatest translator—and they would still think their way was right and ours was wrong." Dan slowly stirred his lukewarm cocoa; he had been on all-night call. "Lia's case ended my idealistic way of looking at the world."

Was the gulf unbridgeable? I kept returning, obsessively, to the Lees' earliest encounters with MCMC during Lia's infancy, when no interpreters were present and her epilepsy was misdiagnosed as pneumonia. Instead of practicing "veterinary medicine," what if the residents in the emergency room had managed to elicit the Lees' trust at the outset—or at least managed not to crush it—by finding out what *they* believed, feared, and hoped? Jeanine Hilt had asked them for their version of the story, but no doctor ever had. Martin Kilgore had tried, but by then it was years too late.

Of course, the Lees' perspective might have been as unfathomable to the doctors as the doctors' perspective was to the Lees. Hmong culture, as Blia Yao Moua observed to me, is not Cartesian. Nothing could be more Cartesian than Western medicine. Trying to understand Lia and her family by reading her medical chart (something I spent hundreds of hours doing) was like deconstructing a love sonnet by reducing it to a series of syllogisms. Yet to the residents and pediatricians who had cared for her since she was three months old, there was no guide to Lia's world *except* her chart. As each of them struggled to make sense of a set of problems that were not expressible in the language they knew, the chart simply grew longer and longer, until it contained more than 400,000 words. Every one of those words reflected its author's intelligence, training, and good intentions, but not a single one dealt with the Lees' perception of their daughter's illness.

Almost every discussion of cross-cultural medicine that I had ever read quoted a set of eight questions, designed to elicit a patient's "explanatory model," which were developed by Arthur Kleinman, a psychiatrist and medical anthropologist who chairs the department of social medicine at Harvard Medical School. The first few times I read these questions they seemed so obvious I hardly noticed them; around the fiftieth time, I began to think that, like many obvious things, they might actually be a work of genius. I recently decided to call Kleinman to tell him how I thought the Lees might have answered his questions after Lia's earliest seizures, before any medications had been administered, resisted, or blamed, if they had had a good interpreter and had felt sufficiently at ease to tell the truth. To wit:

1. What do you call the problem?
Qang dab peg. That means the spirit catches you and you fall down.

2. What do you think has caused the problem?
Soul loss.

3. Why do you think it started when it did?
Lia's sister Yer slammed the door and Lia's soul was frightened out of her body.

4. What do you think the sickness does? How does it work?
It makes Lia shake and fall down. It works because a spirit called a *dab* is catching her.

5. How severe is the sickness? Will it have a short or long course?
Why are you asking us those questions? If you are a good doctor, you should know the answers yourself.

6. What kind of treatment do you think the patient should receive? What are the most important results you hope she receives from this treatment?
You should give Lia medicine to take for a week but no longer. After she is well, she should stop taking the medicine. You should not treat her by taking her blood or the fluid from her backbone. Lia should also be treated at home with our Hmong medicines and by sacrificing pigs and chickens. We hope Lia will be healthy, but we are not sure we want her to stop shaking forever because it makes her noble in our culture, and when she grows up she might become a shaman.

7. What are the chief problems the sickness has caused?
It has made us sad to see Lia hurt, and it has made us angry at Yer.

8. What do you fear most about the sickness?
That Lia's soul will never return.

I thought Kleinman would consider these responses so bizarre that he would be at a loss for words. (When I had presented this same material, more or less, to Neil and Peggy, they had said, "Mr. and Mrs. Lee thought *what*?") But after each answer, he said, with great enthusiasm, "Right!" Nothing surprised him; everything delighted him. From his vantage point, a physician could encounter no more captivating a patient than Lia, no finer a set of parents than the Lees.

Then I told him what had happened later—the Lees' noncompliance with

Lia's anticonvulsant regimen, the foster home, the neurological cat
and asked him if he had any retroactive suggestions for her pediatric

"I have three," he said briskly. "First, get rid of the term 'complianc
a lousy term. It implies moral hegemony. You don't want a command fro
general, you want a colloquy. Second, instead of looking at a model of coer
cion, look at a model of mediation. Go find a member of the Hmong community, or go find a medical anthropologist, who can help you negotiate. Remember that a stance of mediation, like a divorce proceeding, requires compromise on both sides. Decide what's critical and be willing to compromise on everything else. Third, you need to understand that as powerful an influence as the culture of the Hmong patient and her family is on this case, the culture of biomedicine is equally powerful. If you can't see that your own culture has its own set of interests, emotions, and biases, how can you expect to deal successfully with someone else's culture?"

Berry

EMBERSHIP

Farmer, novelist, poet, and essayist Wendell Berry writes about the time his brother John had a heart attack and was rushed to the hospital, and his reflections on medicine as his brother underwent treatment. "In the hospital," Berry notes, "what I will call the world of love meets the world of efficiency—the world, that is, of specialization, machinery, and abstract procedure." The essay questions why these two worlds come together but do not meet.

WENDELL BERRY has been called "America's Tolstoy" by the *Boston Globe.* Berry is the author of more than thirty books, including *The Gift of Good Land, Home Economics,* and *What Are People For?* This essay is taken from a collection of essays titled *Another Turn of the Crank.*

On January 3, 1994, my brother John had a severe heart attack while he was out by himself on his farm, moving a feed trough. He managed to get to the house and telephone a friend, who sent the emergency rescue squad.

The rescue squad and the emergency room staff at a local hospital certainly saved my brother's life. He was later moved to a hospital in Louisville, where a surgeon performed a double-bypass operation on his heart. After three weeks

John returned home. He still has a life to live and work to do. He has been restored to himself and to the world.

He and those who love him have a considerable debt to the medical industry, as represented by two hospitals, several doctors and nurses, many drugs and many machines. This is a debt that I cheerfully acknowledge. But I am obliged to say also that my experience of the hospital during John's stay was troubled by much conflict of feeling and a good many unresolved questions, and I know that I am not alone in this.

In the hospital what I will call the world of love meets the world of efficiency—the world, that is, of specialization, machinery, and abstract procedure. Or, rather, I should say that these two worlds come together in the hospital but do not meet. During those weeks when John was in the hospital, it seemed to me that he had come from the world of love and that the family members, neighbors, and friends who at various times were there with him came there to represent that world and to preserve his connection with it. It seemed to me that the hospital was another kind of world altogether. . . .

Like divine love, earthly love seeks plenitude; it longs for the full membership to be present and to be joined. Unlike divine love, earthly love does not have the power, the knowledge, or the will to achieve what it longs for. The story of human love on this earth is a story by which this love reveals and even validates itself by its failures to be complete and comprehensive and effective enough. When this love enters a hospital, it brings with it a terrifying history of defeat, but it comes nevertheless confident of itself, for its existence and the power of its longing have been proved over and over again even by its defeat. In the face of illness, the threat of death, and death itself, it insists unabashedly on its own presence, understanding by its persistence through defeat that it is superior to whatever happens.

The world of efficiency ignores both loves, earthly and divine, because by definition it must reduce experience to computation, particularity to abstraction, and mystery to a small comprehensibility. Efficiency, in our present sense of the word, allies itself inevitably with machinery, as Neil Postman demonstrates in his useful book, *Technopoly*. "Machines," he says, "eliminate complexity, doubt, and ambiguity. They work swiftly, they are standardized, and they provide us with numbers that you can see and calculate with." To reason, the advantages are obvious, and probably no reasonable person would wish to reject them out of hand.

And yet love obstinately answers that no loved one is standardized. A body, love insists, is neither a spirit nor a machine; it is not a picture, a diagram, a chart, a graph, an anatomy; it is not an explanation; it is not a law. It is precisely and uniquely what it is. It belongs to the world of love, which is a world of living creatures, natural orders and cycles, many small, fragile lights in the dark.

In dealing with problems of agriculture, I had thought much about the difference between creatures and machines. But I had never so clearly understood and felt that difference as when John was in recovery after his heart surgery, when he was attached to many machines and was dependent for breath on a respirator. It was impossible then not to see that the breathing of a machine, like all machine work, is unvarying, an oblivious regularity, whereas the breathing of a creature is ever changing, exquisitely responsive to events both inside and outside the body, to thoughts and emotions. A machine makes breaths as a machine makes buttons, all the same, but every breath of a creature is itself a creature, like no other, inestimably precious.

Logically, in plenitude some things ought to be expendable. Industrial economics has always believed this: abundance justifies waste. This is one of the dominant superstitions of American history—and of the history of colonialism everywhere. Expendability is also an assumption of the world of efficiency, which is why that world deals so compulsively in percentages of efficacy and safety.

But this sort of logic is absolutely alien to the world of love. To the claim that a certain drug or procedure would save 99 percent of all cancer patients or that a certain pollutant would be safe for 99 percent of a population, love, unembarrassed, would respond, "What about the one percent?"

There is nothing rational or perhaps even defensible about this, but it is nonetheless one of the strongest strands of our religious tradition—it is probably the most essential strand—according to which a shepherd, owning a hundred sheep and having lost one, does not say, "I have saved 99 percent of my sheep," but rather, "I have lost one," and he goes and searches for the one. And if the sheep in that parable may seem to be only a metaphor, then go on to the Gospel of Luke, where the principle is flatly set forth again and where the sparrows stand not for human beings but for all creatures: "Are not five sparrows sold for two farthings, and not one of them is forgotten before God?" And John Donne had in mind a sort of equation and not a mere metaphor when he wrote, "If a clod be washed away by the sea, Europe is the less, as well as if a promontory were, as well as if a manor of thy friend's or of thine own were. Any man's death diminishes me."

It is reassuring to see ecology moving toward a similar idea of the order of things. If an ecosystem loses one of its native species, we now know that we cannot speak of it as itself minus one species. An ecosystem minus one species is a different ecosystem. Just so, each of us is made by—or, one might better say, made as—a set of unique associations with unique persons, places, and things. The world of love does not admit the principle of the interchangeability of parts.

When John was in intensive care after his surgery, his wife, Carol, was standing by his bed, grieving and afraid. Wanting to reassure her, the nurse said, "Nothing is happening to him that doesn't happen to everybody."

And Carol replied, "I'm not everybody's wife."

In the world of love, things separated by efficiency and specialization strive to come back together. And yet love must confront death, and accept it, and learn from it. Only in confronting death can earthly love learn its true extent, its immortality. Any definition of health that is not silly must include death. The world of love includes death, suffers it, and triumphs over it. The world of efficiency is defeated by death; at death, all its instruments and procedures stop. The world of love continues, and of this grief is the proof.

In the hospital, love cannot forget death. But like love, death is in the hospital but not of it. Like love, fear and grief feel out of place in the hospital. How could they be included in its efficient procedures and mechanisms? Where a clear, small order is fervently maintained, fear and grief bring the threat of large disorder.

And so these two incompatible worlds might also be designated by the terms "amateur" and "professional"—amateur, in the literal sense of lover, one who participates for love; and professional in the modern sense of one who performs highly specialized or technical procedures for pay. The amateur is excluded from the professional "field."

For the amateur, in the hospital or in almost any other encounter with the medical industry, the overriding experience is that of being excluded from knowledge—of being unable, in other words, to make or participate in anything resembling an "informed decision." Of course, whether doctors make informed decisions in the hospital is a matter of debate. For in the hospital even the professionals are involved in experience; experimentation has been left far behind. Experience, as all amateurs know, is not predictable, and in experience there are no replications or "controls"; there is nothing with which to compare the result. Once one decision has been made, we have destroyed the opportunity to know what would have happened if another decision had been made. That is to say that medicine is an exact science until applied; application involves intuition, a sense of probability, "gut feeling," guesswork, and error.

In medicine, as in many modern disciplines, the amateur is divided from the professional by perhaps unbridgeable differences of knowledge and of language. An "informed decision" is really not even imaginable for most medical patients and their families, who have no competent understanding of either the patient's illness or the recommended medical or surgical procedure. Moreover, patients and their families are not likely to know the doctor, the surgeon, or any of the other people on whom the patient's life will depend. In the hospital, amateurs are more than likely to be proceeding entirely upon faith—and this is a peculiar and scary faith, for it must be placed not in a god but in mere people, mere procedures, mere chemicals, and mere machines.

It was only after my brother had been taken into surgery, I think, that the family understood the extremity of this deed of faith. We had decided—or John had decided and we had concurred—on the basis of the best advice available. But once he was separated from us, we felt the burden of our ignorance. We had not known what we were doing, and one of our difficulties now was the feeling that we had utterly given him up to what we did not know. John himself spoke out of this sense of abandonment and helplessness in the intensive care unit, when he said, "I don't know what they're going to do to me or for me or with me."

As we waited and reports came at long intervals from the operating room, other realizations followed. We realized that under the circumstances, we could not be told the truth. We would not know, ever, the worries and surprises that came to the surgeon during his work. We would not know the critical moments or the fears. If the surgeon did any part of his work ineptly or made a mistake, we would not know it. We realized, moreover, that if we were told the truth, we would have no way of knowing that the truth was what it was.

We realized that when the emissaries from the operating room assured us that everything was "normal" or "routine," they were referring to the procedure and not the patient. Even as amateurs—perhaps *because* we were amateurs—we knew that what was happening was not normal or routine for John or for us.

That these two worlds are so radically divided does not mean that people cannot cross between them. I do not know how an amateur can cross over into the professional world; that does not seem very probable. But that professional people can cross back into the amateur world, I know from much evidence. During John's stay in the hospital there were many moments in which doctors and nurses—especially nurses!—allowed or caused the professional relationship to become a meeting between two human beings, and these moments were invariably moving.

The most moving, to me, happened in the waiting room during John's surgery. From time to time a nurse from the operating room would come in to tell Carol what was happening. Carol, from politeness or bravery or both, always stood to receive the news, which always left us somewhat encouraged and somewhat doubtful. Carol's difficulty was that she had to suffer the ordeal not only as a wife but as one who had been a trained nurse. She knew, from her own education and experience, in how limited a sense open-heart surgery could be said to be normal or routine.

Finally, toward the end of our wait, two nurses came in. The operation, they said, had been a success. They explained again what had been done. And then they said that after the completion of the bypasses, the surgeon had found it necessary to insert a "balloon pump" into the aorta to assist the heart. This possibility had never been mentioned, nobody was prepared for it, and Carol was sorely disappointed and upset. The two young women attempted to reassure her, mainly by repeating things they had already said. And then there was a long moment when they just looked at her. It was such a look as parents sometimes give to a sick or suffering child, when they themselves have begun to need the comfort they are trying to give.

And then one of the nurses said, "Do you need a hug?"

"Yes," Carol said.

And the nurse gave her a hug.

Which brings us to a starting place.

Kay Redfield Jamison

from AN UNQUIET MIND

Psychiatrist Kay Jamison bravely writes of her own manic depression in a book that has been called "one of the best scientific autobiographies ever written." In this excerpt, Jamison, listens as a speaker at a medical conference blandly offers an update on "structural brain abnormalities in bipolar illness." The speaker also shows slides of the brain taken with the newest technologies. Jamison contemplates "the personal side of having manic-depressive illness" and "the professional role of studying and treating it."

KAY REDFIELD JAMISON is the founder of UCLA's Affective Disorder Clinic. She is the author of *Night Fall Fast: Understanding Suicide* and *Touched with Fire: Manic Depressive Illness and the Artistic Temperament.*

Sitting on one of the hard, uncomfortable chairs that are so characteristic of medical conferences, I was semi-oblivious to the world. My mind was on hold after having been lulled into a mild hypnotic state by the click, click, click of the changing of slides in a carousel. My eyes were open, but my brain was swaying gently in its hammock, tucked away in the far back reaches of my skull. It was dark and stuffy in the room, but beautiful and snowing outside. A group of my colleagues and I were in the Colorado Rockies, and anyone with any sense at all was skiing; yet there were more than a hundred doctors in the room, and the slides were going click, click, click. I caught myself thinking, for the hundredth time, that being crazy doesn't necessarily mean being stupid, and what on earth was I doing indoors instead of being out on the slopes? Suddenly, my ears perked up. A flat, numbingly objective voice was mumbling something about giving an "update on structural brain abnormalities in bipolar illness." My structurally abnormal brain came to attention, and a chill shot down my spine. The mumbling continued: "In the bipolar patients we have studied, there is a significantly increased number of small areas of focal signal hyperintensities [areas of increased water concentration] suggestive of abnormal tissue. These are what neurologists sometimes refer to as 'unidentified bright objects,' or UBOs." The audience laughed appreciatively.

I, who could ill afford any more loss of brain tissue—God knows what little chunks of gray matter had crossed the River Styx after my nearly lethal lithium overdose—laughed with somewhat less than total enthusiasm. The speaker went on, "The medical significance of these UBOs is unclear, but we know that they are associated with other conditions, such as Alzheimer's, multiple sclerosis, and multi-infarct dementias." I was right; I should have gone skiing. Against my better judgment, I pointed my head in the direction of the screen. The slides were riveting, and, as always, I was captivated by the unbelievable detail of the structure of the brain that was revealed by the newest versions of MRI techniques. There is a beauty and an intuitive appeal to the brain-scanning methods, especially the high-resolution MRI pictures and the gorgeous multicolored scans from the PET studies. With PET, for example, a depressed brain will show up in cold, brain-inactive deep blues, dark purples, and hunter greens; the same brain when hypomanic, however, is lit up like a Christmas tree, with vivid patches of bright reds and yellows and oranges. Never has the color and structure of science so completely captured the cold inward deadness of depression or the vibrant, active engagement of mania.

There is a wonderful kind of excitement in modern neuroscience, a romantic, moon-walk sense of exploring and setting out for new frontiers. The science is elegant, the scientists dismayingly young, and the pace of discovery absolutely staggering. Like the molecular biologists, the brain-scanners are generally well aware of the extraordinary frontiers they are crossing, and it would take a mind that is on empty, or a heart made of stone, to be unmoved by their collective ventures and enthusiasms.

I was, in spite of myself, caught up by the science, wondering whether these hyperintensities were the cause or the effect of illness, whether they became more pronounced over time, where in the brain they localized, whether they were related to the problems in spatial orientation and facial recognition that I and many other manic-depressives experience, and whether children who were at risk for manic-depressive illness, because one or both of their parents had the disease, would show these brain abnormalities even before they became ill. The clinical side of my mind began to mull about the visual advantages of these and other imaging findings in convincing some of my more literary and skeptical patients that (a) there *is* a brain, (b) their moods are related to their brains, and (c) there may be specific brain-damaging effects of going off their medications. These speculations kept me distracted for a while, as changing gears from the personal side of having manic-depressive illness to the professional role of studying and treating it often does. But, invariably, the personal interest and concerns returned.

When I got back to Johns Hopkins, where I was now teaching, I buttonholed neurology colleagues and grilled my associates who were doing the MRI studies. I scurried off to the library to read up on what was known; it is, after all, one thing to believe intellectually that this disease is in your brain; it is quite another thing to actually see it. Even the titles of some of the articles were a bit ungluing: "Basal Ganglia Volumes and White Matter Hyperintensities in Patients with Bipolar Disorder," "Structural Brain Abnormalities in Bipolar Affective Disorder: Ventricular Enlargement and Focal Signal Hyperintensities," "Subcortical Abnormalities Detected in Bipolar Affective Disorders, Using Magnetic Resonance Imaging"; on and on they went. I sat down to read. One study found that "Of the 32 scans of the patients with bipolar disorder, 11 (34.4%) showed hyperintensities, while only one scan (3.2%) from the normal comparison group contained such abnormalities."

After an inward snort about "normal comparison group," I read on and found that, as usual in new fields of clinical medicine, there were far more questions than answers, and it was unclear what any of these findings really meant: they could be due to problems in measurement, they could be explained by dietary or treatment history, they could be due to something totally unrelated to manic-depressive illness; there could be any number of other explanations. The odds were very strong, however, that the UBOs meant *something*. In a strange way, though, after reading through a long series of studies, I ended up more reassured and less frightened. The very fact that the science was moving so quickly had a way of generating hope, and, if the changes in the brain structure did turn out to be meaningful, I was glad that first-class researchers were studying them. Without science, there would be no such hope. No hope at all.

And, whatever else, it certainly gave new meaning to the concept of losing one's mind.

Robert Coles

A YOUNG PSYCHIATRIST LOOKS AT HIS PROFESSION

from The Mind's Fate

In this essay, a young doctor in psychiatric and psychoanalytic training is looking at the profession he has just entered. First published in the *Atlantic Monthly* in 1961 when he was just beginning his psychiatry practice, Robert Coles wrote that those involved in psychiatry must strive to avoid "a death of the heart," to avoid becoming numbed by the work they do; instead, they must keep their hearts alive, vitally engaged with and by those they treat.

ROBERT COLES'S most recent works include a literary anthology titled *Growing Up Poor* and *Lives of Moral Leadership*. This essay is taken from a collection of Coles's essays titled *The Mind's Fate*.

Recently, in the emergency ward of the Children's Hospital in Boston, an eight-year-old girl walked in and asked to talk to a psychiatrist about her "worries." I was called to the ward, and when we ended our conversation I was awake with sorrow and hope for this young girl, but also astonished at her coming. As a child psychiatrist, I was certainly accustomed to the troubled mother who brings her child to a hospital for any one of a wide variety of emotional problems. It was the child's initiative in coming which surprised me. I recalled a story my wife had told me. She was teaching a ninth-grade English class, and they were starting to read the Sophoclean tragedy of *Oedipus*. A worldly thirteen-year-old asked the first question: "What is an Oedipus complex?" Somehow, in our time, psychiatrists have become the heirs of those who hear the worried and see the curious. I wondered, then, what other children in other times did with their troubles and how they talked of the Greeks. I wondered, too, about my own profession, its position and its problems, and about the answers we might have for ourselves as psychiatrists.

We appear in cartoons, on television serials, and in the movies. We are "applied" by Madison Avenue, and we "influence" writers. Acting techniques, even schools of painting are supposed to be derived from our insights, and Freud has become what Auden calls "a whole climate of opinion." Since children respond so fully to what is most at hand in the adult world, there should have been no reason for my surprise in that emergency ward. But this quick acceptance of us by children and adults alike is ironic, tells us something about this world, and is dangerous.

The irony is that we no longer resemble the small band of outcasts upon whom epithets were hurled for years. One forgets today just how rebellious Freud and his contemporaries were. They studied archaelogy and mythology, were versed in the ancient languages, wrote well, and were a bit fiery, a bit eccentric, a bit troublesome, even for one another. Opinionated, determined, oblivious of easy welcome, they were fighters for their beliefs, and their ideas fought much of what the world then thought.

This is a different world. People today are frightened by the memory of concentration camps, by the possibility of atomic war, by the breakdown of old empires and old ways of living and believing. Each person shares the hopes and terrors peculiar to this age, not an age of reason or of enlightenment, but an age of fear and trembling. Every year brings problems undreamed of only a decade ago in New York or Vienna. Cultures change radically, values are different, even diseases change. For instance, cases of hysteria, so beautifully described by Freud, are rarely found today. A kind of innocence is lost; people now are less suggestible, less naive, more devious. They look for help from many sources, and chief among them, psychiatrists. Erich Fromm, in honor of Paul Tillich's seventy-fifth birthday, remarked: "Modern man is lonely, frightened, and hardly capable of love. He wants to be close to his neighbor, and yet he is too unrelated and distant to be able to be close. . . . In search for closeness he craves knowledge; and in search for knowledge he finds psychology. Psychology becomes a substitute for love, for intimacy. . . ."

Now Freud and his knights are dead. Their long fight has won acclaim and increasing protection from a once reluctant society, and perhaps we should expect this ebb tide. Our very acclaim makes us more rigid and querulous. We are rent by rivalries, and early angers or stubborn idiosyncrasies have hardened into a variety of schools with conflicting ideas. We use proper names of early psychiatrists—Jung, Rank, Horney—to describe the slightest differences of emphasis or theory. The public is interested, but understandably confused. If it is any comfort to the public, so are psychiatrists, at times. Most of us can recall our moments of arrogance, only thinly disguised by words which daily become more like shibboleths, sound hollow, and are almost cant.

Ideas need the backing of institutions and firm social approval if they are to result in practical application. Yet I see pharisaic temples being built everywhere in psychiatry; pick up our journals and you will see meetings listed almost every week of the year and pages filled with the abstracts of papers presented at them. These demand precious time in attendance and reading, and such time is squandered all too readily these days. Who of us, even scanting sleep, can keep up with this monthly tidal wave of minute or repetitive studies? And who among us doesn't smile or shrug, as he skims the pages, and suddenly leap with hunger at the lonely monograph that really says something? As psychiatrists we need to be in touch not only with our patients but with the entire range of human activity. We need time to see a play or read a poem, yet daily we sit tied to our chairs, listening and talking for hours on end. While this is surely a problem for all professions, it is particularly deadening for one which deals so intimately with people and which requires that its members themselves be alive and alert.

It seems to me that psychiatric institutions and societies too soon become bureaucracies, emphasizing form, detail and compliance. They also breed the idea that legislation or grants of money for expansion of laboratories and buildings will provide answers where true knowledge is lacking. Whereas we desperately need more money for facilities and training for treatment programs, there can be a vicious circle of more dollars for more specialized projects producing more articles about less and less, and it may be that some projects are contrived to attract money and expand institutions rather than to form any spontaneous intellectual drive. We argue longer and harder about incidentals, such as whether our patients should sit up or lie down; whether we should accept or reject their gifts or answer their letters; how our offices should be decorated; or how we should talk to patients when they arrive or leave. We debate for hours about the difference between psychoanalysis and psychotherapy; about the advantages of seeing a person twice a week or three times a week; about whether we should give medications to people, and if so, in what way. For the plain fact is that, as we draw near the bureaucratic and the institutionalized, we draw near quibbling. Maybe it is too late, and much of this cannot be stopped. But it may be pleasantly nostalgic, if not instructive, to recall Darwin sailing on the *Beagle*, or Freud writing spirited letters of discovery to a close friend, or Sir Alexander Fleming stumbling upon a model of penicillin in his laboratory—all in so simple and creative a fashion, and all with so little red tape and money.

If some of psychiatry's problems come from its position in the kind of society we have, other troubles are rooted in the very nature of our job. We labor with people who have troubled thoughts and feelings, who go awry in bed or in the office or with friends. Though we talk a great deal about our scientific interests, man's thoughts and feelings cannot be as easily understood or manipulated as atoms. The brain is where we think and receive impressions of the world, and it is in some ultimate sense an aggregate of atoms and molecules. In time we will know more about how to control and transform all cellular life, and at some point the cells of the brain will be known in all their intricate functions. What we now call "ego" or "unconscious" will be understood in terms of cellular action or biochemical and biophysical activity. The logic of the nature of all matter predicts that someday we will be able to arrange and rearrange ideas and feelings. Among the greatest mysteries before us are the unmarked pathways running from the peripheral nervous system to the thinking areas in the brain. The future is even now heralded by machines which think and by drugs which stimulate emotional states or affect specific moods, like depressions. Until these roads are thoroughly surveyed and the brain is completely understood, psychiatry will be as pragmatic or empirical as medicine.

Social scientists have taught us a great deal about how men think and how they get along with one another and develop from infancy to full age. We have learned ways of reaching people with certain problems and can offer much help to some of them. Often we can understand illnesses that we cannot so readily treat. With medicines, we can soften the lacerations of nervousness and fear, producing no solutions, but affording some peace and allowing the mind to seek further aid. Some hospitals now offer carefully planned communities where new friendships can arise, refuges where the unhappy receive individual medical and psychiatric attention. Clinics, though harried by small staffs and increasing requests, offer daily help for a variety of mental illnesses. Children come to centers devoted to the study and treatment of early emotional difficulties. If the etiologies are still elusive, the results of treatment are often considerable. Failures are glaring, but the thousands of desperate people who are helped are sometimes overlooked because of their very recovery. Indeed, it is possible that our present problems may give way to worse ones as we get to know more. The enormous difficulties of finding out about the neurophysiology of emotional life may ultimately yield to the Orwellian dilemma of a society in which physicists of the mind can change thoughts and control feelings at their will.

However, right now I think our most pressing concern is less the matter of our work than the manner of ourselves. For the individual psychiatrist, the institutional rigidities affect his thoughts and attitudes, taint his words and feelings, and thereby his ability to treat patients. We become victims of what we most dread; our sensibilities die, and we no longer care or notice. We dread death of the heart—any heart under any moon. Yet I see Organization Men in psychiatry, with all the problems of deathlike conformity. Independent thinking by the adventurous has declined; psychiatric training has become more formal, more preoccupied with certificates and diplomas, more hierarchical. Some of the finest people in early dynamic psychiatry were artists, like Erik Erikson, schoolteachers, like August Aichhorn, or those, like Anna Freud, who had no formal training or occupation but motivations as personal as those of a brilliant and loyal daughter. Today we are obsessed with accreditation, recognition, levels of training, with status as scientists. These are the preoccupations of young psychiatrists. There are more lectures, more supervision, more examinations for specialty status, and thus the profession soon attracts people who take to these practices. Once there were the curious and bold; now there are the carefully well-adjusted and certified.

When the heart dies, we slip into wordy and doctrinaire caricatures of life.

Our journals, our habits of talk become cluttered with jargon or the trivial. There are negative cathects, libido quanta, "presymbiotic, normal-autistic phases of mother-infant unity," and "a hierarchically stratified, firmly cathected organization of self-representations." Such dross is excused as a short cut to understanding a complicated message by those versed in the trade; its practitioners call on the authority of symbolic communication in the sciences. But the real test is whether we best understand by this strange proliferation of language the worries, fears, or loves in individual people. As the words grow longer and the concepts more intricate and tedious, human sorrows and temptations disappear, loves move away, envies and jealousies, revenge and terror dissolve. Gone are strong, sensible words with good meaning and the flavor of the real. Freud called Dostoevski the greatest psychologist of all time, and long ago Euripides described in *Medea* the hurt of the mentally ill. Perhaps we cannot expect to describe our patients with the touching accuracy and poetry used for Lady Macbeth or Hamlet or King Lear, but surely there are sparks to be kindled, cries to be heard, from people who are individuals.

If we become cold, and our language frosty, then our estrangement is complete. Living in an unreliable world, often lonely, and for this reason attracted to psychiatry as a job with human contacts, we embrace icy reasoning and abstractions, a desperate shadow of the real friendships which we once desired. Estrangement may, indeed, thread through the entire fabric of our professional lives in America. Cartoons show us pre-empted by the wealthy. A recent study from Yale by Doctor Redlich shows how few people are reached by psychiatrists, how much a part of the class and caste system in America we are. Separated from us are all the troubled people in villages and farms from Winesburg to Yoknapatawpha. Away from us are the wretched drunks and the youthful gangs in the wilderness of our cities. Removed from us are most of the poor, the criminal, the drug addicts. Though there are some low-cost clinics, their waiting lists are long, and we are all too easily and too often available to the select few of certain streets and certain neighborhoods.

Whereas in Europe the theologian or artist shares intimately with psychiatrists, we stand apart from them, afraid to recognize our common heritage. European psychiatry mingles with philosophers; produces Karl Jaspers, a psychiatrist who is a theologian, or Sartre, a novelist and philosopher who writes freely and profoundly about psychiatry. After four years of psychiatric training in a not uncultured city, I begin to wonder whether young psychiatrists in

America are becoming isolated by an arbitrary definition of what is, in fact, our work. Our work is the human condition, and we might do well to talk with Reinhold Niebuhr about the "nature and destiny of man," or with J. D. Salinger about our Holden Caulfields. Perhaps we are too frightened and too insecure to recognize our very brothers. This is a symptom of the estranged.

In some way our hearts must live. If we truly live, we will talk clearly and avoid the solitary trek. In some way we must manage to blend poetic insight with a craft and unite intimately the rational and the intuitive, the aloof stance of the scholar with the passion and affection of the friend who cares and is moved. It seems to me that this is the oldest summons in the history of Western civilization. We can answer this request only with some capacity for risk, dare, and whim. Thwarting us at every turn of life is the ageless fear of uncertainty; it is hard to risk the unknown. If we see a patient who puzzles us, we can avoid the mystery and challenge of the unique through readily available diagnostic categories. There is no end to classifications and terminologies, but the real end for us may be the soul of man, lost in these words: "Name it and it's so, or call it and it's real." This is the language of children faced with a confusion of the real and unreal, and it is ironic, if human, to see so much of this same habit still among psychiatrists.

Perhaps, if we dared to be free, more would be revealed than we care to admit. I sometimes wonder why we do not have a journal in our profession which publishes anonymous contributions. We might then hear and feel more of the real give-and-take in all those closed offices, get a fuller flavor of the encounter between the two people, patient and psychiatrist, who are in and of themselves what we call psychotherapy. The answer to the skeptic who questions the worth of psychotherapy is neither the withdrawn posture of the adherent of a closed system who dismisses all inquiry as suspect, nor an eruption of pseudoscientific verbal pyrotechnics. Problems will not be solved by professional arrogance or more guilds and rituals. For it is more by being than by doing that the meaningful and deeply felt communion between us and our patients will emerge. This demands as much honesty and freedom from us as it does from our patients, and as much trust on our part as we would someday hope to receive from them.

If the patient brings problems that may be understood as similar to those in many others, that may be conceptualized and abstracted, he is still in the midst of a life which is in some ways different from all others. We bring only ourselves; and so each morning in our long working day is different, and our methods of treatment will differ in many subtle ways from those of all of our colleagues. When so much of the world faces the anthill of totalitarian living, it is important for us to affirm proudly the preciously individual in each human being and in ourselves as doctors. When we see patients, the knowledge and wisdom of many intellectual ancestors are in our brains, and, we hope, some life and affection in our hearts. The heart must carry the reasoning across those inches or feet of office room. The psychiatrist, too, has his life and loves, his sorrows and angers. We know that we receive from our patients many of the irrational, misplaced, distorted thoughts and feelings once directed at parents, teachers, brothers, and sisters. We also know that our patients attempt to elicit from us many of the attitudes and responses of these earlier figures. But we must strive for some neutrality, particularly in the beginning of treatment, so that our patients may be offered, through us and their already charged feelings toward us, some idea of past passions presently lived. Yet, so often this neutrality becomes our signal for complete anonymity. We try to hide behind our couches, hide ourselves from our patients. In so doing we prolong the very isolation often responsible for our patients' troubles, and if we persist, they will derive from the experience many interpretations, but little warmth and trust.

I think that our own lives and problems are part of the therapeutic process. Our feelings, our own disorders and early sorrows are for us in some fashion what the surgeon's skilled hands are for his work. His hands are the trained instruments of knowledge, lectures, traditions. Yet they are, even in surgery, responsive to the artistry, the creative and sensitive intuition of the surgeon as a man. The psychiatrist's hands are himself, his life. We are educated and prepared, able to see and interpret. But we see, talk, and listen through our minds, our memories, our persons. It is through our emotions that the hands of our healing flex and function, reach out, and finally touch.

We cannot solve many problems, and there are the world and the stars to dwarf us and give us some humor about ourselves. But we can hope that, with some of the feeling of what Martin Buber calls "I-Thou" quietly and lovingly nurtured in some of our patients, there may be more friendliness about us. This would be no small happening, and it is for this that we must work. Alert against dryness and the stale, smiling with others and occasionally at ourselves, we can read and study; but maybe wince, shout, cry, and love, too. Really, there is much less to say than to affirm by living. I would hope that we would dare to accept ourselves fully and offer ourselves freely to a quizzical and apprehensive time and to uneasy and restless people.

Abraham Verghese

from THE TENNIS PARTNER

David Smith was an Australian tennis player who quit playing the sport in order to become a doctor and study medicine at Texas Tech. There, Smith met Abraham Verghese. The two became friends and played tennis together. But Smith was addicted to cocaine and eventually died. Verghese's book is an account of their tennis playing, their friendship, and, in this excerpt, a heartfelt warning against the loneliness of the doctor's world.

ABRAHAM VERGHESE is a professor of medicine at Texas Tech University. He is also the author of *My Own Country*, an excerpt from which also appears in this anthology.

I cannot help but believe that David's aloneness, his addiction, was worse for being in the medical profession—and not just because of ease of access, or stress, or long hours, but because of the way our profession fosters loneliness.

Despite all our grand societies, memberships, fellowships, specialty colleges, each with its annual dues and certificates and ceremonials, we are horribly alone. The doctor's world is one where our own feelings—particularly those of pain, and hurt—are not easily expressed, even though *patients* are encouraged to express them. We trust our colleagues, we show propriety and reciprocity, we have the scientific knowledge, we learn empathy, but we rarely expose our own emotions.

There is a silent but terrible collusion to cover up pain, to cover up depression; there is a fear of blushing, a machismo that destroys us. The Citadel quality to medical training, where only the fittest survive, creates the paradox of the humane, empathetic physician, like David, who shows little humanity to himself. The profession is full of "dry drunks," physicians who use titles, power, prestige, and money just as David used drugs; physicians who are more comfortable with their work identity than with real intimacy. And so it is, when one of our colleagues is whisked away, to treatment, and the particulars emerge, the first response is "I had no idea."

It is not individual physicians who are at fault as much as it is the system we have created. So many doctors and medical students came to my office after David's death, cried with me, expressed concern for me as if I were the grieving widow. Over a hundred people showed up at the funeral home for David's memorial service, all of them deeply affected by his death, sitting as one body behind his sisters and his father. . . .

Mine was the only eulogy at the service. I blush to remember how nakedly in that eulogy I expressed my sorrow, my shame. But I am proud too that I celebrated his life, consecrated our friendship. It would have amazed David, but perhaps not have saved him, to know that at the end, even as I stumbled through my last words, my voice breaking, that so many others wept for him.

David Loxtercamp

FACING OUR MORALITY: THE VIRTUE OF A COMMON LIFE

This gentle reflection asks health care practitioners to consider virtue, medical ethics, and the nature of one's relationships with other people. David Loxtercamp wonders about how physicians respond to patients "in mood and action." He advocates collaboration not just with other physicians, but with all those one meets in the course of one's life, and explores the application of medical ethics in everyday practice.

DAVID LOXTERCAMP is a family practitioner living in Belfast, Maine, and author of *A Measure of My Days: The Journal of a Country Doctor.*

Last week I admitted Mr. M. in the predawn hours of an evolving MI [myocardial infarcation]. I had forgotten his name. Erased the particulars of our prickly past until we came face-to-face behind closed curtains in the emergency department. Through sleep-deprived eyes I saw clearly what time had veiled. Thankfully, there was business to conduct, orders to write, and the beat of a clinical guideline to march us along.

Throughout his uncomplicated recovery, I dwelt in the indigo moods of my inaugural year, the day especially when I botched his outpatient operation. A general surgeon was called to complete it. No lasting harm came except to the doctor's pride and the prospects for our relationship. Mr. M. saw the surgeon in follow-up. We never again spoke of that afternoon, or my regrets, or the gravitation of his family's care to my partners.

Instead, we sank roots into the community. Stayed obliquely aware of the other's passing through guarded glances in the waiting room or grocery aisle or post office parking lot. Each time our eyes met I flushed with feelings of ineptitude. Patients came and went, other successes and failures blotted the memory, and "complications" became a stubborn but accepted fact.

But it changed me, this stinging appreciation for the stakes of my authority. Had I really informed Mr. M. before claiming his consent? Did I exceed the bounds of my training? Could I admit to errors and make amends? In the recesses of the physician's black bag, beneath the armamentarium of drugs and instruments of power and the very best of our intentions, we bear the weight of multitudinous mistakes. They amount to more than misapplication of judgment or fact. We blunder, as William Carlos Williams often reminds us, in our big and hurried ways: a heavy-handed exam, the voltage of our anger, each neglected kindness.

The ethical dilemmas in medicine are no longer about distributive justice or physician-assisted suicide: these we have surrendered to the stockholders and politicians. For the battle-worn physician, our Waterloo waits in the stack of messages at the end of the day, or in the denied insurance claim we let lapse. We recognize it in unwritten cards of condolence, our cowardice to confront addiction or abuse, the contempt we feel for self-destructive patients, and the encounters we crimp with a blood test or prescription when another five minutes with the doctor would do. How we respond to patients—in mood and action—reflects the core of the physician we are striving to become.

Recently books on virtue began drifting to my desk like the flotsam and jetsam of a discipline in distress. A thin text by Smith and Churchill was joined by those of Pellegrino and Coles, John Drane and Stanley Hauerwas. Their works flow from an ancient and venerable tradition, one largely neglected in an era of decision making by cookbook and committee. Yet here is ethics in a digestible form, one that appeals to the appetites, whose juices of repulsion and attraction whet the clinical day. In bold type and chapter headings are words like benevolence, compassion, trust, honesty, and justice. These are the elements of a virtuous physician.

Virtue has a voice, one that whispers (in the words of Abraham Lincoln) to the better angels of our nature and impels us through the drama of lives literary and real, ordinary and heroic. It is neither pious nor Pollyannish but remains largely empiric, always testing the adage that "Virtue has its own reward." Its attributes are ingrained by repetition until they become habit and attitude and self-image. They press upon everyday acts but withhold judgment until careers draw to a close.

Virtue has a heart, as Smith and Churchill distill from their commentary on the Gospel story of the good Samaritan. "[He] tends to look like a philanthropist. What usually goes unnoticed is that [he] acts out of compassion. He does not act out of altruism or *noblesse oblige*, nor does he see his help as fulfillment of a duty or an ideal or even a free and noble act. We are told, rather, that he is 'moved by compassion' upon seeing the man in the road."[1]

But the heart exposed is also vulnerable, as we know from young love, and equally from John Berger's classic tale of rural general practice. The protagonist, Dr. Eskell, confronted "far more nakedly than many doctors, the suffering of his patients and the frequent inadequacy of his ability to help them. . . ."[2] The price of "facing, trying to understand, hoping to overcome the extreme anguish of other persons five or six times a week" was isolation, cyclical depression, and eventual ruin. It is with irony and truth that Berger entitled his story *A Fortunate Man*.

Perhaps this is why doctors are not trained to be tender. We are clinical commandos who target the chief complaint with skill, knowledge, and the force of authority. Patients who refuse to be cured, who remain fundamentally needy, and who return each week unchanged or destined to die, must be bandaged by our welcome. Like Jonah, we enter the whale's belly of boredom, pain, fantasy, fear. Access is granted to those who dress the leper's wound, forswear judgment, and peer where others refuse to gaze. We are relief workers in a refugee camp, supplied with an insufficient stockpile of loyalty, friendship, and love. It is ordinary human relationship we engage in, no matter how much is made of the gap in power or degree of intimacy. Differences disappear: we become the patient, and our business is simultaneously the world and a neighbor in need.

Medical ethics, if it can ever become a practical art, must guide us over the land mines of muddled relationship. It mustn't be made a bore or the privileged pursuit of specialists. It should hold us accountable, not rarely or remotely like the spectacle of malpractice, but daily in our devotion to patient care. Against the insularity of professionalism, Dickens offers his timeless antidote:

"But you were always a good man of business, Jacob [Marley]," faltered Scrooge, who now began to apply this to himself.

"Business!" cried the ghost, wringing its hands again. "Mankind was my business. The common welfare was my business; charity, mercy, forbearance, and benevolence were, all, my business. The dealings of my trade were but a drop of water in the comprehensive ocean of my business!"[3]

I reaffirm that relationships are the bedrock of medical practice. We are not risk managers or information brokers, entrepreneurs or bureaucrats. We are *nobody's* agent except the sickly who entrust us with their care. Our actions are not unerring, never easy. Thus the well-intentioned physician needs a moral compass, a sense of solid footing, and the stamina to carry on. These are the fruits of living in community.

A decade ago, Pellegrino challenged the New York Medical Society with his vision of medicine as a moral community.[4] Sadly, who can agree? No centripetal force draws us together as one body. Real communities are centered on service to others, not pecuniary zeal. They do not fence their membership or boundaries but promote a sense of common cause. Time is needed, unbillable time, time enough for conversation or coming to an understanding. More time than is required for a procedure and its recovery, a clinical clerkship, or a granting cycle. What endures is loyalty and trust, such as you find in lasting friendships.

The purpose of community (because, in an affluent age, we no longer need it for physical survival) is to remind us who we are. This message is refreshed every Saturday morning at public market, along the Fourth of July parade route, at yard sales, benefit suppers, community plays, and YMCA runs. Today's archenemy is tomorrow's teammate, our auto mechanic, my daughter's dentist, or the crucial vote in an upcoming election. However difficult it might be to shed the role of "doctor" when I leave the office, my work is blessed by the roles I bring back: husband, father, runner, gardener, singer, churchgoer. They nourish and enlarge me: they ensure access to honest advice, gentle reproves, words that can mend and mold me.

It is a shame, really, that doctors spend so little time in the communities where they practice. If we did, we might come to see our patients from a different angle, as real people on equal terms, capable of returning more than they receive. With greater depth of field, we might more easily grasp their worries and woes, and recognize our failure to help them. We might be fed by their gratitude, motivated by friendship instead of their demands or our sense of sacred duty or the lure of the almighty dollar. Perhaps our panel of patients, and those who assist us in their care, are the communities we seek.

Fourteen years have passed. I cope more easily now with the small but niggling regrets of the daily grind, surrendering these and their moral burden to my Thursday morning meeting of partners. Here, for an hour each week, we air our dirty laundry, search our foibles, sift through soured interactions and missed opportunities that would otherwise fall through the cracks. Following Dr. Williams's suggestion, we exchange "heart-to-heart stories," knowing that "the more open we are about what gets our moods going and how those moods affect our work, the more likely we are to catch hold of ourselves—in the nick of time."[5]

Within a few short years, I have learned to walk on two empiric legs. First is the knowledge that doctors rise to their best by serving the least of their patients—the least insured, the least curable, the least attractive, responsible, or grateful. The least like us. Second is my belief that personal and clinical contributions to the patient's well-being are an indivisible act—fused in their timing, their import, and the totality of patients' expectations.

Virtue is about the everyday responsibility of living in community. It is not the province of heroes and saints, whom we idolize and elevate and leave holding the bag. We must overcome fear and false modesty in order to reclaim virtue and in the process a fuller sense of ourselves.

If there are any heroes or saints left in the world, they are each of us at our best, responding to the worst that the world imposes. Like a photo mosaic, our lives create the ethereal outline of virtue. But it is in the individual faces, or parts thereof, that virtue becomes most worthy of emulation.

Mr. M. and I did not undo the past. We stumble forward as best we can, two lives mingled by fate and pulled on providential leash. Happily, I didn't botch my second chance. I realize now that its very possibility depended on living in a community where the doctor's fallibility and faithfulness are a matter of record. Yes, occasionally I'm a hero in the small town. But more importantly, I am moored to my patients' predicament, their fleshed-in lives, and the unflinching fact that we are interchangeable. Commoners all. Located by the real things we live by.

NOTES

1. Smith H., Churchill L. *Professional Ethics and Primary Care Medicine*. Durham, NC: Duke University Press; 1986: 50.
2. Berger J., Mohr J. *A Fortunate Man*. New York, NY: Vintage International Edition; 1997: 105–106.
3. Dickens C. *A Christmas Carol*. Boston, Mass: Atlantic Monthly Press.
4. Pellegrino, ed. The medical profession as a moral community. *Bull N Y Ac Med*. 1990; 66: 221–232.
5. Coles R. *The Call of Stories*. Boston, Mass: Houghton Mifflin; 1989: 117–118.

PERMISSIONS

We are grateful for permission to reproduce copyrighted material:

"Outpatient" by Rosalind Warren. © Rosalind Warren. Used by her permission.

Excerpt from "First Sermon on Reverence for Life," from *A Place for Revelation*, by Albert Schweitzer, translated by David Larrimore Holland. Copyright © 1989 by Macmillan Publishing Company. Used by permission of Simon & Schuster, Inc.

"Like a Prayer," from *The Poetry of Healing: A Doctor's Education in Empathy, Identity, and Desire*, by Raphael Campo. Copyright © 1997 by Raphael Campo. Used by permission of W. W. Norton & Company, Inc., and Georges Borchardt, Inc., for the author.

"The Body Flute," by Cortney Davis, from *Between the Heartbeats: Poetry and Prose by Nurses*, edited by Cortney Davis and Judy Schaefer. Copyright © 1995. Used by permission of the University of Iowa Press.

Excerpt from "Can You Teach Compassion?" from *The Midnight Meal and Other Essays about Doctors, Patients, and Medicine*, by Jerome Lowenstein, M.D. Copyright © 1997. Used by permission of Yale University Press.

"1852: J. Marion Simms Perfects a Repair for Vesicovaginal Fistula," from *How Do You Feel?* By Kirsten Emmott (Victoria BC: Sono Nis Press). © 1992. Used by permission of Kirsten Emmott.

Excerpt from *The Nazi Doctors*, by Robert Jay Lifton. Copyright © 1986 by Robert Jay Lifton. Reprinted by permission of Basic Books, a member of Perseus Books, L.L.C.

"The Lie," by Lawrence D. Grouse, M.D., from *A Piece of My Mind: A Collection of Essays from the Journal of the American Medical Association*, edited by Bruce B. Dan. Copyright © 1988 by the American Medical Association. Used by permission of Alfred A. Knopf, a division of Random House, Inc.

"The Wound Dresser," from *Leaves of Grass*, by Walt Whitman.

"The Good Doctor" by Susan Onthank Mates. Copyright © 1994 by Susan Onthank Mates. Used by permission of the University of Iowa Press.

"Baptism by Rotation," from *A Country Doctor's Notebook,* by Mikhail Bulgakov, published by the Harvill Press. English translation © Michael Glenny, 1975. Used by permission of the Harvill Press.

"Who Owns the Libretto?" by Judy Schaefer, from *Between the Heartbeats: Poetry and Prose by Nurses,* edited by Cortney Davis and Judy Schaefer. Copyright © 1995. Used by permission of the University of Iowa Press.

"The Tallis Case," by David T. Nash, M.D., from *Journal of the American Medical Association,* vol. 249, no. 7 (2/18/83), p. 879f. © 1983. Used by permission of the American Medical Association.

Excerpt from *My Own Country,* by Abraham Verghese. Copyright © 1994 by Abraham Verghese. Used by permission of Simon & Schuster and The Orion Publishing Group.

"What the Doctor Said," from *A New Path to the Waterfall,* by Raymond Carver. Copyright © 1989 by the Estate of Raymond Carver. Used by permission of Grove/Atlantic, Inc.

"This Red Oozing," from *Breathless,* by Jeanne Bryner, RN, GA, CEN (Kent State University Press). Used by permission of Jeanne Bryner.

Excerpt from *In the Country of Hearts: Journeys in the Art of Medicine* (Delacorte), by John Stone. Copyright © 1990 by John Stone. Used by his permission.

"Large Woman, Half," by Alyson Porter, from *Journal of the American Medical Association,* vol. 262, no. 9 (9/1/99), p. 823. © Alyson Porter. Used by her permission.

"The Knee," by Constance J. Meyd, from *A Piece of My Mind: A Collection of Essays from the Journal of the American Medical Association,* edited by Bruce B. Dan. Copyright © 1988 by the American Medical Association. Used by permission of Alfred A. Knopf, a division of Random House, Inc.

"Voice Offstage," from *The Diving Bell and the Butterfly,* by Jean-Dominique Bauby, translated by Jeremy Leggat. Copyright © 1997 by Alfred A. Knopf, a division of Random House, Inc. Used by permission of Alfred A. Knopf, a division of Random House, Inc., and Fourth Estate, a division of HarperCollins Publishers (UK).

"Letter from the Rehabilitation Institute," from *Intensive Care,* by Lucia Cordell Getsi. Copyright © 1992. Used by permission of New Rivers Press.

"Breast Cancer: Power vs. Prosthesis," from *The Cancer Journals,* by Audre Lorde (San Francisco: Aunt Lute Books). Copyright © 1980 by Audre Lorde. Used by permission of The Charlotte Sheedy Literary Agency.

"A Small Good Thing," from *Cathedral,* by Raymond Carver. Copyright © 1983 by Raymond Carver. Used by permission of Alfred A. Knopf, a division of Random House, Inc., and International Creative Management, Inc.

"Pies," by Timothy J. Fisher, M.D. © Timothy J. Fisher. Used by his permission.

"Communion," by Sarah Lentz, from *Academic Medicine*, vol. 73, no. 2. © Sarah Lentz. Used by her permission.

"The Nature of Suffering and the Goals of Medicine," by Eric J. Cassell, M.D., from *The New England Journal of Medicine*, vol. 306, no. 11. Copyright © 1982 Massachusetts Medical Society. All rights reserved.

"Repose," by Matt Dugan. © Matt Dugan. Used by his permission.

"The Girl with the Pimply Face," from *The Collected Stories of William Carlos Williams.* Copyright © 1938 by William Carlos Williams. Used by permission of New Directions Publishing Corp. and Carcanet Press Limited.

"Healers: The Physician and the Mori," by Michael Weingarten, from *Patients and Doctors*, edited by Jeffrey M. Borkan. © 1999. Used by permission of The University of Wisconsin Press.

"Poverty Medicine," from *Not All of Us Are Saints*, by David Hilfiker. Copyright © 1994 by David Hilfiker. Used by permission of Hill and Wang, a division of Farrar, Staus and Giroux, LLC.

"In Terror of Hospital Bills," from *Shall We Gather at the River,* by James Wright. Copyright © 1968 by James Wright. Used by permission of Wesleyan University Press.

"Another Case of Chronic Pelvic Pain," from *Rehab at the Florida Avenue Grill*, by Veneta Masson. Copyright © 1999 by Veneta Masson. Used by permission of Sage Femme Press, Washington DC.

"Rez Dogs and Crow Dreams," from *The Scalpel and the Silver Bear*, by Lori Arviso Alvord M.D., and Elizabeth Cohen Van Pelt. Copyright © 1999 by Lori Arviso Alvord and Elizabeth Cohen Van Pelt. Used by permission of Bantam Books, a division of Random House, Inc.

"Unwed," from *How Do You Feel?* By Kirsten Emmott (Victoria BC: Sono Nis Press, 1992). Used by permission of Kirsten Emmott.

Excerpts from *A Wise Birth*, by Penny Armstrong and Sheryl Feldman. © 1990 by Penny Armstrong and Sheryl Feldman. Used by permission of HarperCollins Publishers, Inc., and The Martell Agency.

"The Eight Questions," from *The Spirit Catches You and You Fall Down*, by Anne Fadiman. Copyright © 1997 by Anne Fadiman. Reprinted by permission of Farrar, Straus and Giroux, LLC.

Excerpt from *Another Turn of the Crank*, by Wendell Berry. Copyright © 1995 by Wendell Berry. Used by Permission of Counterpoint Press, a member of Perseus Books, L.L.C.

Excerpt from *An Unquiet Mind*, by Kay Redfield Jamison. Copyright © 1995 by Kay Redfield Jamison. Used by permission of Alfred A. Knopf, a division of Random House, Inc.

"A Young Psychiatrist Looks at His Profession," from *The Mind's Fate: Ways of Seeing Psychiatry and Psychoanalysis*, by Robert Coles. Copyright © 1975, 1995 by Robert Coles. Used by permission of Little, Brown and Company, Inc.

Excerpt from *The Tennis Partner*, by Abraham Verghese. Copyright © 1998 by Abraham Verghese. Used by permission of HarperCollins Publishers Inc. and Mary Evans Inc.

"Facing Our Mortality: The Virtue of a Common Life," by David Loxtercamp, M.D., from *Journal of the American Medical Association*, vol. 282, no. 10 (9/8/1999), p. 923f. © 1999. Used by permission of the American Medical Association.